CAMBRIDG
HISTORY OF PO

JOHN KNOX
On Rebellion

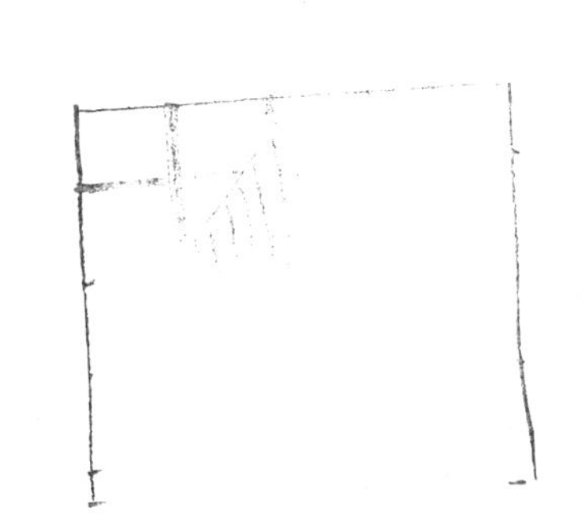

CAMBRIDGE TEXTS IN THE HISTORY OF POLITICAL THOUGHT

Cambridge Texts in the History of Political Thought is now firmly established as the major student textbook series in political theory. It aims to make available to students all the most important texts in the history of western political thought, from ancient Greece to the early twentieth century. All the familiar classic texts will be included but the series does at the same time seek to enlarge the conventional canon by incorporating an extensive range of less well-known works, many of them never before available in a modern English edition. Wherever possible, texts are published in complete and unabridged form, and translations are specially commissioned for the series. Each volume contains a critical introduction together with chronologies, biographical sketches, a guide to further reading and any necessary glossaries and textual apparatus. When completed, the series will aim to offer an outline of the entire evolution of western political thought.

For a list of titles in the series, please see end of book

JOHN KNOX

On Rebellion

EDITED BY

ROGER A. MASON

University of St Andrews

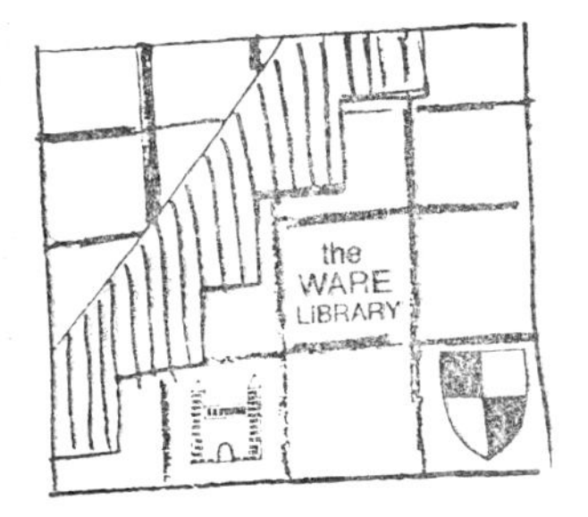

Published by the Press Syndicate of the University of Cambridge
The Pitt Building, Trumpington Street, Cambridge CB2 1RP
40 West 20th Street, New York, NY 10011–4211, USA
10 Stamford Road, Oakleigh, Melbourne, 3166, Australia

First published 1994

Printed in Great Britain at the University Press, Cambridge

A catalogue record for this book is available from the British Library

Library of Congress cataloguing in publication data

Knox, John, 1505–1572.
John Knox on rebellion / edited by Roger A. Mason.
p. cm. – (Cambridge texts in the history of political thought)
Includes bibliographical references.
Contents: pt. 1, the 1558 Tracts. The First Blast of the Trumpet – The Letter to the Regent – The Appellation to the Nobility and Estates – The Letter to the Commonalty – Summary of the Second Blast of the Trumpet – pt. 2. Knox and Scotland, 1557–1564.
ISBN 0 521 39089 3 (hardback). – ISBN 0 521 39988 2 (pbk.)
1. Reformation – Scotland – Sources. 2. Scotland – Church history – 16th century – Sources. 3. Church and state – Scotland – History – 16th century – Sources. I. Mason, Roger A. II. Title. III. Series.
BR385.K65 1993 93–19944
274.11'06 – dc20 CIP

ISBN 0 521 39089 3 hardback
ISBN 0 521 39988 2 paperback

Contents

Preface

As the introduction makes clear, to talk of the 'political works' of John Knox is to give a misleading impression of the style and substance of the writings of a man who saw himself, first and foremost, as a preacher and a prophet. Nevertheless, Knox did write extensively on the theme of resistance to political authority and the purpose of this edition is to bring together in a single volume those of his works in which the problem of rebellion is discussed at length. Part I, therefore, contains the four tracts of 1558 – *The First Blast of the Trumpet against the Monstrous Regiment of Women*, *The Letter to the Regent of Scotland*, *The Appellation to the Scottish Nobility and Estates* and *The Letter to the Commonalty of Scotland* – in which he addressed the issue most directly. Part II contains a body of related material, mostly drawn from Knox's *History of the Reformation in Scotland*, which sheds light both on the development of Knox's ideas before 1558 and on how they were applied in the context of the Scottish 'Reformation-Rebellion' of 1559 and its aftermath.

It is a great pleasure to be able to acknowledge here the numerous debts I have accumulated in compiling this edition. It would not have been possible without the help of the staff of the National Library of Scotland, Edinburgh University Library and St Andrews University Library. I am particularly grateful to the Keeper of Rare Books at St Andrews, Christine Gascoigne, and her predecessor, Geoffrey Hargreaves, for their unstinting courtesy and helpfulness. In the early stages of the project, the technical assistance of Lorna Weatherill was invaluable and it would have taken much longer to complete but for the patience and stamina of Carol Edington who took time off from her own research on Knox's coeval, Sir David Lindsay of the Mount, to commit the original texts of the 1558 tracts to disk. Thanks are also due to John Durkan, Roger Green, Angus MacKay and Andrew Pettegree for their help with specific queries, and particularly to Jane Dawson who willingly shared with me her own very considerable knowledge of Knox and his period and kindly found time, at very short notice, to read and comment on the introduction. Since embarking on the project, my colleagues in the Department of Scottish History at St Andrews, particularly Norman Macdougall and Chris Smout, have been as supportive of me as they have been tolerant of Knox. Their forbearance has been surpassed only by that of my wife, Ellen, whose affection for her adopted homeland has been sorely tested (but fortunately never broken) by close acquaintance with one of its spiritual fathers. The completion of this edition owes a great deal to the tact and understanding she has shown towards an increasingly distracted husband. Finally, I owe a long-standing debt to my parents for their support over many years; it is not a debt that can ever be repaid, but it is one that I acknowledge here with grateful thanks.

Introduction

I

There was little in John Knox's background to suggest that as a self-styled instrument of God he was destined to wield considerable influence over the course of the Reformation in Britain. Of his early life, in fact, very little is known. Even the date of his birth – *c.*1514 – is conjectural, though we can say that he was born of humble parentage in the Scottish burgh of Haddington in East Lothian and was probably educated at the local grammar school before attending St Andrews University. There is no record of his graduating from St Andrews, but he did take holy orders in the later 1530s and, unable to obtain a benefice, eked out a living as a notary apostolic (a minor legal official) and a tutor to the children of the gentry. The date of his conversion to Protestantism is similarly obscure, but it must have occurred in the early 1540s as Knox was closely involved with the ministry of George Wishart who returned to Scotland in 1543 after five years of exile in England and on the continent. Wishart's return appears to have been prompted by the Protestant and anglophile policies pursued by the Regent Arran following the death of James V in 1542 and the accession to the Scottish throne of the infant Mary Stewart. If so, it proved a fatal miscalculation. The powerful Catholic and pro-French party, led by the queen mother, Mary of Guise, and ably seconded by the archbishop of St Andrews, Cardinal David Beaton, ensured that Arran's 'godly fit' was short-lived. Wishart was arrested in January 1546 and burned at the stake outside the cardinal's castle at St Andrews two months later.

It was fear of suffering the same fate as his mentor that drove

Knox to seek refuge in the castle the following year. There he joined the Protestant lairds who had avenged Wishart's death by murdering the cardinal and who were now under siege vainly awaiting relief from England. It was in these inauspicious circumstances, during a prolonged armistice, that in April 1547 Knox preached his first Protestant sermon. According to his own account, however, he did so only reluctantly, at first refusing 'to run where God had not called him'. It was only when publicly summoned in the face of the congregation and after several days of soul-searching that he became convinced that this was a 'lawful vocation' which he could not deny. It is surely significant that, while he tells us nothing about his conversion in his *History*, Knox describes the circumstances of his calling in such detail (Laing, vol. I, pp. 185–93; Dickinson, vol. I, pp. 81–86). If he suffered a conversion experience, it paled into insignificance when set beside the public drama – and personal trauma – of discovering his vocation. Nor is this surprising. For it was precisely the fact of having been singled out by God through the agency of the congregation which justified for Knox the very public role which he thereafter assumed. Throughout his career as a reformed preacher, it was to his vocation that he constantly referred to legitimise his public actions and utterances.

It was a vocation, moreover, which he repeatedly identified with that of the Old Testament prophets. Knox was not alone among Protestant preachers in turning to the prophets for inspiration and example, but his sense of kinship with them was unusually strong. Time and again in his writings he had recourse to the careers of Isaiah, Ezekiel and particularly Jeremiah to justify his conduct. In part, this stemmed from a kind of biblical 'legalism' to which we shall return in a moment. But it was also founded on Knox's deep-rooted conviction that, like his biblical predecessors, he had an 'extraordinary' vocation which bound him to proclaim the divine will and warn the disobedient of the fearful consequences of their iniquity. Not unnaturally, the vehemence of his prophesying varied in proportion to the adversity he faced. Exiled from England during Mary Tudor's reign, he indulged in an orgy of prophetic denunciation quite unrestrained in its violent abuse of Catholicism. Yet while his identification with the Old Testament prophets was only fully realised in exile, it was firmly rooted in the conviction – dating from 1547 – that he was indeed a chosen instrument of God.

In 1547, however, Knox's future as a prophet looked decidedly bleak. Within months of his debut in the pulpit, St Andrews castle fell to the French and he was to spend almost two years as a prisoner on a French galley. He was released in March 1549, but rather than return to Scotland, where English military intervention had failed to prevent Mary Stewart being sent to Catholic France and to an eventual French marriage, he settled in Protestant England. There he was licensed to preach by Edward VI's reforming privy council and ministered to congregations at Berwick and Newcastle before his growing reputation as a preacher led to his appointment as a royal chaplain and the offer (which he declined) of the bishopric of Rochester. His years in England were in retrospect probably among the happiest of his career. But at the time Knox was less than satisfied with the slow pace of reform. While the offer of a bishopric is evidence of his growing stature within the English church, his rejection of it testifies to his refusal to conform with a moderate ecclesiastical establishment. His opposition to kneeling at communion, and hence to Cranmer's 1552 Prayer Book, clearly aligned Knox with the radicals in the English Protestant movement. At the same time, it betrayed a reluctance to deviate from biblical precept and precedent which is the most fundamental feature of his thought.

If sixteenth-century Protestantism was pre-eminently the religion of the Word, Knox was one of those who pressed the doctrine of *sola scriptura* to extremes. Certainly, in the *First Blast*, he shored up his argument with any authority – legal, classical or patristic – which came to hand. But this is the exception that proves the rule. For Knox took such authorities seriously only when they accorded with the will of God as revealed in the Word. Indeed, it was in the *First Blast* that he declared that the fundamental authority was 'the law moral . . . the constant and unchangeable will of God to the which the Gentile is no less bound than was the Jew' (p. 30). The effect of this biblical literalism was to turn the Scriptures – particularly the Old Testament – into a source book of 'legal' precedents which were as binding on the kingdoms of England and Scotland as they had been on Israel and Judah. At its most arid, this could give rise, as in the *First Blast*, to an obscure discussion of Jewish inheritance practices as evidenced by the daughters of Zelophehad (pp. 38–9). More generally, however, it meant that when Knox identified himself with Jeremiah, or Mary Tudor with Jezebel, he was doing much more than invoking convenient scriptural parallels or paradigms. He was appealing to biblical 'case law' to establish precedents which were universally binding because they revealed to man the immutable laws of God.

In the England of Edward VI, however, the immediate focus of Knox's biblical literalism was the Roman Catholic mass. Manifestly, he argued, the mass was a human invention and *ipso facto* an idolatrous ceremony repugnant to the divine law he had been called to proclaim. As a preacher and a prophet, Knox was bound in conscience to warn the people of the hideous consequences of participating in what he knew to be the most perverted ceremony of an antichristian church. 'For so odious and abominable I know the mass to be in God's presence', he wrote in 1550, 'that unless ye decline from the same, to life can ye never attain. And therefore, Brethren, flee from that idolatry rather than from the present death' (Laing, vol. III, pp. 69–70). With the accession in July 1553 of a Catholic sovereign to the throne of England, such advice was to strike sharply home among those Protestants who – unlike Knox – were in no position to seek solace and sanctuary in continental exile.

II

For those Protestants who did remain in England, Mary Tudor's accession, and the Catholic reaction she initiated, created an agonising dilemma. It posed in the acutest possible way the problem of whether the allegiance of the faithful was owed to the commands of God or to those of man. Knox himself, of course, had no doubt which was the sovereign authority. After arriving in Dieppe early in 1554, he wrote a series of letters to his former congregations in England whose leading theme was the absolute necessity 'as ye purpose and intend to avoid God's vengeance', of eschewing 'as well in body as in spirit, all fellowship and society with idolaters in their idolatry' (Laing, vol. III, p. 166). While such an uncompromising stance was fairly predictable, the main argument which Knox deployed in its support was not. For it was in this context that he made use for the first time of the idea that to participate in the mass was irrevocably to violate 'the league and covenant of God' which 'requires that we declare ourselves enemies to all sorts of idolatry' (Laing, vol. III, p. 193). Formulated in terms of a renewed Mosaic covenant, the avoidance of idolatry was transformed from a simple scriptural precept into a clause in a formal 'contract' drawn up between God and the elect. Moreover, according to Knox, just as the reward for fulfilling the terms of the covenant was eternal salvation, so the penalty for their infraction was eternal damnation. In effect, in the context of Mary Tudor's reign, this crudely conditional interpretation of the covenant rendered civil disobedience a precondition of salvation.

While Knox had thrust the covenant firmly into the political arena, it is important to emphasise that he did not at this stage view forcible resistance to ungodly rule as one of its terms. Certainly, when formulated in terms of a binding contract, the injunction to obey God rather than man represented a formidable challenge to power structures founded on human rather than biblical precepts. Nevertheless, Knox expressly warned his English brethren 'that ye presume not to be revengers of your own cause, but that ye resign over vengeance unto Him' (Laing, vol. III, p. 244). Such a policy of non-resistance was as distasteful to Knox as it was dangerous for his fellow Protestants in England. But in 1554 it was the only option available to him. For just as his belief that allegiance was owed to God rather than man had an impeccable biblical source (Acts 5.29), so too did the claim that the powers that be were ordained by God and whoever resisted them resisted the ordinance of God and would suffer eternal damnation (Romans 13.1–7). The latter Pauline injunction was the most influential biblical precept of the age and, beyond advocating a policy of passive disobedience in all things repugnant to the law of God, Knox was in no position to deny it.

His stance conformed, moreover, with the views of the leading lights of European Protestantism. Knox's attempt during a tour of the Swiss churches early in 1554 to elicit a more aggressive response from John Calvin and Heinrich Bullinger proved unsuccessful. Bullinger responded cautiously that, while it *might* be possible to justify rebellion in the cause of God and the Word, the great danger was that baser motives would masquerade under the cloak of religious zeal. Of Calvin's response we know only that it differed little from Bullinger's and offered Knox no great encouragement. Given their emphatic belief in the divine nature of political authority and their anxiety to distance themselves from the excesses of the Anabaptist sects, Calvin and his associates were ill-equipped to forge any justification of resistance in the early 1550s. Knox became more sensitive to these constraints as he fell directly under Calvin's influence during his exile. As a result, he continued to urge on the faithful in England the orthodox Calvinist policy of disobedience in all things repugnant to the law of God, but passive acceptance of any persecution that such a stance might bring upon them.

Gradually Knox did learn how to interpret St Paul's injunction to obey in such a way as to admit the possibility of armed resistance to an idolatrous ruler. But he did so only with significant reservations. After all, as Calvin surely made clear to him, to admit the general principle of resistance was to provide also the means of challenging those very powers to whom he looked for the imposition of godly rule. Knox was no more a radical antinomian than he was a popular constitutionalist. His aim was the establishment of a godly commonwealth ruled by a godly prince in strict accordance with the law of God. It was against the background of a Calvinist ideal of a severely disciplined society, a society in which obedience to the temporal power was of paramount importance, that his theory of resistance was evolved. To understand its development, however, we must see it in the context, not just of Knox's relations with Marian England, but also of his complex reaction to events in contemporary Scotland.

III

Knox spent the winter of 1554–5 ministering to the English congregation at Frankfort and locked in a bitter dispute over his radical liturgical views. Forced to leave Frankfort, he spent the summer months in Geneva before returning to Berwick in the autumn of 1555 to marry the Englishwoman, Marjory Bowes, to whom he had been betrothed before his flight to the continent. While there, he ventured into Scotland and was astonished at the warm reception he received. Although Mary of Guise had formally assumed the regency the previous year (buying off the earl of Arran, a former supporter of reform, with the French duchy of Châtelherault), her hostility to her Protestant subjects was tempered by her need to win their acquiescence in the marriage of her daughter to the French dauphin. Unlike their English counterparts, therefore, Scottish Protestants were not being actively persecuted and, during the winter of 1555–6, Knox was able to undertake a hastily improvised mission criss-crossing the country ministering to congregations assembled in the houses of sympathetic brethren. He returned to Geneva in July 1556, but not before the Scottish bishops, increasingly alarmed at his activities, summoned him to Edinburgh to face a charge of heresy. The trial never took place. Unwilling to risk a confrontation with her Protestant subjects, Mary of Guise had the proceedings quashed.

It is indicative of the impact of his mission that, after his departure, the Scottish bishops did condemn Knox as a heretic and publicly burned his effigy. As he preached mostly in private and to audiences already sympathetic to his cause, he can have done little to extend the existing base of Protestant support. But his rapid movement around the country lent the scattered congregations a sense of common purpose which they had never previously experienced. For the first time both Knox and the lay leaders of the localised Protestant cells became aware of the possibility of adding a concerted political dimension to what had hitherto been a haphazard spiritual movement. In this respect, the most crucial aspect of his visit was his success in establishing contact with sympathetic noblemen. For it was these men – the future lords of the Congregation – who were to turn the fledgling movement for reform into a significant political force. In securing the support of such notables as Lord James Stewart and the earls of Glencairn and Argyll, Knox had laid the foundations of the organised Protestant party which within a few years was to embark on revolution. If he still remained reticent as to the legitimacy of resistance, he had gone some way towards consolidating a movement capable of armed rebellion.

But Knox's reticence may only have applied to his public utterances. It is likely that privately he did broach the possibility of some form of organised resistance with the nobility. Certainly, they appeared to be acting with the foreknowledge of his approval when, in March 1557, they wrote to him in Geneva asking that he return once again to Scotland and assuring him that they were now prepared 'to jeopard lives and goods in the forward setting of the glory of God' (pp. 133–4). Knox duly responded to the call, but he had travelled only as far as Dieppe before he received further letters intimating that the nobles had changed their minds. Understandably incensed, on 27 October 1557 he wrote an indignant reply upbraiding them for their irresolution and affirming that, as noblemen, their 'office and duty' bound them 'to vindicate and deliver your subjects from all violence and oppression to the uttermost of your power' (p. 137).

It is tempting to read into this letter the full-blown theory of armed rebellion which Knox was to set out in the *Appellation* the following year. As we shall see, however, the *Appellation* is much less radical in the demands it makes of the Scottish nobility than is commonly supposed. The same applies to Knox's correspondence of 1557. Although an earlier letter in which he explained what he expected of the nobility was 'lost by negligence and troubles' (p. 137), in one of 17 December, he made it plain that, while they were duty bound to defend their brethren from persecution, they were under no circumstances to deny 'lawful obedience' to the regent (pp. 147–8).

Paradoxically, however, it was while advising the Scottish nobility to respect the authority of Mary of Guise, that Knox began to write his classic diatribe against the very principle of female government itself. Although not published until he returned to Geneva in the spring of 1558, Knox began work on the *First Blast* in Dieppe in the latter months of 1557. Here there was none of the caution evident in his Scottish correspondence. Writing in the style of the schools, but enlivening his scholastic reasoning with outbursts of prophetic invective, Knox took as his starting-point the wholly unambiguous proposition that nature and the Scriptures, both of which were revelations of the divine will, demanded the total exclusion of women from power. He then proceeded to marshal an array of authorities, ranging from Aristotle to Augustine and from the civil law to secular history, to support his claim. But he was patently more at home when he turned to biblical 'case law' and was able to exercise his exegetical talents on the precedents set by such exemplars of vicious female rule as Athaliah and Jezebel. Well armed with scriptural references, he had no difficulty in proving that 'the regiment of a woman is a thing most odious in the presence of God'. Less predictably, however, he then concluded that those who 'have most heinously offended against God, placing in authority such as God by His Word hath removed from the same ... ought without further delay to remove from authority all such persons as by usurpation, violence or tyranny do possess the same' (pp. 43–4). This was, without doubt, an unequivocal call to revolution.

Although its conclusion was extreme, in terms of sixteenth-century attitudes to women, the premises on which the *First Blast* was based were hardly exceptional. Knox was merely articulating, albeit in his characteristic language of imperatives, a prejudice common among his contemporaries. But it was not a view which was to commend itself to Protestants in Scotland or England over the next few years. With the accession of Elizabeth only months later, the publication of the *First Blast* proved a source of acute embarrassment to those – including Knox and the Scottish Congregation – who were to look to the English queen for aid. Subsequently, in an interview with Mary Stewart, Knox refused to retract the principles expounded in the *First Blast*, but argued that 'that book was written most especially against that wicked Jezebel of England', Mary Tudor (p. 177). He was substantially correct. For although God's law was universal and immutable, Knox chose in the *First Blast* to apply it only to England. He was certainly aware that Scotland too was ruled by a female regent on behalf of a female sovereign, but it was only the English whom he explicitly instructed to fulfil the divine ordinance and destroy the 'monster' who reigned over them (p. 46). That this was not an oversight, but was based on a deliberate distinction between the two countries, is borne out by the *Appellation*, but it is also evident in the very different attitude that Knox displayed towards Mary of Guise in the *Letter to the Regent*.

As published in the summer of 1558, the *Letter to the Regent* was a revised version with substantial additions of an appeal which Knox had addressed to Mary of Guise while in Scotland in May 1556. To some extent, this explains the difference in tone between it and the *First Blast*. In 1556, Knox thought it possible that the regent might be persuaded to extend her policy of conciliating Protestants to one of formal toleration and perhaps even to embrace the 'true religion' herself. It would have been a dereliction of his duty not to warn her of the terrible fate she was courting by continuing to participate in idolatry. But his central purpose was to instruct her in her duty to reform religion in accordance with the Word of God. If Knox was far from confident of success, in 1556 he at least wrote more in sorrow than in anger. By 1558, however, his attitude had hardened and the additions to the original text betray a less temperate spirit. A discordant note is introduced by citing the untimely death of the regent's husband and two male children as evidence of 'the anger and hot displeasure of God' (p. 66), while more pertinently, in an echo of the *First Blast*, she is reminded that 'seldom it is that women do long reign with felicity and joy' (p. 65). Yet this was as close as Knox came in the *Letter to the Regent* to pronouncing against Mary of Guise the sentence he had already pronounced against Mary Tudor. That this was not simply a matter of expediency – the faint and fading hope that the regent might yet be persuaded to forsake idolatry – is apparent from the *Appellation*. For there it becomes clear that the contrasting agendas which Knox was setting for Scotland and England rested on compelling ideological foundations.

IV

The *Appellation* is the most important as well as the most easily misconstrued of Knox's political writings. Taking shape in his mind as he wrote the *Letter to the Regent*, it was published in Geneva in July 1558 together in a single volume with its companion piece, the *Letter to the Commonalty*, and a summary of the questions which he intended to address in his *Second Blast of the Trumpet*. The latter was never written, but the former three were clearly intended by Knox to be read as one. Having defined the duties of a godly prince, it was his purpose now to make clear those of the nobility and estates (in effect, the Scottish landed elite) and finally those of the common people.

As its title suggests, the *Appellation* is an appeal to the Scottish nobility and estates against 'the cruel and most injust sentence' which the Scottish clergy had pronounced against Knox in 1556. In this, it has much in common with the *Letter to the Regent* where Mary of Guise was similarly implored to protect the preacher from the bishops' wrath and allow him to defend himself against the charge of heresy. Underlying this argument lay the Erastian contention that the authority of the church was subject at all times to that of the crown. As a whole, Knox's writings hardly suggest consistent support for the idea of the royal supremacy. But the belief in the primacy of the civil sword is fundamental to the case he presented in 1558. On the basis of such precedents as the subjection of Aaron to the authority of Moses, he argued in the *Appellation* that, just as the civil magistrate was duty bound to reform religion, so he possessed the authority to discipline the clergy. This applied, however, not simply to the supreme magistrate – the crown – but also to the inferior magistrates of the realm – the nobility. It was a crucial extension of the principle. For it was in pursuing this argument that Knox finally established the grounds which, without denying the authority of Romans 13, allowed him nevertheless to elaborate a theory of aristocratic resistance to ungodly rule.

The key element in this theory was the idea that, as St Paul had said that the 'powers' (plural) were ordained by God, there must exist in each kingdom alternative – albeit inferior – magistrates whose office was, like a king's, of divine institution, and whose duty it was, again like a king's, to reform the religion in accordance with the law of God. The inferior magistrates of Scotland were, primarily, the nobility. It was to them, therefore, as 'lawful powers by God appointed' (p. 72), that Knox addressed his *Appellation*. That his reasoning was squarely based on Romans 13 is revealed by a passage where, after quoting the appropriate verses, he went on to explain to the nobility that 'if you be powers ordained by God (and that I hope all men will grant), then by the plain words of the Apostle is the sword given unto you by God for maintenance of the innocent and for punishment of malefactors' (p. 85). Like a godly prince, the godly nobility were to wield the sword of justice in the cause of Christian discipline. Even when the superior power commanded the contrary, the inferior magistrates were bound to fulfil the function assigned to them by God. That being so, Knox could now insist that a godly Protestant magistrate was duty bound to protect the innocent elect from a godless Catholic prince. Moreover, from this position it was but a short step to the more radical conclusion that those 'whom God hath raised up to be princes and rulers . . . whose hands He hath armed with the sword of His justice' were also 'appointed to be as bridles to repress the rage and insolency of your kings whensoever they pretend manifestly to transgress God's blessed ordinance' (p. 102). Apparently, unlike in 1557, this was a step which Knox was now prepared to take.

Yet it was not a step which he could base solely on the expedient of pluralising the Pauline maxim that the powers are ordained by God. Of itself, the idea of an inferior magistracy did nothing to counter the injunction to obey in Romans 13. On the contrary, it confused the issue by positing a plurality of powers to each and all of whom obedience was theoretically due. It was, of course, palpably absurd to invite a situation in which divinely ordained magistrates were opposed to a divinely ordained prince, both of whom were demanding obedience in accordance with the divine will. But how was such a scenario to be avoided without denying that *all* the powers are ordained by God and must not be resisted? According to Knox, the answer lay in distinguishing between a prince acting according to God's ordinance and a prince acting *ultra vires*. When faced with the contention that the powers are to be obeyed 'be they good or be they bad', Knox retorted that, when kings acted wickedly, God 'hath commanded no obedience, but rather He hath approved, yea, and greatly rewarded, such as have opponed themselves to their ungodly commandments and blind rage' (p. 95). Although not fully articulated here, Knox was working towards the conclusion that there was a great difference between the power ordained by God and the person who wielded that power. As a divine ordinance, the former was perfect and unchallengeable, but the latter was prone to all the imperfections stemming from man's fallen nature. In the General Assembly debate of 1564, Knox made the distinction much more explicitly in defending the proposition 'that the prince may be resisted and yet the ordinance of God not violated' (pp. 191–2). But it is already present in embryo in the *Appellation*. In addition to having located a magistracy empowered to resist an ungodly prince, Knox had found a way of sanctioning rebellion without negating the divine ordinance of obedience to the royal office.

Knox's use of these ideological devices was crucial to the radicalisation of his political thought. It should be stressed, however, that they were by no means original to him. Knox's theory was a variation on the constitutionalist case for resistance developed by Lutheran theologians in the 1520s and 1530s. Radical French reformers like Pierre Viret and Theodore Beza had already learned to tap this tradition and Knox, together with his fellow Marian exiles, John Ponet and Christopher Goodman, was to do the same. A key document here was the Magdeburg *Confession* of 1550 which, drawn up by the city's Lutheran pastors to vindicate their defiance of the emperor, summed up many of the ideas on resistance promulgated by previous generations of Protestants in their struggles with Charles V. It was to prove a valuable source for militant Calvinists whose own leaders were unable to provide ideological backing for their revolutionary schemes. Although there is no proof that Knox was aware of its existence before 1564 (p. 204), the *Confession* does contain the key elements of the theory set out in the *Appellation*. As with the *First Blast*, however, it is important to distinguish between the general principles espoused by Knox and the particular circumstances in which he thought them applicable. For, whatever the source of his theory, at no point in the *Appellation* did he instruct the Scottish nobility to act on it against duly constituted authority. On the contrary, it was only the inferior magistrates of England who received such explicitly radical instructions.

What lay behind this distinction was the belief that, while England was a covenanted nation, Scotland was not. 'I fear not to affirm', Knox wrote in the *Appellation*, 'that the Gentiles (I mean every city, realm, province or nation amongst the Gentiles embracing Christ Jesus and His true religion) be bound to the same league and covenant that God made with His people Israel' (p. 103). In the case of England where, under Edward VI, the magistrates and people had 'solemnly avowed and promised to defend' God's truth, Knox insisted that the terms of such a covenant still applied. Consequently, he had no compunction about arguing that there it was 'lawful to punish to the death such as labour to subvert the true religion' – including 'Mary that Jezebel whom they call their queen' (p. 104). Unlike the English, however, the Scots had never officially embraced Protestantism and were not bound under the covenant in the same way. Knox's instructions to the Scottish nobility, therefore, fall far short of demanding the execution of their sovereign, Mary Stewart, or of her representative, Mary of Guise. In contrast to the remarks which immediately precede it, his advice to the Scottish nobility was aimed at the punishment, not of the crown, but only of the Catholic clergy: 'if ye know that in your hands God hath put the sword . . . then can ye not deny but that the punishment of obstinate and malapert idolaters (such as all your bishops be) doth appertain to your office' (pp. 104–5).

While it is true that there is no explicit mention of the covenant in the *First Blast*, the way it is used in the *Appellation* does help to resolve the puzzle of the different programmes of action which Knox set out for Scotland and England in the 1558 tracts. But where does it leave the claim that in the *Letter to the Commonalty* Knox developed a populist theory of resistance? It is certainly the case that his colleague, Christopher Goodman, propounded such a theory in his *How Superior Powers Ought to be Obeyed*, also published in Geneva in 1558. But there is nothing in the *Letter to the Commonalty* to suggest that Knox accepted Goodman's extreme views. Admittedly, there are undeveloped references in the *Appellation* to a people's obligation under the covenant to punish idolaters and revenge the injuries committed against God's majesty. But on each occasion Knox introduced a note of ambiguity by adding such qualifying phrases as 'according to the vocation of every man' (pp. 99–102). The implications of this are explained neither in the *Appellation* nor in the *Letter to the Commonalty*. The latter, in fact, goes no further than to advise the people to demand true preachers of their superiors, themselves to establish and defend them if necessary, and 'to withhold the fruits and profits' – the tithes – 'which your false bishops and clergy most injustly receive of you' (pp. 123–4). This hardly amounts to a radically populist theory of resistance. As with the other tracts of 1558, the *Letter to the Commonalty* suggests that Knox's Scottish agenda was far less extreme than is often supposed.

V

This interpretation of the 1558 tracts is borne out by the development of Knox's views after he returned to Scotland in May 1559 and threw his weight behind the Congregation's armed defiance of the regent. It was the marriage of Mary Stewart to the French dauphin in April 1558, followed six months later by the accession of Elizabeth to the English throne, which led Mary of Guise to abandon her conciliatory policy towards her Protestant subjects and which made some form of confrontation inevitable. But it was Knox who brought matters to a head when, immediately on his arrival in Scotland, he preached a sermon against idolatry which led to a wave of iconoclastic rioting. The rebellion had effectively begun and Knox had found an arena in which his theory of resistance could be tested in practice.

Although there is no proof that Knox wrote the series of public documents issued by the rebels in the course of 1559, the imprint of his ideas on the Congregation's propaganda is unmistakable. At the outset of the rebellion, a justification of resistance was deployed which, heavily reliant on the distinction between the office and the person of a prince, is strikingly similar to that developed in the *Appellation* (pp. 153–4). There was, however, no attempt to use this theory to justify the regent's overthrow. By August, in an attempt to broaden their appeal, the Congregation had abandoned their exclusively religious demands in favour of a wholesale indictment of her administration designed to tap the Scots' fear of French military occupation (pp. 159–65). But at the same time, in response to the regent's assertion that the preachers were encouraging disobedience to the 'higher powers', it was claimed that they had always maintained that 'they ought to be honoured, feared, obeyed, even for conscience sake, provided that they command nor require nothing expressly repugning to God's commandment and plain will, revealed in His Holy Word' (p. 166). Certainly, if wicked rulers commanded wicked things, then those who 'may and do bridle' them 'cannot be accused as resisters of the authority, which is God's good ordinance' (p. 166). But if this passage was written by Knox, it is as close as he came in 1559 to pressing on the Scots the extreme solution to the problem of ungodly rule which he had earlier urged on the English.

There were, of course, sound tactical reasons for sparing Mary of Guise the full rigour of the death sentence which he had pronounced against Mary Tudor. Not only would it have proved too extreme for the Scottish political community to stomach, but it would have done nothing to encourage Elizabeth to lend the Congregation her much-needed support. Consequently, when in October 1559 the Congregation formally 'suspended' Mary of Guise from the regency, they did so on the grounds that she was an enemy of the commonwealth rather than because she was a Catholic idolatress (pp. 171–4). Tactical considerations aside, however, Knox's attitude to Mary of Guise still appears remarkably moderate. In the debate among the Congregation which preceded her suspension, while agreeing with John Willock's views on the legitimacy of resistance, he added significant reservations: firstly, that her suspension should not detract from the obedience owed to Mary Stewart and her husband; secondly, that it should not be motivated by 'malice and private envy'; and thirdly, that 'upon her known and open repentance, and upon her conversion to the commonwealth and submission to the nobility, place should be granted unto her of regress to the same honours from the which, for just causes, she justly might be deprived' (pp. 170–1). While the second condition is reminiscent of Bullinger's fears regarding rebellion, the others reflect a pragmatism far removed from the imperatives which Knox thought binding on a covenanted nation.

Knox's attitude underwent a marked change, however, once the intervention of Elizabeth had ensured the Congregation's success and the Reformation Parliament of August 1560 had given a Protestant settlement statutory backing. Although never ratified by Mary Stewart, the acts renouncing papal authority, abolishing the mass and adopting a Protestant Confession of Faith were assumed to have the force of law. Scotland had publicly embraced the 'true religion' and, like England under Edward VI, had entered into a covenant with God. It is not surprising, therefore, that Mary Stewart's return to Scotland in August 1561 was met by Knox with a furious tirade against the reintroduction of the mass to the heart of the realm. It threatened apostasy on a scale equal only to that of England under Mary Tudor. It also led to the first of a series of 'reasonings' with the queen during which he refused to retract the arguments against female rule laid down in the *First Blast*. Although, as we have seen, he maintained that it was directed primarily against Mary Tudor, he otherwise conceded only that, if the realm found 'no inconvenience from the regiment of a woman', he would be 'as well content to live under your Grace as Paul was to live under Nero' (p. 176). Moreover, he added that, irrespective of their gender, when 'princes exceed their bounds . . . and do against that wherefore they should be obeyed, it is no doubt but that they may be resisted, even by power' (p. 178). Knox was thinking here of princes who actively persecuted the faithful. Nevertheless, it was an argument capable of much broader interpretation.

If Knox's interviews with the queen were intended to charm him into silence, they did not succeed. He continued to denounce her mass from his Edinburgh pulpit and to demand that the nobility deprive her of it. Indeed, preaching on Romans 13 during a meeting of the General Assembly in June 1564, he finally applied to Scotland the arguments which in the *Appellation* he had reserved only for England. When asked the following day to defend his views in a debate with William Maitland of Lethington, he reaffirmed that the distinction between the office and the person of a prince empowered men to 'oppone themselves to the fury and blind rage of princes; for so they resist not God, but the devil, who abuses the sword and authority of God' (p. 192). Now, however, he did not hesitate, as he had before, to apply this in Scotland to its fullest extent. Asked by Lethington 'whether that we may and ought to suppress the Queen's mass?', Knox replied without equivocation that 'Idolatry ought not [only] to be suppressed, but the idolater ought to die the death' (p. 195). As with 'the carnal seed of Abraham', in the time of their Egyptian bondage the Scots had been obliged only to avoid idolatry, but having taken full possession of the land of Canaan they were now duty bound to suppress it (pp. 196–7). Like the English before them, they had entered into a covenant with God which bound them to fulfil the divine injunction that idolaters – including royal idolaters – must die the death.

VI

It would have marked a fitting climax to Knox's career had Mary Stewart been deposed in 1567 for her manifest idolatry rather than her alleged adultery. As it was, though he advocated her execution from the pulpit, he was already on the political sidelines and was to remain there throughout the ensuing years of civil war, revising and extending his *History*, until his death in 1572. To expect consistency in a writer as unsystematic as Knox, whose works were all written in haste and in response to rapidly changing circumstances, would be to expect too much. Nevertheless, it is possible to discern a clear logic in the development of his ideas on rebellion and, just as importantly, in the limits of their application. Throughout his career, these limits were set, as his political vision was defined, by the intense biblicism which is the true hallmark of his thought. It is conceivable that, had he written his *Second Blast of the Trumpet*, he might have developed a secular theory of the accountability of kings to their subjects akin to that which he attributes in the General Assembly debate to his colleague John Craig (pp. 206–8). Yet it hardly seems likely. When a fellow member of the General Assembly, George Buchanan, published his theory of contractual monarchy in 1579, his solution to the problem posed by Romans 13 was to dismiss Paul's words as relevant only to the historical context in which they were written. Such a blatant disregard for the immutable will of God was wholly alien to the closed world of biblical precept and precedent inhabited by John Knox.

A note on the texts

General

In keeping with the requirements of the series, I have tried to produce versions of Knox's writings which are at once accessible to the modern reader and as faithful as that allows to the original texts. Thus, while spelling and punctuation have been modernised and new paragraphing has been introduced, I have not sought to eradicate all traces of sixteenth-century diction or vocabulary (a glossary of archaic and less familiar words will be found on pp. lxiv–lxviii). On occasions when sense demanded the insertion of words or phrases not in the original texts, these are indicated by square brackets. This extends to the sidenotes, though here some additional explanation is necessary. Biblical references have been standardised according to modern conventions. Versions of the Bible prior to the publication of the Geneva edition in 1560 were not divided into verses and Knox refers only to chapters. Where possible, and particularly where Knox is quoting, these references have been silently expanded to include both chapter and verse. (It should be borne in mind that Knox was often quoting – or paraphrasing – from memory, and his version of the text concerned is frequently inexact. Although no systematic analysis has been undertaken here, he is likely to have been most familiar with the Latin Vulgate version and the English Great Bible, first published in 1539, revised in 1540, and frequently reissued thereafter.) Where appropriate, I have also added in square brackets biblical references which Knox omitted. Generally Knox gives only abbreviated names and titles in his references to classical and patristic sources; these have been silently expanded according to the format of the editions cited in the list of abbreviations and references. Major discrepancies with these editions have been footnoted. Otherwise footnotes have been kept to a minimum, although additional information is included in the biographical notes.

The Tracts of 1558

All the tracts printed in Part I were published in Geneva in 1558. *The Appellation* and *The Letter to the Commonalty* (including the summary of the proposed *Second Blast of the Trumpet*) formed a single volume together with another pamphlet not reprinted here by Knox's fellow Marian exile Anthony Gilby (*An Admonition to England and Scotland to call them to repentance* (see Laing, vol. IV, pp. 541–71)). Only the *Letter to the Regent* identifies the printers – Jacques Poullain and Antoine Reboul, French Protestant refugees who worked together in Geneva in 1557–8 – but common initial letters and other internal evidence suggest that all the tracts were products of the same press. The versions printed here are based on the original editions of 1558 (STC nos. 15063 (*The Appellation*, etc.), 15067 (*Letter to the Regent*) and 15070 (*The First Blast of the Trumpet*)).

Knox and Scotland

All but one (the letter to the Scottish nobility of 17 December 1557) of the texts in Part II are extracted from Knox's *History of the Reformation in Scotland* and are based on the earliest surviving manuscript of the *History*, now generally known as the Laing MS, in Edinburgh University Library (Laing MSS, III, 210). The MS, written by a number of scribes between 1566 and 1571 but bearing many indications of Knox's personal supervision and/or dictation, formed the basis of the version of the *History* printed in Laing, vols. I–II, and is described in detail in Dickinson, vol. I, pp. xcv-cix. Generally speaking, Laing's transcription is remarkably accurate and there are only minor errors (invariably repeated, incidentally, in Dickinson's modernised version) which have been silently corrected here. The MS contains a number of sidenotes which refer to the time of writing rather than to the time of the events being described; these have been omitted here to avoid unnecessary explanatory footnotes. In the latter part of the MS – the account of the General Assembly debate of 1564 – where the hand deteriorates markedly and there are many more scribal errors and omissions, I have relied on Laing's collation of this manuscript with later manuscript and printed versions (these are described in detail in Laing, vol. I, pp. xxix–xliii); words and phrases derived from sources other than the Laing MS have been placed in square brackets. The letter from Knox to the Protestant nobility of 17 December 1557, for which no manuscript original appears to have survived, is a modernised version of the text as printed in Laing, vol. IV, pp. 276–86.

Further reading

The standard edition of Knox's writings is *The Works of John Knox*, ed. David Laing (6 vols., Wodrow Society, 1846–64). Though a remarkable achievement for its time, a modern critical edition of Knox's complete works is badly needed. His *History of the Reformation in Scotland* is available in a fine modernised version by William Croft Dickinson (2 vols., London and New York, 1949), but the tracts of 1558 are ill-served by Marvin Breslow's edition of *The Political Writings of John Knox* (Folger Books; Washington, 1985) where the transcription of the texts is riddled with inaccuracies and the critical apparatus is at best sketchy. For a provisional attempt to catalogue all Knox's publications, see Ian Hazlett, 'A Working Bibliography of Writings by John Knox' in Robert V. Schnucker (ed.), *Calviniana: Ideas and Influence of Jean Calvin* (Kirksville, Mo., 1988), pp. 185–93.

There are numerous biographies of Knox, though none can be considered definitive. Among the best are Eustace Percy, *John Knox*, 2nd edn (London, 1964); Jasper Ridley, *John Knox* (Oxford, 1968); and W. Stanford Reid, *Trumpeter of God: A Biography of John Knox* (New York, 1974). The only full-length study of his thought as a whole is Richard G. Kyle's useful if rather mechanical *The Mind of John Knox* (Lawrence, Kansas, 1984), but there is also much to be learned from the series of essays by Richard L. Greaves (most of them previously published elsewhere) brought together in his *Theology and Revolution in the Scottish Reformation: Studies in the Thought of John Knox* (Grand Rapids, Michigan, 1980).

Knox's views on resistance feature prominently in Quentin Skinner's magisterial survey, *The Foundations of Modern Political Thought* (2 vols., Cambridge, 1979), vol. II, chapter 7. But for a recent corrective to Skinner's exaggerated view of Knox's radicalism, see Robert M. Kingdon, 'Calvinism and Resistance Theory 1550–1580', in J. H. Burns and Mark Goldie (eds.), *The Cambridge History of Political Thought 1450–1700* (Cambridge, 1991), pp. 194–200. Both Kyle and Greaves discuss Knox's political views at some length in the works cited above, but it is still well worth consulting older studies such as John R. Gray, 'The Political Theory of John Knox', *Church History*, 8 (1939), 132–42, and particularly two articles by J. H. Burns: 'The Political Ideas of the Scottish Reformation', *Aberdeen University Review*, 36 (1955–6) 251–68, and most useful of all 'John Knox and Revolution 1558', *History Today*, 8 (1958), 565–73. My own understanding of the development of Knox's views on rebellion was first expressed in an article entitled 'Knox, Resistance and the Moral Imperative', *History of Political Thought*, 1 (1980–1), 411–36, but has since been considerably influenced and refined by the approach adopted in Jane Dawson's important article 'The Two John Knoxes: England, Scotland and the 1558 Tracts', *Journal of Ecclesiastical History*, 42 (1991), 555–76.

Two other articles by Jane Dawson are also useful in establishing the immediate context in which Knox was writing and in providing a basis of comparison with his fellow exiles: 'Revolutionary Conclusions: The Case of the Marian Exiles', *History of Political Thought*, 11 (1990), 257–72, and 'Resistance and Revolution in Sixteenth-Century Thought: The Case of Christopher Goodman', in J. Van Den Berg and P. G. Hoftijzer (eds.), *Church, Change and Revolution* (Leiden, 1991), pp. 69–79. Constance Jordan, 'Women's Rule in Sixteenth-Century British Political Thought', *Renaissance Quarterly*, 40 (1987), 421–51, discusses the debate on women's rule to which Knox's *First Blast* was an important contribution, while two articles by Richard G. Kyle explore other aspects of Knox's thought touched on in the introduction: 'The Church–State Patterns in the Thought of John Knox', *Journal of Church and State*, 30 (1988), 71–87, and 'John Knox's Methods of Biblical Interpretation: An Important Source of his Intellectual Radicalness', *Journal of Religious Studies*, 12 (1986), 57–70.

The Scottish Reformation is best approached through Jenny Wormald's lively treatment of the period in *Court, Kirk and Community:*

Scotland 1470–1625 (London, 1981) and Ian Cowan's duller but solid study *The Scottish Reformation: Church and Society in Sixteenth-Century Scotland* (London, 1982). Generally speaking, Scottish historians of the period have concentrated on institutions rather than ideology, but James Kirk's collection of essays *Patterns of Reform: Continuity and Change in the Reformation Kirk* (Edinburgh, 1989) contains much of interest on both, while the Congregation's propaganda campaign of 1559 is analysed in my 'Covenant and Commonweal: The Language of Politics in Reformation Scotland', in Norman Macdougall (ed.), *Church, Politics and Society: Scotland 1408–1929* (Edinburgh, 1983), pp. 97–126.

Principal events in Knox's life

1514 Probable date of birth, Haddington, East Lothian.
1542 Death of James V in December and accession of Mary Stewart to Scottish throne; regency of Arran.
1543 George Wishart returns to Scotland.
1546 Wishart arrested and executed.
1547 Knox takes refuge in St Andrews castle and preaches his first Protestant sermon in April; castle falls to the French in July and Knox is consigned to a French galley.
1549 Released from imprisonment and settles in England; minister at Berwick.
1551 Minister at Newcastle.
1552 Moves to London under Northumberland's patronage; appointed royal chaplain and offered bishopric of Rochester. Dispute over Prayer Book.
1553 Death of Edward VI, brief 'reign' of Protestant successor, Lady Jane Grey, followed by recognition of Mary Tudor as queen.
1554 Knox flies to Dieppe and then travels to Geneva and Zurich before settling in Frankfort where he is appointed minister of the English congregation. Writes *A Godly Letter of Warning* and *A Faithful Admonition* to his former English congregations.
1555 Forced to leave Frankfort following a dispute over the liturgy amongst the English exiles; settles briefly in Geneva where he is appointed pastor of the English congregation there, before

returning to Berwick to be married; begins improvised mission in Scotland.

1556 Charged with heresy in Scotland and forced to return to Geneva in July, but addresses *Letter to the Regent*, Mary of Guise, in May.

1557 Receives request from Scottish nobility in March asking him to return to Scotland; travels to Dieppe but receives further letters in October that delay his departure.

1558 Returns to Geneva where the *First Blast* is published in the spring, followed by the revised version of the *Letter to the Regent* and the *Appellation* and the *Letter to the Commonalty*. Receives further request that he return to Scotland following the marriage of Mary Stewart to the dauphin in April. Travels to Dieppe where he learns of the death of Mary Tudor and the accession of Elizabeth in England in November.

1559 Refused entry into England, he returns to Scotland where his preaching against idolatry precipitates the outbreak of the Congregation's rebellion in May.

1560 Elizabeth's intervention in Scotland in March is rapidly followed by the death of Mary of Guise in June, the signing of the Treaty of Edinburgh in July and the meeting of the Reformation Parliament in August.

1561 Return of Mary Stewart to Scotland in August; Knox, principal minister in Edinburgh, preaches against her mass and has personal 'interview' with the queen.

1564 Meeting of General Assembly at which the question of resistance is debated at length.

1565 Marriage of Mary Stewart to Lord Darnley.

1567 Murder of Darnley; marriage of Mary Stewart to earl of Bothwell; revolution of Confederate Lords leads to the queen's imprisonment.

1568 Mary Stewart escapes confinement but flees to England on losing battle of Langside.

1572 Knox dies in Edinburgh on 24 November.

Biographical notes

AARON. Elder brother of MOSES and high priest or spiritual leader of the Jews. Two of his sons, NADAB and ABIHU, died as a result of transgressing the temple laws, but a third, ELEAZAR, continued the priestly function in Aaron's family. In the *Appellation*, Knox was concerned to argue that Aaron's priestly authority was subordinate to the 'civil' power of Moses.

ABEL. Second son of ADAM and EVE and brother of CAIN. According to Genesis 4, he was a shepherd and his offering of the firstlings of his flock was accepted by God. He was subsequently murdered by his brother whose own offering was rejected.

ABIATHAR. High priest during the reign of DAVID who conspired to prevent SOLOMON succeeding him as king and was expelled from office, thus ending the line of ELI. In the *Appellation*, Knox cites Abiathar's expulsion from office as an example of the clergy's subjection to the civil power.

ABIHU. Son of AARON who, with his brother NADAB, transgressed the temple laws and died as a result.

ABRAHAM. Descendent of Shem and son of Terah. The ancestor of the Jews and founder of Jewish monotheism. His faith in God was tested and proved by his willingness to sacrifice his son ISAAC.

ADAM. The first man who, at the prompting of EVE, ate the fruit of the tree of knowledge and suffered expulsion from paradise. Father of CAIN and ABEL.

AEGESIPPUS. See HEGESIPPUS.

AHAB. Seventh king of Israel (*c.*874–852 BC), his reign was distinguished by the idolatry encouraged by his wife JEZEBEL. After his own death in battle against the Syrians, his wife and family were destroyed by JEHU.

AHIMELECH. Priest of Nob, slain by Doeg on the orders of SAUL for his support of DAVID.

AMAZIAH. Son of JOASH whom he succeeded as king of Judah (800 BC). Defeat at the hands of the Israelites led to the plundering of the temple and to his own capture. He was eventually assassinated.

AMBROSE, St (*c.*339–97). Bishop of Milan and theologian who exerted enormous moral and political authority over the developing Christian church and its relations with the Roman empire. Knox quotes selectively from his writings to support his case against female rulers in the *First Blast* and alludes in the *Appellation* to his importance in redefining the relationship between church and state.

ANANIAS. Member of the primitive church of Jerusalem whose contribution to the common fund was less than he pretended. Both he and his wife, Sapphira, fell dead when their dishonesty was exposed.

ARGYLL, Archibald Campbell, fourth earl of (d. 1558). Leading Scottish Protestant nobleman with whom Knox stayed at Castle Campbell during his mission of 1555–6. He was subsequently among the signatories of the First Band in December 1557 and continued to press reforming policies on Mary of GUISE until his death the following year.

ARGYLL, Archibald Campbell, fifth earl of (*c.*1538–73). Eldest son of Archibald Campbell, fourth earl of ARGYLL, and like his father a staunch supporter of the Protestant cause. He first made contact with Knox in 1555 and, as Lord Lorne, was among those who invited him to return to Scotland in March 1557 and was one of the signatories of the First Band in December 1557. On his father's death in 1558, he inherited the earldom of Argyll and, after initially seeking to negotiate a peaceful settlement on behalf of Mary of GUISE, joined the Congregation in rebellion in May 1559. Although he remained a Protestant, he became disillusioned with the pro-English policies pursued by MORAY and LETHINGTON after 1561, and fought for MARY STEWART during the civil war precipitated by her deposition in 1567.

ARISTOTLE (384–324 BC). After Plato, the most famous of all the Greek philosophers and, rediscovered by Western European thinkers in the eleventh and twelfth centuries, providing the basis of late medieval scholasticism. Knox could hardly have been unaware of his writings, but makes only passing reference in the *First Blast* to his criticisms of Spartan women in the *Politics*.

ARIUS (*c.*250–336). Christian priest whose denial of the full divinity of Christ gave rise to what became known as the Arian heresy. His teachings were condemned by the council of Nicaea in 325.

ARRAN, James Hamilton, second earl of. See CHÂTELHERAULT.

ASA. Third king of Judah (*c.*911–870 BC). His religious zeal was made apparent in his cleansing of the land of idolatry and his willingness to remove his mother, Maachah, from the queenship for making an idol.

ATHALIAH. Daughter of AHAB, her son, Ahaziah, was killed by JEHU. In order to retain power for herself, she in turn attempted to murder all her grandchildren, though the year-old baby JOASH escaped by hiding in the temple. Athaliah's six-year reign was finally brought to an end when the high priest JEHOIADA proclaimed Joash king and had his grandmother executed. Often bracketed with JEZEBEL, Athaliah was for Knox a prime example of wicked female rule.

ATHANASIUS, St (*c.*298–373). Bishop of Alexandria, theologian and church father. In the *Appellation*, Knox alludes to his determination to ensure adherence to the decrees of the council of Nicaea despite the rival claims of such councils as the pro-Arian synod of Tyre of 335.

AUGUSTINE, St (354–430). Bishop of Hippo and greatest of the early Christian theologians. His voluminous writings had an incalculable influence on the development of Christian thought in the West. Knox quotes selectively from his writings in the *First Blast* in support of his arguments against female rule and invokes his authority in the *Appellation* to persuade the nobility that they have power in ecclesiastical affairs.

AYLMER, John (1521–94). English Protestant and one-time tutor to Lady Jane GREY who was forced to flee to the continent on the failure of Wyatt's rebellion in 1554. While in exile in Strasburg and then Zurich, he wrote a reply to Knox's *First Blast* entitled *An Harborowe for Faithfull and Trewe Subjectes*, published in Strasburg in 1559. On his return to England following the accession of ELIZABETH, he was closely involved in working out the new ecclesiastical settlement and finally was consecrated bishop of London in 1577.

AZARIAH. High priest who withstood the attempts of King UZZIAH to offer incense in the temple.

BAAL. Ancient Hebrew deity whose cult, despite being repeatedly outlawed as idolatrous, rivalled the worship of Yahweh throughout Israelite history.

BAASHA. King of Israel (*c.*900–880 BC), he seized the throne after assassinating the son of JEROBOAM whose entire family he exterminated. Despite this, however, he continued the idolatrous practices of his predecessors and incurred the wrath of JEHU the prophet who foretold his imminent destruction as well as that of his son ELAH and his whole house.

BARAK. Military commander who led the Israelites to victory against the Canaanite general, SISERA. He consented to act only on condition that DEBORAH accompanied him into battle, for which reason he was told that not he, but a woman, would finally kill Sisera.

BARON, James. Prominent Edinburgh merchant and regular member of the town council. Together with James SIM, in 1557 he delivered a letter to Knox in Geneva inviting him to return to Scotland. He remained a prominent member of the Protestant party in Edinburgh until his death in 1569.

BARUCH. Faithful attendant (or, as Knox preferred, scribe) of JEREMIAH who wrote down his master's prophecies and read them to the people. Several apocryphal books are attributed to him.

BASILIUS MAGNUS. Basil of Caesarea (*c.*329–79), called 'the Great'. Bishop of Caesarea and Christian theologian, his writings had a far-reaching impact on both Eastern and Western Christianity.

BEATON, David (*c.*1494–1546). Leading Scottish Catholic at the court of JAMES V, he was made a cardinal in 1538 and archbishop of St Andrews the following year. On the king's death in 1542, he led the pro-French and papal party in opposition to the anglophile policies pursued by the Regent ARRAN and was successful in orchestrating the Scottish parliament's rejection of the Treaties of Greenwich in 1543. His persecution of Protestants and execution of George WISHART in 1546 earned him the undying enmity of reformers like Knox and led to his assassination by a group of Fife lairds in his castle at St Andrews in May 1546.

BEATON, James, archbishop of Glasgow (*c.*1523–1603). A nephew of Cardinal David BEATON whom he succeeded as commendator of Arbroath before becoming archbishop of Glasgow in 1551. A close ally of Mary of GUISE (it was in his presence that she mocked Knox's *Letter to the Regent* as a 'pasquil'), he supported her during the Congregation's rebellion of 1559 and, following the triumph of the reformers, acted as an agent in France for both MARY STEWART and James VI.

BENJAMIN. Youngest son of JACOB who gave his name to the tribe of Benjaminites (or Benjamites, as Knox prefers). Renowned for courage and clannishness, the Benjaminites resisted the national demand for justice in the matter of the Levite's concubine with disastrous consequences and subsequently they gave allegiance to the kings of Judah.

BUCER, Martin (1491–1551). German Protestant reformer who exerted a formative influence on the reformed faith from his base at Strasburg. In the 1530s and 1540s, he sought unsuccessfully to mediate between Catholics and Protestants and in 1549 he moved to England at the invitation of Thomas CRANMER. Although invoked by LETHINGTON in the General Assembly debate of 1564 in support of non-resistance to magistrates, Bucer's views on the duties of an inferior magistracy appear similar to those propounded by Knox in his *Appellation*.

BUCHANAN, George (1506–82). The most distinguished Scottish humanist of the sixteenth century, he spent most of his career on the continent, particularly France, before returning to Scotland in 1561 very possibly in the entourage of MARY STEWART. On his return, he converted to Protestantism and held office in the reformed kirk. Following the queen's deposition in 1567, he acted as tutor to James VI and in his *De jure regni apud Scotos* (1579) and *Rerum Scoticarum historia* (1582) set out a radical political theory of resistance to tyranny.

BULLINGER, Heinrich (1504–75). Swiss–German Protestant reformer who succeeded Zwingli as pastor in Zurich in 1531 and remained there until his own death. An enormously productive and influential theologian, his opinions were generally moderate and he made great efforts to build bridges between the various Protestant churches.

CAIN. First son of ADAM and EVE and brother of ABEL. According to Genesis 4, he was a farmer and his offering of the fruit of the ground was rejected by God. He subsequently murdered his brother. God punished him by sending him to become a wanderer; to prevent him being slain, a 'mark' was placed upon his forehead.

CALVIN, John (1509–64). French theologian, author of *The Insti-*

tutes of the Christian Religion (1536) and one of the most influential Protestant reformers of the sixteenth century. Exiled from France, he eventually settled in Geneva where he established a godly regime which Knox considered 'the most perfect school of Christ that ever was in earth since the days of the Apostles'. Knox's theological thinking owed a great deal to Calvin, but their views on the legitimacy of resistance gradually diverged, the more cautious Calvin distancing himself from the revolutionary implications of works like the *First Blast*.

CARDAILLAC-SARLABOUS, Corbeyran de (*c.*1515–84). Gascon military officer who commanded the French garrison at Dunbar during the Congregation's rebellion. He is later alleged to have participated in the assassination of Admiral Coligny during the St Bartholemew's Day massacre of 24 August 1572.

CHÂTELHERAULT, James Hamilton, second earl of Arran and duke of (*c.*1516–75). Heir presumptive to the Scottish throne, he was appointed regent or governor in 1543. His pursuit of pro-English and Protestant policies brought him into conflict with Mary of GUISE and Cardinal BEATON and, under the influence of his half-brother, John HAMILTON, he was led to abandon the reforming cause. Created duke of Châtelherault by the French king in 1549, he was forced to resign the regency in favour of Mary of Guise in 1554. He joined the Congregation in September 1559, but played no very distinguished part in the rebellion. Seeing his own dynastic ambitions thwarted by MARY STEWART's marriage to Lord Darnley in 1565, he joined MORAY in an unsuccessful rebellion which led to his exile until 1569.

CHRYSOSTOM (*c.*354–407). Bishop of Constantinople, father of the Eastern church, orator and biblical commentator. Knox makes selective use of his writings in arguing against female rule in the *First Blast* and again in the *Appellation* in support of the view that the clergy are subject to the authority of the civil power.

CICERO, Marcus Tullius (106–43 BC). Lawyer, politician and leading figure of the Roman republic. His writings were enormously influential in the middle ages and particularly during the Renaissance when his moral and rhetorical works proved increasingly popular. Their impact on Knox was minimal, however, and he makes only one casual reference to *De officiis* in the *First Blast*.

CIRCE. Sorceress of classical mythology whose magic potions

turned Ulysses and his companions into swine. Knox alludes to the legend in the *First Blast.*

COCHRANE, Thomas (or Robert). Familiar of James III of Scotland who was allegedly hanged by the nobility at Lauder Bridge in 1482 for dispensing evil counsel to the king.

CONIAH. See JEHOIACHIN.

CRAIG, John (1512–1600). Scottish Dominican friar who in the 1530s fell under suspicion of heresy and fled first to England and then to Rome. He subsequently in the 1550s became rector of the Dominican convent at Bologna, but his reforming tendencies led him to be condemned to death for heresy. He escaped and returned to Scotland in 1560 where two years later he became Knox's colleague as minister in Edinburgh. At the 1564 General Assembly, he gave an account of a disputation he had attended at Bologna in which the right of the people to depose a prince was upheld. Later in his career, however, he was able sufficiently to moderate his opinions to win the trust of James VI.

CRANMER, Thomas (1489–1556). Cambridge theologian whose support for HENRY VIII's divorce proceedings led to his appointment as archbishop of Canterbury in 1533. His increasingly Protestant outlook found favour under EDWARD VI, but fell foul of the Catholic regime of MARY TUDOR after her accession in 1553. In 1556, he was burned as a heretic.

CYPRIAN, St (*c.*205–58). Bishop of Carthage and theologian who suffered martyrdom under the Emperor Valerian. In the *Letter to the Commonalty*, Knox cites him along with TERTULLIAN and LACTANTIUS in support of the view that antiquity and custom cannot justify religious error.

CYRUS II (the Great). King of Persia (*c.*559–530 BC) and, through his conquests, founder of the Persian empire. Generally perceived as a sympathetic ruler, having subdued Babylonia, he allowed exiled Jews to return to their homeland and to restore the temple.

DANIEL. Prophet of the sixth century BC who served in the government of NEBUCHADNEZZAR (who took him as a captive to Babylon) and DARIUS. His prophetic and apocalyptic visions, contained in the book which bears his name, appealed greatly to Knox.

DARIUS. In the *Letter to the Regent*, Knox mistakenly associates DANIEL the prophet with the reign of Darius the Persian emperor

(423–408 BC). In fact, it was Darius the Mede who ruled the kingdom of Chaldea in the early sixth century BC and employed Daniel in his government.

DAVID. Son of Jesse and king of Israel (1010–970 BC) in succession to SAUL who pursued him relentlessly for displacing him on the throne. Thought to have been the author of the Psalms as well as the ancestor of Jesus.

DEBORAH. Wife of Lapidoth. Prophetess who commanded BARAK to lead the Israelites against the oppressive rule of JABIN and SISERA. At Barak's insistence, she accompanied him in battle and the result was a crushing defeat for Sisera and the liberation of the Israelites. In the *First Blast*, Knox insists that, while she was a great prophetess, she wielded no temporal authority over the people of Israel.

DONATUS. Fourth-century Numidian bishop (d. 355) who gave his name to the Donatist movement in the North African church. Despite both imperial persecution and the opposition of Christian theologians such as AUGUSTINE, the Donatists' insistence on the purity and holiness of the church and priesthood remained influential until the seventh century.

DOUGLAS, John (*c.* 1494–1574). Rector of St Andrews University 1551–73 and a convert to Protestantism. He supported the rebellion of the Congregation in 1559 and was appointed along with Knox and others to draw up the *First Book of Discipline.* He was present at the General Assembly debate of 1564 where, like John WINRAM, he argued that the nobility might oppose the queen in defence of their religion, but doubted whether they might deprive her of the mass by force.

EBEDMELECH. An Ethiopian servant of ZEDEKIAH, king of Judah, who rescued JEREMIAH when he was threatened with death by the king and his council. As a reward for his faith, his life was spared when Jerusalem was sacked by NEBUCHADNEZZAR IN 587 BC.

EDWARD VI (1537–53), king of England (1547–53) in succession to his father, HENRY VIII. Scholarly, intelligent and with pronounced Protestant leanings, Edward was viewed favourably by reformers (including Knox) in search of a 'godly prince'. Their hopes were only partially fulfilled, however, for (still a minor) Edward's reign was dominated by factional struggles. The regency council which governed in his name was led initially by his uncle Edward Seymour, duke of SOMERSET, but came to be dominated by John Dudley, duke of NORTHUMBERLAND. The king's health, never robust, began to fail in 1552 and shortly before his death he was persuaded by Northumberland to exclude his half-sisters MARY and ELIZABETH TUDOR from the succession in favour of Northumberland's daughter-in-law, Lady Jane GREY.

ELAH. Son of BAASHA whom he succeeded as king of Israel. His brief reign of two years (880–878 BC) ended when he was assassinated during a drunken orgy. Following his death, in fulfilment of the prophecy of JEHU, the whole house of Baasha was destroyed.

ELEAZAR. Third son of AARON whom he succeeded as chief priest after his elder brothers, NADAB and ABIHU, suffered death for transgressing the temple laws. Frequently associated with MOSES and later JOSHUA as a leader of the Israelites.

ELI. Priest in Israel for forty years whose long service was marred only by the scandalous conduct of his sons which led to a curse being placed on them and their descendants.

ELIJAH. Prophet of Israel in the ninth century BC. His denunciation of the worship of BAAL in the reign of AHAB brought him into conflict with the latter's wife, JEZEBEL.

ELISHA. Prophet of Israel in the ninth century BC, a younger contemporary of ELIJAH whose mantle he inherited. He was responsible for commissioning JEHU to destroy the house of AHAB and his wife JEZEBEL.

ELIZABETH TUDOR (1533–1603). Daughter of HENRY VIII and Anne Boleyn, she succeeded to the English throne on the death of her half-sister, MARY TUDOR, in 1558. Brought up a Protestant, she reversed her predecessor's religious policies, but remained deeply suspicious of the radical wing of the Protestant movement. The publication of the *First Blast* on the eve of her accession did nothing to endear Knox to her and, for this and other reasons, she intervened on behalf of the Congregation in 1560 only with great reluctance. Although her intervention did not result in the Anglo-Scottish union looked for by many Scottish Protestants, it did prove decisive in ensuring the establishment of a reformed church in Scotland.

EPHRAIM. Second son of JOSEPH who gave his name to one of the tribes of Israel. He and his elder brother MANASSEH were both blessed by JACOB, but Ephraim received the blessing from Jacob's right hand, signifying the greater prosperity of his descendants.

ERSKINE, John, of Dun (*c.* 1508–91). Leading Scottish Protestant laird, an early and steadfast convert to the reformed cause. Knox stayed with him at Dun in the Mearns in 1555 and he was among those who wrote to Knox in March 1557 inviting him to return to Scotland. One of the five signatories of the First Band of December 1557, he played a leading role in the rebellion of the Congregation in 1559. He was ordained to the ministry in 1561 and subsequently remained an active, though moderating, influence in the reformed kirk for many years.

ESAU. The elder of the twin sons of ISAAC. Although his father's favourite, he was defrauded of his birthright by his brother JACOB. Subsequently, he fathered the Edomites whose relations with the seed of Jacob, the Israelites, were always strained.

EVE. The first woman, wife of ADAM and cause of the fall of man. She succumbed to the serpent's wiles, ate of the fruit of the tree of knowledge and persuaded her husband to do the same. As a consequence, both were expelled from paradise, but God further punished Eve by condemning her to bear children in pain and to be ruled over by Adam.

EZEKIEL. Prophet of the early sixth century BC and author of the Book of Ezekiel. Deported from Jerusalem when NEBUCHADNEZZAR took the city in 597 BC, most of his prophecies were uttered in exile and concern the iniquities of the corrupt and rebellious house of Israel. Along with his close contemporary JEREMIAH, he was probably Knox's favourite and most frequently cited Old Testament prophet.

FESTUS. Porcius Festus, procurator of Judaea, who according to Acts 24–26 was prevailed upon by the Jews to try St PAUL for heresy and then to hand him over to the Jewish authorities for retrial and almost certain death. In the *Appellation*, with his own case in mind, Knox makes much of Paul's appeal to the civil authority of Caesar to protect him from the high priests of Jerusalem.

GAD. Seventh son of JACOB who gave his name to one of the twelve tribes of Israel.

GIDEON. Judge who delivered Israel from the Midianites. A humble man, he refused the people's offer of the kingship.

GLENCAIRN, Alexander Cunningham, fifth earl of (d. 1574). Prominent Scottish Protestant nobleman and among the first to lend his support to the Congregation at the outset of the rebellion of 1559. He first made contact with Knox during the latter's visit to Scotland in 1555–6, was among those who invited him to return to Scotland in March 1557 and was one of the five signatories of the First Band. Subsequently, he was one of the leaders of the Confederate Lords who overthrew MARY STEWART in 1567.

GOODMAN, Christopher (*c.*1520–1603). English reformer who became professor of divinity at Oxford in 1548. On MARY TUDOR's accession in 1553 he fled to the continent and eventually settled in Geneva where, along with Knox, he became pastor of the English congregation in 1555. In 1558, the same year that saw the publication of Knox's major political writings, Goodman published his *How Superior Powers Ought to be Obeyed* in which he advocated, in terms more radical than anything penned by his Scottish colleague, popular rebellion against ungodly rule. His extreme views prevented his return to England on the accession of ELIZABETH and he spent six years in Scotland and four more in Ireland before returning permanently to England in 1570.

GRATIAN of Bologna. Italian canon lawyer who compiled (*c.*1140) the first systematically organised collection of ecclesiastical law entitled the *Concordia discordantium canonum* (Concord of discordant canons), better known as Gratian's *Decretals*. It came to form the first part of the body of canon law (*Corpus iuris canonici*) to which the *Decretals* of Pope GREGORY IX were also added.

GREGORY IX, Pope (1227–41). Celebrated for his continuation of the papal struggle with the Holy Roman Empire, Gregory was also a distinguished canon lawyer and commissioned the first complete and authoritative codification of ecclesiastical law. His *Decretals*, added to those of GRATIAN, came to comprise a substantial part of the official body of ecclesiastical law, the *Corpus iuris canonici*.

GREY, Lady Jane (1537–54). Known to Knox as Jane Dudley because of her forced and unhappy marriage to Guildford Dudley, son of the duke of NORTHUMBERLAND. A great-granddaughter of Henry VII as well as being a pious Protestant, her father-in-law proclaimed her queen on the death of EDWARD VI in 1553. Her 'reign' lasted only nine days and she was executed by the Marian regime after the failure of Wyatt's rebellion in 1554.

GUISE, Charles of (1524–74). Brother of Mary of GUISE and, from 1547, cardinal of Lorraine. Influential figure at the court of

Henry II of France whom he encouraged in his anti-Protestant policies and in his support for his sister's pro-French and Catholic regime in Scotland.

Guise, Mary of (1515–60). Daughter of Claude, duke of Guise, married James V in 1538. On her husband's death in 1542, following hard on the heels of that of her two baby sons in 1541, her daughter Mary Stewart succeeded to the Scottish throne when still barely one week old. The dowager queen played an active part in the political manoeuvrings which ensued and succeeded in maintaining the Scottish kingdom's traditional alliances with France and the papacy despite the close attention and military intervention of England. In 1554 she was formally appointed governor on behalf of her daughter during the latter's continued absence in France. The recipient of Knox's *Letter to the Regent* in 1558, she was also the 'authority' against whom the Protestant Congregation rebelled in 1559.

Hamilton, Gavin (*c.*1515–71). Made commendator of Kilwinning in 1550 and a lord of session in 1555. As a member of the Hamilton family, he was held in deep suspicion by Protestants like Knox and played a cautious role in the rebellion of 1559–60. He was later to be a prominent supporter of Mary Stewart during the civil war which followed her deposition in 1567 and was killed during a skirmish with the King's Men in 1571.

Hamilton, John (1512–71). A bastard son of James Hamilton, first earl of Arran, he succeeded David Beaton as archbishop of St Andrews in 1547 and was a major influence over his half-brother, James Hamilton, second earl of Arran and duke of Châtelherault. During the Congregation's rebellion of 1559, he was a cautious supporter of Mary of Guise and tried unsuccessfully to prevent Châtelherault from joining the Protestants. Subsequently, he was imprisoned by Mary Stewart in 1563 for saying mass, but joined her party after her deposition in 1567. He was hanged after the fall of Dumbarton Castle in 1571.

Hay, George (*c.*1530–88). Scottish Protestant minister who endorsed Knox's views on the legitimacy of resistance during the General Assembly debate of 1564. In 1562, together with Knox, he had been involved in a celebrated disputation with Quintin Kennedy, abbot of Crossraguel, and was subsequently, in 1576, engaged in further controversy with the Jesuit, James Tyrie.

HEGESIPPUS or Aegesippus. Supposed author of a fourth-century Latin adaptation of the *Jewish War* of JOSEPHUS. The seven books of Josephus are compressed into five, but more information is added from Josephus's *Jewish Antiquities* and from other Roman historians. Largely concerned with the destruction of Jerusalem in AD 70, the edition used here (Paris, 1511) has the running title *Excidii Hierosolymitani*.

HENRY II (1519–59), king of France (1547–59). Son of Francis I whom he succeeded in 1547. He continued his father's policy of war with Spain while pursuing an increasingly repressive policy towards Protestantism in France. In both respects, he was aided by the Guise family, whom he raised to favour and who helped to ensure that France's (and their own) interests in Scotland were not forgotten. In 1558, MARY STEWART married the French king's son and heir, Francis, and the latter succeeded to the throne the following year when Henry was accidentally killed during a tournament held to celebrate the signing of the Treaty of Cateau-Cambrésis which had at last brought Franco-Spanish hostilities to a close.

HENRY VIII (1491–1547), king of England (1509–47). The latter half of Henry's reign was dominated by his obsession with producing a male heir to the throne. The refusal of the papacy to grant him a divorce from Catherine of Aragon (who had borne him only a daughter, MARY) led to his repudiation of papal authority and assumption of the headship of the church in England. By subsequent marriages, he had two children, ELIZABETH and EDWARD. His break with Rome led to increasing Anglo-Scottish tension which the death of JAMES V in 1542 promised to resolve through the marriage of Prince Edward to MARY STEWART, the infant queen of Scots. In retrospect, reformers such as Knox were to lament the breakdown of the marriage negotiations as a lost opportunity to create a Protestant British kingdom. In 1543, however, after initially agreeing to the proposed marriage, the Scots almost immediately reneged. Henry vented his rage in a series of punitive military campaigns known as the 'Rough Wooing', but despite (or because of) these military reprisals, the majority of Scots remained unreconciled to the prospect of union with England and married their queen into the French royal house.

HEROD. Herod Antipas, son of Herod the Great on whose behalf he ruled the Galilean portion of his father's kingdom. Chiefly remembered for his part in the execution of JOHN the Baptist and for his meeting with Jesus when the latter was sent to him by Pontius Pilate for judgement.

HEZEKIAH. Fourteenth king of Judah (*c.*729–700 BC). Of outstanding piety himself, his reign was marked by successful attempts to reform religious practices and re-establish true worship. Like JOSIAH and JEHOSHAPHAT, he was for Knox a model of godly kingship.

HILKIAH. High priest in the reign of JOSIAH who found an ancient book of the law which was presented to HULDAH the prophetess for her judgement. Hilkiah was later involved in putting Josiah's religious reforms into effect.

HOSEA. Prophet of Israel in the late eighth century BC and author of the Book of Hosea. Blamed Israel's defeat at the hands of the Assyrians on the worship of pagan deities and the breaking of the covenant with God.

HULDAH. Prophetess, wife of Shallum, who was consulted by HILKIAH the chief priest on behalf of JOSIAH following the discovery of an ancient book of laws. She accepted the book as the Word of God and prophesied judgement against Jerusalem and Judah following Josiah's death. In the *First Blast*, Knox is concerned to argue that, like DEBORAH, Huldah was simply a prophetess who exercised no temporal authority.

IRENE (*c.*752–803). Wife of Byzantine emperor Leo IV. On her husband's death, she became guardian and co-emperor with her ten-year-old son, Constantine VI. Her attempts to increase her personal control led to a conspiracy against Constantine who was blinded on his mother's orders in 797. Knox simply mentions her name in a sidenote to the *First Blast*, citing SABELLICUS as his source.

ISAAC. Son of ABRAHAM and father of ESAU and JACOB. His survival of his father's attempt to sacrifice him as a child confirmed God's promise to Abraham and his seed.

ISAIAH. A prophet of the eighth century BC greatly admired and frequently cited by Knox. Although reputedly of royal blood himself, Isaiah was a stern critic of those kings – UZZIAH, Jotham, Ahaz and HEZEKIAH – who ruled in Judah during his lifetime.

JABIN. King of Canaan who tyrannised the Israelites for twenty years after they had been reduced to vassalage because of their idolatry. Liberation was finally achieved when BARAK and DEBORAH defeated

Jabin's general SISERA, a notable victory immortalised in the Song of Deborah.

JACOB. Son of ISAAC and ancestor of the Jews (from his twelve sons descended the twelve tribes of Israel) who lived in the eighteenth century BC. Inherited Isaac's position by defrauding his elder twin brother ESAU of his birthright. Fleeing from Esau's wrath, he had a vision of a ladder between heaven and earth and of the God of his family standing above it – confirmation of God's promise made to his grandfather, ABRAHAM.

JAMES V (1512–42). The son of James IV and Margaret Tudor, he succeeded to the Scottish throne on his father's death at the battle of Flodden in 1513. Then barely one year old, he did not take personal control of the kingdom until 1528. Thereafter, despite the efforts of his uncle, HENRY VIII, to persuade him to break the Scottish crown's traditional alliances with France and the papacy, he remained loyal to both, exacting in return considerable financial rewards from the church and two brides with appropriately large dowries from the French king, Francis I. By his second wife, Mary of GUISE, he had three children, but the death of his two male heirs in 1541, followed by military defeat at the hands of the English in 1542, contributed to his own early death, aged thirty, later the same year. He was succeeded by his sole surviving legitimate child, the week-old MARY STEWART.

JEHOIADA. High priest of the temple who sheltered JOASH during the usurpation of ATHALIAH and finally engineered the latter's destruction.

JEHOIACHIN (also Jeconiah and, in Jeremiah, Coniah). Son of JEHOIAKIM whom he succeeded as king of Judah in 598 BC. His reign lasted only a few months, however, and on the fall of Jerusalem to NEBUCHADNEZZAR, he was taken as a royal hostage to Babylon.

JEHOIAKIM. Son of JOSIAH whom he succeeded as eighteenth king of Judah (609–598 BC). Despite the warnings of JEREMIAH, he allowed the reforms of his father to lapse and reverted to idolatrous practices. Forced to submit to NEBUCHADNEZZAR in 604 BC, he subsequently rebelled against him and died shortly before Jerusalem fell to the Babylonian king in 597 BC.

JEHORAM. Son of AHAB and JEZEBEL and ruler of Israel (852–841 BC). At the instigation of the prophet ELISHA, he was killed by JEHU in fulfilment of the prophecy against his parents and their house.

JEHOSHAPHAT. Fourth king of Judah (*c.*873–849 BC). Apart from his efforts to improve relations with Israel through the marriage of his son to ATHALIAH, daughter of AHAB, Jehoshaphat is notable chiefly for his strict adherence to the law of God and his attempts to purify worship by eradicating idolatrous practices. It was to his role as a religious reformer that Knox most frequently referred, often bracketing him with JOSIAH and HEZEKIAH.

JEHU. Prophet who foresaw the end of the dynasty of BAASHA and also criticised JEHOSHAPHAT.

JEHU. King of Israel (*c.*842–815 BC) and son of JEHOSHAPHAT. He was anointed by a prophet appointed by ELISHA and was commissioned to destroy the line of AHAB and his idolatrous wife JEZEBEL. Although he then proceeded to stamp out the worship of BAAL, Jehu himself later reverted to the sinful practices first introduced to Israel by JEROBOAM.

JEREMIAH. Prophet of Judah in the late seventh and early sixth centuries BC. Lived through one of the most turbulent periods of Judah's history, witnessing the religious reforms of JOSIAH, Judah's rebellion against NEBUCHADNEZZAR under JEHOIAKIM, the seizure of Jerusalem in 597 BC and its destruction in 587 BC in the reign of ZEDEKIAH, the last king of Judah, who badly mistreated the prophet. Knox identified strongly with Jeremiah, frequently citing him and (particularly in the *Appellation*) using him as a model for his own conduct in adversity.

JEROBOAM. First king of Israel following the partition of Israel and Judah (*c.*930 BC). Incurred God's wrath (and that of Knox) by introducing idolatrous practices derived from the cult of BAAL. Nevertheless, he set a pattern for his royal successors many of whom transgressed in a similar way.

JEZEBEL. Wife of AHAB, her devotion to BAAL led her to insist that her god have equal rights with the God of Israel and brought her into conflict with the prophet ELIJAH. After her husband's death in battle against Syria, she remained a powerful figure in Israel until executed by JEHU. Her name became a byword for apostasy and idolatry and Knox repeatedly identifies Mary of GUISE and particularly MARY TUDOR with her. As he frequently reminds his readers, according to 2 Kings 9, after her death her carcase was consumed by dogs.

JOAN I (1326–82). Queen of Naples (1343–82) who was implicated in a plot which culminated in the assassination of her husband,

Andrew, in 1345. In the *First Blast*, Knox asserts in a sidenote that she 'hanged her husband'. It is possible that, like the reference to IRENE, this derives from SABELLICUS.

JOASH. Eighth king of Judah (*c*.837–800 BC). Narrowly escaped death at the hands of ATHALIAH, but proclaimed king in her stead by the high priest JEHOIADA when still only seven years old. With Jehoiada's help he rebuilt the temple, but later allowed pagan practices to re-emerge. He was eventually killed in a plot to overthrow him.

JOHN the Baptist. Called to prepare the people for the coming of Jesus, he is presented in the New Testament as the forerunner of Christ. He was imprisoned and put to death by HEROD Antipas.

JOHN, the Apostle. Son of Zebedee, closely associated with PETER in the early history of the Christian church, he is traditionally credited with the authorship of the Gospel and Epistles which bear his name.

JONATHAN. Eldest son and heir of SAUL, he antagonised his father by remaining loyal to DAVID when the latter succeeded to the throne of Israel.

JOSEPH. Eleventh and favourite son of JACOB who was sold into slavery in Egypt by his jealous brothers. There he prospered and, through his practical approach to the threat of famine, won favour from the Pharaoh.

JOSEPHUS, Flavius (*c*.37–100). The single most important Jewish historian of the early Roman period. Participated in the Jewish uprising against Rome which began in AD 66 and ended with the destruction of Jerusalem four years later. Subsequently, he worked in Rome under imperial patronage on a number of major historical works including the seven-book *Jewish War* and the twenty-book *Jewish Antiquities*.

JOSHUA. Chosen by MOSES as his personal assistant and his successor as military leader, co-ordinate with the priestly authority of ELEAZAR.

JOSIAH. Seventeenth king of Judah (*c*.640–609 BC). His reign was distinguished by religious reforms and a renewal of the covenant with God. Encouraged by the discovery by HILKIAH of an ancient book of laws as well as by the prophecies of JEREMIAH, Josiah cleansed the temple of idolatry and restored purity of worship. Together with HEZEKIAH and JEHOSHAPHAT, he is frequently portrayed by Knox as a model of godly kingship.

JUDAH. Fourth son of JACOB who gave his name to the tribe of

Judah. He shared in the early action against the Benjaminites when the latter resisted the national demand for justice in the matter of the Levite's concubine.

JUDAS Iscariot. One of Jesus's twelve disciples, he betrayed his master and later, filled with remorse, committed suicide.

JULIAN the Apostate. Flavius Claudius Julianus (*c.*331–63), half-brother of Constantine the Great, was the last Roman emperor to attempt to replace Christianity by a revived Greco-Roman polytheism. Although brought up a Christian, his initial tolerance of the faith degenerated into suppression and persecution.

LACTANTIUS. Lucius Caecilius Firmianus Lactantius (*c.*240–320). Early Christian apologist whose most famous work, the *Divinae institutiones*, was primarily an attack on pagan superstition. It was probably this work which Knox had in mind when he cited him, together with TERTULLIAN and CYPRIAN, in the *Letter to the Commonalty.*

LATIMER, Hugh (*c.*1485–1555). Protestant preacher patronised by Thomas Cromwell in the 1530s and elevated to the bishopric of Worcester. Too radical for the Henrician regime – he was forced to resign his see in 1539 – he came into his own in the reign of EDWARD VI, but inevitably fell foul of the Catholic reaction initiated by MARY TUDOR in 1553. He was burned at the stake, together with Nicholas RIDLEY, in 1555.

LETHINGTON, William Maitland of (*c.*1525–73). A secretary to Mary of GUISE in 1558, he joined the Protestant Congregation in rebellion in October 1559 largely because of his commitment to Anglo-Scottish unity. With MORAY, he continued to pursue this policy as secretary to MARY STEWART after 1561. At best a moderate in religious affairs, he was held in suspicion by radicals like Knox and it was primarily with Lethington that Knox engaged in a debate on the legitimacy of resistance to ungodly rulers at the General Assembly of 1564. His pro-English policies were wrecked by the queen's marriage to Lord Darnley in 1565 and he was implicated in the latter's murder in 1567. Subsequently, however, he fought on the queen's side in the civil war that followed her deposition and he died, possibly through poison, after the fall of Edinburgh Castle in 1573.

LEVI. Third son of JACOB and ancestor of the Levite tribe, noted for their priest-like functions.

LORNE. See ARGYLL, Archibald Campbell, fifth earl of.

LOT. Nephew of ABRAHAM who settled in the Jordan valley close to Sodom. He and his two daughters escaped the destruction of Sodom and Gomorrah through the intervention of two angels.

LUTHER, Martin (1483–1546). The son of a Saxon miner, he studied and taught theology at the university of Wittenberg. His search for personal spiritual fulfilment led eventually to his rejection of the theological foundations of medieval Catholicism and to the elaboration of a reformed theology which would form the basis of the Protestant faith.

MCGILL, Sir James, of Nether Rankeillor (d. 1579). Scottish Protestant laird and lawyer who served as clerk register from 1554. He does not appear to have participated in the Congregation's rebellion of 1559 and took a moderate stance in a debate which took place in his house in 1561 over whether MARY STEWART might be deprived of the mass. He referred to this episode in the course of the General Assembly debate of 1564 at which he was also present. He was dismissed from office in 1566 by the queen, but was reinstated by MORAY in 1567 and was subsequently involved in presenting the case against the queen at the York–Westminster conference in 1568.

MAHOMET (570–632) or Mahommed. The great prophet of the Moslem faith. From 622 onwards he established both military and spiritual authority over a wide area of Arabia. His prophecies are contained in the Koran or, as Knox preferred, the Alcoran.

MAITLAND, Robert (d. 1579). Scottish Protestant minister who became dean of Aberdeen about 1560 and subsequently was a frequent member of the General Assembly, including that of 1564 when he was present at the debate between Knox and LETHINGTON on the legitimacy of resistance to ungodly rulers.

MAITLAND, William. See LETHINGTON.

MANASSEH. Elder brother of EPHRAIM, JACOB blessed him with his left hand, signifying the loss of his birthright to his younger brother. Gave his name to the tribe of Manasseh which was renowned for its valour.

MANASSEH. Son of HEZEKIAH and ruler of Judah for fifty-five years, initially as co-regent with his father (696–686 BC) and then as sole ruler (686–642 BC). His reign was characterised by a return to idolatrous practices.

MARY STEWART (1542–87). Daughter of JAMES V and Mary of

GUISE, she came to the throne in 1542 when barely seven days old. Largely through her mother's efforts, she was sent to France in 1548 where she was brought up a Catholic and married to the French dauphin, Francis, in April 1558. The following year Francis succeeded to the French throne on the death of his father, HENRY II. His reign was short-lived, however, and his own death in December 1560 led Mary to return to Scotland in August 1561 to reclaim her native kingdom and to pursue further her interest in the throne of England. The latter claim was based on the Catholic view of ELIZABETH TUDOR's illegitimacy and it was largely for dynastic reasons that Mary was reluctant to renounce the mass and give royal sanction to the Protestant revolution which had occurred in Scotland in 1559–60. The return of their Catholic queen caused increasingly deep divisions in the Scottish Protestant movement between those like MORAY and LETHINGTON who were prepared to tolerate the queen's private mass and those like Knox who saw it as an affront to the law of God. The situation was finally resolved when Mary was effectively deposed in 1567 following the murder of her second husband, Lord Darnley, and her marriage to a third, the earl of Bothwell. Although she escaped confinement in 1568, her flight to England after her defeat at the battle of Langside led only to a lengthy period of imprisonment before her final execution at the hands of Elizabeth in 1587.

MARY TUDOR (1516–58), queen of England (1553–8). Daughter of HENRY VIII and Catherine of Aragon, Mary succeeded her half-brother, EDWARD VI, after rallying support against the Protestant claimant, Lady Jane GREY. A devout Catholic, she successfully quelled the rebellions sparked off by her marriage to PHILIP II of Spain in 1554 and set about reversing the Protestant settlement established by her predecessor. Her persecution of Protestants (some 300 lost their lives during her reign, while many others fled to the continent) earned her the undying hatred of Knox whose *First Blast* is directed primarily against Mary, the English JEZEBEL.

MAXWELL, John, master of (*c.*1512–83). Became fourth Lord Herries through marriage but better known as master of Maxwell, heir presumptive to Robert, fifth Lord Maxwell. Initially a staunch supporter of the Protestant cause, he was active in the ranks of the Congregation during the rebellion of 1559. Relations with Knox cooled during the personal rule of MARY STEWART, however, and he supported the treason charges against him in 1563 and sided with

LETHINGTON in the General Assembly debate of 1564. After 1565, he emerged as one of the queen's most loyal supporters.

MELANCHTHON, Philip (1497–1560). Professor of Greek at Wittenberg where he espoused the theology of LUTHER which he subsequently did much to refine and propagate.

MICAH of Moresheth. Author of Book of Micah in the late eighth and early seventh centuries BC. Younger contemporary of ISAIAH, he prophesied during the reigns of Jotham, Ahaz and HEZEKIAH, kings of Judah.

MICAIAH. Prophet in Israel in the days of AHAB who foretold the king's death at the hands of the Syrians.

MOLECH (or Moloch). Ancient deity to whom the Israelites, in times of apostasy, sacrificed children. Like the worship of BAAL, the worship of Molech was repeatedly outlawed in the Old Testament.

MORAY, James Stewart, earl of (1531–70). Bastard son of JAMES V and thus half-brother of MARY STEWART. Commendator of St Andrews Priory from 1538, but an early convert to Protestantism. As Lord James Stewart, he first met Knox during the latter's mission to Scotland in 1555–6 and was subsequently among those who invited him to return to Scotland in March 1557. In 1559, he initially sought to negotiate a peaceful settlement on behalf of Mary of GUISE, but joined the Congregation in May and emerged as its leader. The leading counsellor of MARY STEWART between 1561 and 1565 (he was created earl of Moray in 1562), his relations with Knox and the radical wing of the Protestant movement became increasingly strained. The queen's marriage to Lord Darnley in 1565 undermined his policy of *rapprochement* with England and led him into rebellion. A leader of the Confederate Lords who deposed Mary in 1567, he acted as regent for James VI until his assassination in 1570.

MORTON, James Douglas, fourth earl of (*c.*1516–81). Although a signatory of the First Band of December 1557, he did not openly support the Congregation's rebellion of 1559 until their victory was assured. A firm supporter of the pro-English policy of MORAY and LETHINGTON, he was made chancellor in 1562 and in that capacity attended the General Assembly debate of 1564. He was among the Confederate Lords who deposed MARY STEWART in 1567 and subsequently acted as regent between 1572 and 1578. Accused of complicity in the murder of Lord Darnley, he was executed in 1581.

MOSES (*c.*1350–1230 BC). The great Jewish leader and lawgiver who was called by God to lead the children of Israel out of Egypt and bring them within sight of the land promised to their ancestors. As a baby he narrowly escaped execution by the terms of a pharaonic edict requiring the execution of Hebrew male children. As a young man, he slew an Egyptian overseer who had been beating a Jew and was forced to flee into the wilderness. There he received his call from God in a vision of a burning bush which was not consumed. Together with his brother AARON, and with the help of a series of miracles, he persuaded the PHARAOH to permit the Jews to leave Egypt. Through the miraculous parting of the Red Sea, Moses was able to lead the Jews from Egypt to Sinai where, standing alone on Mount Sinai, he received the Ten Commandments, the basis of the Jewish people's covenant with God. It was the terms of this covenant, and the punishment meted out by God to those who broke them, which particularly concerned Knox.

MUSCULUS, Wolfgang (1497–1563). Protestant reformer and theologian who studied under BUCER at Strasburg before becoming a professor of theology at Berne.

NADAB. Eldest son of AARON who, with his brother ABIHU, transgressed the temple laws and died as a result.

NEBUCHADNEZZAR. King of Babylon from 605 to 562 BC, he defeated the Egyptians at the battle of Carchemish on the eve of his accession to the throne and thus established his pre-eminent power in Western Asia. Strained relations with the kings of Judah led him to capture Jerusalem in 597 BC and to sack and destroy it ten years later. Many of these events were witnessed by JEREMIAH, EZEKIEL and DANIEL whose prophetic writings are constantly referred to by Knox.

NERO (37–68). Nephew of Caligula who became Roman emperor in 54. Notorious for his fickle behaviour as well as for his persecution of Christians, St PAUL was among his victims.

NICEPHORUS CALLISTUS (*c.*1265–1325). Nikephoros Kallistos Xanthopolous, Byzantine theologian and church historian, author of a Greek ecclesiastical history in eighteen books covering the period from the birth of Christ to 610. Knox was evidently familiar with an early sixteenth-century Latin edition of the work and quotes an anecdote from it in the *Letter to the Regent*.

NIMROD. Warrior and hunter whose kingdom (according to Genesis 10) included Babylon, Erech and Akkad and who is said to have founded Nineveh. His name was a byword for tyranny.

NOAH. Last of the antediluvian patriarchs and hero of the Flood. His three sons and their wives accompanied Noah and his wife in the ark and were responsible for repopulating the earth once the waters withdrew.

NORTHUMBERLAND, John Dudley, duke of (*c.* 1502–53). A powerful member of EDWARD VI's regency council, he overthrew Protector SOMERSET in 1551 and became virtual ruler of England. His Protestantism was matched (or surpassed) by personal ambition and he persuaded the king to name his daughter-in-law, Lady Jane GREY, as successor to the throne. Although proclaimed queen on Edward's death in 1553, Lady Jane's 'reign' proved short-lived and, despite his attempts to save his life by announcing his conversion to Catholicism, Northumberland was executed by the triumphant Marian regime.

OYSEL, Henri Cleutin, sieur d'. French ambassador in Scotland from 1546 to 1560 and principal adviser to Mary of GUISE during the period of French domination which culminated in the Congregation's rebellion of 1559. He left Scotland in 1560 and died in Rome in 1566.

PASQUILLUS. *Pasquillo* or *Pasquino* was the name given to a mutilated statue disinterred at Rome in 1501 where it was re-erected by Cardinal Caraffa. It became customary to post satirical Latin verses on it on St Mark's day, though Knox was clearly not amused at having his own *Letter to the Regent* dismissed as a 'pasquil'.

PAUL, St. Following his miraculous conversion on the road to Damascus, Saul of Tarsus changed his name to Paul and devoted the remainder of his life to preaching the Gospel in the Eastern Mediterranean and Rome. He finally suffered martyrdom under NERO (*c.* 67). His Epistles laid the foundations of developed Christian theology.

PETER, St. First of the Apostles whose denial of Christ was forgiven and whose martyrdom at Rome led to the belief that he was the bishop of Rome. The Epistles of Peter in the New Testament are traditionally ascribed to him.

PHARAOH. The Pharaoh associated with MOSES and the Exodus

was most probably Rameses II who ruled in Egypt in the first half of the thirteenth century BC.

PHILIP II (1527–98). King of Spain (1558–98) and of England (1554–58) through his marriage to MARY TUDOR. The marriage was extremely unpopular as it drew England into war with France in 1557, leading to the loss of Calais (the last English possession on the continent) the following year.

PLATO (*c.*427–*c.*347 BC). The most famous of the Greek philosophers, a pupil of Socrates and the teacher of ARISTOTLE. Knox makes passing reference to his best known work on politics, *The Republic*, in the General Assembly debate of 1564.

PONET, John (*c.*1514–56). English Protestant theologian who was made bishop of Rochester in 1550 and of Winchester the following year. On the accession of MARY TUDOR in 1553, he took refuge on the continent, settling in Strasburg where he published in the year of death his *Short Treatise of Politike Power*.

REUBEN. First son of JACOB who gave his name to one of the twelve tribes of Israel.

RIDLEY, Nicholas (*c.*1503–55). Cambridge academic, his Protestant leanings brought him to the attention of Thomas CRANMER in the 1530s and led to ecclesiastical preferment culminating in 1550 in his appointment as bishop of London. He supported the claim of Lady Jane GREY to succeed EDWARD VI and was arrested once MARY TUDOR was securely on the throne. He was burned at the stake, along with Hugh LATIMER, in 1555.

ROMILDA. Wife of Gisulf II, duke of Friuli, who was killed during the Avar invasion of Lombardy *c.*610. After her husband's death, Romilda is alleged to have developed such a passion for the Avar leader that she surrendered the city to him in return for being his wife for a night. Perhaps drawing on SABELLICUS, Knox cites her betrayal in the *First Blast* as an instance of women's inability to control their passions.

RUBAY, Yves de. One of a number of Frenchmen elevated to high office in Scotland – in this case keeper of the great seal – by Mary of GUISE. He is described in contemporary French documents as a king's councillor.

RUTHVEN, Patrick, third Lord (*c.*1520–66). Scottish Protestant nobleman who, as provost of Perth, played an active role in the defiance of Mary of GUISE which initiated the rebellion of the Congregation in 1559. He subsequently took a leading part in the murder of MARY STEWART's secretary David Riccio in 1566 and was forced to flee to England where he died the same year.

SABELLICUS (1436–1506). Marcantonio Cocci (Coccius) of Vicovaro. Italian humanist and historian whose most ambitious work was a massive universal history from the Creation under the title *Enneados seu rhapsodiae historiarum*. Knox appears to have quarried from it some examples of female misrule (IRENE, ROMILDA, JOAN) for use in the *First Blast*.

SAMUEL. Last of the judges and first of the prophets; with divine guidance he was instrumental in establishing the Israelite monarchy, first anointing SAUL and later, following Saul's disobedience, anointing DAVID in his place.

SAPPHIRA. See ANANIAS.

SAUL. The first king of Israel (*c.* 1000 BC), chosen by God to institute monarchical rule over His people, he three times proved disobedient to God's will and was eventually replaced by DAVID, against whom he thereafter pursued a relentless vendetta.

SENNACHERIB. King of Assyria (705–681 BC) who besieged Jerusalem during the reign of HEZEKIAH. According to 2 Kings 19, his forces were destroyed by the angel of the Lord and he himself was later assassinated by his own sons.

SHALMANESER V, king of Assyria (727–722 BC) to whom Hoshea, king of Israel, was forced to pay tribute.

SHALLUM. Son of JOSIAH whom he succeeded as eighteenth king of Judah in 609 BC. He was deposed after a brief reign of three months.

SIM, James. Edinburgh apothecary with whom Knox lodged during his mission of 1555 and who in 1557, together with James BARON, delivered a letter to Knox in Geneva inviting him to return to Scotland.

SIMON MAGUS. Magician who professed to have been converted to Christianity and was baptised. He continued, however, to view the Apostles as fellow magicians and sought to buy their secrets from them until sternly rebuked by PETER.

SINCLAIR, Henry (1508–65). Scottish lawyer and ecclesiastic who became president of the college of justice in 1558 and was made bishop of Ross in 1561. Knox considered him a hypocrite and enemy of religious truth despite Sinclair's role in acquitting him of a trumped-up treason charge in 1563. He died at Paris in 1565.

SISERA. The military commander whose defeat at the hands of BARAK and DEBORAH ended the tyranny exercised by JABIN over the Israelites. In fulfilment of a prophecy of Deborah, he was subsequently murdered by a woman, Jael.

SOLOMON. Son of DAVID and third king of Israel (*c.*971–931 BC). Of legendary wisdom, he was responsible for building the temple in Jerusalem, but his foreign marriages drew criticism as they introduced idolatrous forms of worship to Israel. Although this and other breaches of the covenant went unpunished during Solomon's reign, his son and successor, Rehoboam, was to reap a bitter harvest.

SOMERSET, Edward Seymour, first earl of Hertford and duke of (*c.*1506–52). Brother of Jane Seymour, third wife of HENRY VIII, and thus uncle of EDWARD VI. As Hertford, he commanded the English forces which ravaged Scotland during the 'Rough Wooing' campaigns of 1544–5 and, as Somerset, following Henry VIII's death and his own assumption of the regency during Edward VI's minority, he extended this policy to one of military occupation following his crushing defeat of the Scots at the battle of Pinkie in 1547. Although, as Lord Protector, he was able to advance the cause of Protestant reform in England, his Scottish policy proved an expensive failure and led finally to his overthrow in 1551 and execution by NORTHUMBERLAND in 1552.

STEWART, Lord James. See MORAY, James Stewart, earl of.

STOBAEUS. John of Stobi in Macedonia, compiler in the fifth century AD of a collection of fragments of ancient writings from which much of our knowledge of pre-Socratic philosophy is derived. Knox was evidently familiar with an early sixteenth-century edition of his *Florilegium* or *Sermones* from which he quotes a saying of Democritus in the *Letter to the Regent*.

TERTULLIAN. Born in Carthage around 160, he converted to Christianity *c.*195 and through his prolific writings exerted a profound influence on the subsequent development of Christian thought. Knox refers to his famous *Apology* in both the *Letter to the Regent* and the *Letter to the Commonalty* and to a number of his other works in the *First Blast*.

UZZIAH. Tenth king of Judah who reigned *c.*791–739 BC. In the *Letter to the Regent*, and again in the debate at the General Assembly of 1564, Knox alludes to his having been struck with leprosy for violating the laws of the temple.

WALLACE, Adam. Scottish Protestant who was burned as a heretic in 1550. Knox describes his trial at some length in his *History* (Laing, vol. I, pp. 237–41).

WILLOCK, John (d. 1585). Scottish Dominican friar who converted to Protestantism and fled to England in 1539 where he became a preacher. On the accession of MARY TUDOR he took refuge on the continent and settled at Emden. He returned to Scotland in 1558 and was an active supporter of the Congregation, openly advocating the right of the people to depose a prince in the debate over the regent's suspension in October 1559. An influential figure in the new reformed kirk, he was moderator of the General Assembly of 1564.

WINRAM, John (*c.*1492–1582). Initially a reforming Catholic, he was present at Knox's first sermon at St Andrews in 1547 and engaged in a disputation with him immediately afterwards. The date of his conversion to Protestantism is unknown, but he attended the Reformation Parliament in 1560 and was appointed, along with Knox and others, to draw up the *First Book of Discipline*. He attended the 1564 General Assembly where he supported the view that the nobility might oppose the queen in defence of their religion, but doubted whether she might be deprived of the mass by force.

WISHART, George (*c.*1513–46). Scottish Protestant reformer who returned to Scotland in 1543 after fleeing to England in 1538 and the continent the following year to avoid facing heresy charges. He preached widely in Scotland in 1544–5, during which time Knox became closely associated with his mission, before being arrested by Cardinal David BEATON and burned at the stake in St Andrews in March 1546.

WISHART, Sir John, of Pittarrow (d. 1585). Scottish Protestant laird with whom Knox probably established contact during his mission to Scotland in 1555–6 and to whom he wrote from Dieppe in 1557. Subsequently, Wishart played an active part in the Congregation's rebellion of 1559 and remained a firm Protestant throughout the personal rule of MARY STEWART whose deposition he supported.

WYATT, Sir Thomas (*c.*1521–54). Leader of an unsuccessful

rebellion against MARY TUDOR in 1554, triggered by the queen's marriage to PHILIP II of Spain, and aimed at placing ELIZABETH on the throne. His execution shortly after the rebellion turned him into a patriot and martyr for those opposed to Mary Tudor's anti-Protestant policies.

ZADOK. A descendant of ELEAZAR the third son of AARON and priest along with ABIATHAR at the court of DAVID. He took part in the anointing of SOLOMON which Abiathar opposed, and he and his successors remained as priests in Solomon's temple until its destruction in 587 BC.

ZEDEKIAH. Third son of JOSIAH and twenty-first, and last, king of Judah (*c.* 597–587 BC). He was placed on the throne by NEBUCHADNEZZAR, but despite the warnings of JEREMIAH later rebelled against the Babylonian ruler. The result was the siege and eventual destruction of Jerusalem, following which Zedekiah was blinded and taken as a captive to Babylon.

ZELOPHEHAD. Son of Hepher of the tribe of Manasseh and father of five daughters. On his death, having no male issue, his property passed to his daughters. In the *First Blast*, Knox is concerned to argue that the law which thus originated applied only to property and not to the strictly male preserves of offices and authority. Likewise, with one eye on the contemporary scene, he underlines that by the same law it was laid down that women should marry only within their own tribes.

Abbreviations and references

The following includes full details of the editions used in checking Knox's references and of other works cited in the notes and introductory material.

Ambrose	*Commentarius in Epistulas Paulinas*, ed. H. J. Vogel, Corpus Scriptorum Ecclesiasticorum Latinorum [CSEL] (3 vols., Vienna, 1966–9).
	Hexameron in *Sancti Ambrosii opera pars prima*, ed. C. Schenkl, CSEL (Vienna, 1897).
Aristotle	*The Politics of Aristotle*, ed. and trans. Ernest Barker (Oxford, 1946).
Augustine	*The Works of Aurelius Augustine, Bishop of Hippo*, ed. Marcus Dods (15 vols., Edinburgh, 1871).
	De ordine in *Aurelii Augustini opera*, Pars II, 2, Corpus Christianorum Series Latina XXIX (Turnhout, 1970).
	Pseudo-Augustini quaestiones Veteris et Novi Testamenti CXXVII, ed. A. Souter, CSEL (Vienna, 1908).
	Retractationes, ed. P. Knoll, CSEL (Vienna, 1902).
	Epistulae, ed. A. Goldbacher, CSEL (4 vols., Vienna, 1895–1923).
Basilius Magnus	*Basilius Magnus . . . opera . . . omnia* (2 vols., Basle, 1540).
Chrysostom	*Homilies on the Minor Pauline Epistles*, ed. P. Schaff, The Nicene and Post-Nicene Fathers XIII (New York, 1894).

	Homilies on the Epistles of Paul to the Corinthians, ed. P. Schaff, The Nicene and Post-Nicene Fathers XII (New York, 1893).
	Homilies on the Gospel of St John, Library of the Fathers (2 vols., Oxford, 1848–52).
	Homilies on the Gospel of St Matthew, Library of the Fathers (3 vols., Oxford, 1843–51).
	Homilies on the Epistle of St Paul to the Romans, Library of the Fathers (Oxford, 1841).
	In S. Geneseos librum enarrationes (Antwerp, 1547).
Cicero	*On Duties* [*De officiis*], ed. M. T. Griffin and E. M. Atkins, Cambridge Texts in the History of Political Thought (Cambridge, 1991).
Cyprian	*On the Vanity of Idols*, in *The Writings of Cyprian*, ed. and trans. R. E. Wallis, Ante-Nicene Christian Library (2 vols., Edinburgh, 1868–9), vol. II, pp. 443–51.
Dickinson	*John Knox's History of the Reformation in Scotland*, ed. W. C. Dickinson (2 vols., London and New York, 1949).
Digest	*The Digest of Justinian*, Latin text ed. T. Mommsen with P. Krueger and English trans. by A. Watson (4 vols., Philadelphia, 1985).
Gratian	*Decretals*, in *Corpus iuris canonici*, ed. A. Friedberg (2 vols., Leipzig, 1879–81), vol. I.
Gregory IX	*Decretals*, in *Corpus iuris canonici*, ed. A. Friedberg (2 vols., Leipzig, 1879–81), vol. II.
Hegesippus	*Aegisippi . . . Historia de bello Judaico* (Paris, 1511).
Josephus	*The Complete Works*, ed. and trans. W. Whiston (London and Glasgow, 1981).
Justin Martyr	*Discourse to the Greeks*, in *Justin Martyr and Athenagoras*, ed. A. Roberts and J. Donaldson, Ante-Nicene Christian Library II (Edinburgh, 1867).
Lactantius	*The Divine Institutes*, in *The Works of Lactantius*, ed. and trans. W. Fletcher, Ante-Nicene Christian Library (2 vols., Edinburgh, 1871), vol. I.
Laing	*The Works of John Knox*, ed. David Laing (6 vols., Wodrow Society, 1846–64).

Laing MS	'John Knox's History of the Reformation in Scotland', Edinburgh University Library, Laing MSS. III. 210.
Sabellicus	*Opera* (2 vols., Basle, 1538).
STC	A. W. Pollard, G. R. Redgrave *et al.* (eds.), *A Short-Title Catalogue of Books Printed in England, Scotland and Ireland and of English Books Printed Abroad 1475–1640* (3 vols., London, 1976–91).
Stobaeus	*Joannis Stobaei sententiae, ex thesauris Graecorum delectae* (Lyon, 1609).
Tertullian	*Tertulliani opera*, Corpus Christianorum, Series Latina (2 vols., Turnhout, 1954).

Glossary

accompt	account
addebted	indebted
adduce	cite
advert	warn, take note
affection	feeling, emotion
againstand	resist
aggrege	exaggerate, emphasise
appellation	appeal
approbation	approval, proof
arrayment	raiment, clothing
attaint	accuse, convict
attour	in addition
auditure	auditor, audience
bairns	children
band	bond, covenant
before-speak	foretell, prophesy
Bononia	Bologna
brook	possess
bruit	report, rumour
bud	bribe
but	without
cankered	infected, corrupted
carcagies	carcasses
cassin	cast

claw-back	sycophant, flatterer
coact	compel, force
commonalty	common people
commonty	community, commonwealth
complease	gratify, delight
compt	reckoning, reason
conjuration	conspiracy
conjure	conspire, band together by oath
conqueiss	acquire
consuetude	usage, custom
contemn	scorn
contemner	scorner
contumely	insulting, contemptuous
convent	convene
croppin	crept
cunzie	coin, coinage
danton	daunt
decept	deceit
decore	embellish, adorn
depauperate	impoverished
dolour	pain, grief
downthring	overthrow
dreddour	dread
embase	degrade, humiliate, humble
embassade	embassy
empire	rule, government
endamage	injure
engine	wit, genius
entres	entrance, beginning
esperance	hope
Ethnic	pagan, heathen
expone	expose, explain
fact	deed, action
facund	eloquent
file	defile
forsamekle	in as much

fort	fortify
frack	resolute
frenetic	delirious, mad
furnitour	supplier
garniss	furnish
girnall	granary
glistering	sparkling, brilliant
Helvetia	Switzerland
indifference	impartiality
indifferent	impartial
indurate	stubborn
induration	obduracy
ingenerate	engender, generate
innocency	innocence
insensible	unfeeling
intromission	interference
jeopard	hazard, jeopardise
layit	alloyed
lenity	mildness, gentleness
let	hinder, obstruct
lippin	look, expect
list	care to
malapert	forward, impudent
malediction	curse
mansworn	perjured
mekill	much, great(ly)
mekle	much
mell	meddle
monstriferous	monster-bearing
nor	than
oblation	gift, offering

oppone	oppose
opprobries	reproaches
oppugn	attack
or	before
pasquil	pasquinade, lampoon, satire
perfurnish	furnish, supply
pined	afflicted, distressed
policy	polity, constitution
Polonia	Poland
port	gate, gateway
probation	proof
purgation	purging, acquittal
puissance	power
quod	quoth, said
rang	reigned
reciproce	reciprocal
reft	spoiled, robbed
regiment	government
remanent	remainder, rest
remeid	remedy, redress
ring	reign
rive	take away, seize, tear
rooms	lands, inheritance
rounged	worn away, filed
ruth	pity
scripped	mocked, derided
scruiff	scruff, base money
sensyne	since then
sentence	opinion
shamefastness	modesty
sicle	shekel
slake	assuage, satisfy
sleuth	sloth, neglect
solicitate	solicit
solist	solicitous

spulzie	spoil, despoil
stark	strong
sture	stir, trouble
suffrage	support, assistance
suppone	suppose
supposts	followers, supporters
tane	taken, made
testification	proof, testimony
till	to, for
transitorious	transitory
travail	work, labour
tred	path, line of argument
vendicate	vindicate, claim
verity	truth, Word of God, the Scriptures
vility	wretchedness, worthlessness
vivers	food, victuals
waring	expense
wat	wot, know
while	until

PART I
THE 1558 TRACTS

THE FIRST BLAST OF THE TRUMPET

against the Monstrous Regiment of Women

Veritas temporis filia

M.D.LVIII

[THE PREFACE]

THE KINGDOM APPERTAINETH TO OUR GOD.

Wonder it is that amongst so many pregnant wits as the Isle of Great Britanny hath produced, so many godly and zealous preachers as England did sometime nourish, and amongst so many learned and men of grave judgement as this day by Jezebel are exiled, none is found so stout of courage, so faithful to God, nor loving to their native country, that they dare admonish the inhabitants of that Isle how abominable before God is the empire or rule of a wicked woman, yea, of a traitress and bastard, and what may a people or nation, left destitute of a lawful head, do by the authority of God's Word in electing and appointing common rulers and magistrates. That Isle, alas, for the contempt and horrible abuse of God's mercies offered, and for the shameful revolting to Satan from Christ Jesus and from His Gospel once professed, doth justly merit to be left in the hands of their own counsel and so to come to confusion and bondage of strangers.

But yet I fear that this universal negligence of such as sometimes were esteemed watchmen shall rather aggravate our former ingratitude than excuse this our universal and ungodly silence in so weighty a matter. We see our country set forth for a prey to foreign nations; we hear the blood of our brethren, the members of Christ Jesus, most cruelly to be shed; and the monstrous empire of a cruel woman

Negligence of watchmen.

(the secret counsel of God excepted) we know to be the only occasion of all these miseries; and yet, with silence we pass the time as though the matter did nothing appertain to us. But the contrary examples of the ancient Prophets move me to doubt of this our fact. For Israel did universally decline from God by embracing idolatry under Jeroboam, in which they did continue even unto the destruction of their commonwealth. And Judah with Jerusalem did follow the vile superstition and open iniquity of Samaria. But yet ceased not the Prophets of God to admonish the one and the other, yea, even after that God had poured forth His plagues upon them. For Jeremiah did write to the captives in Babylon, and did correct their errors, plainly instructing them who did remain in the midst of that idolatrous nation. Ezekiel, from the midst of his brethren, prisoners in Chaldea, did write his vision to those that were in Jerusalem and, sharply rebuking their vices, assured them that they should not escape the vengeance of God by reason of their abominations committed. The same Prophets, for comfort of the afflicted and chosen saints of God, who did lie hid amongst the reprobate of that age (as commonly doth the corn amongst the chaff), did prophesy and before-speak the changes of kingdoms, the punishments of tyrants, and the vengeance which God would execute upon the oppressors of His people. The same did Daniel and the rest of the Prophets every one in their season. By whose examples, and by the plain precept which is given to Ezekiel, commanding him that he shall say to the wicked: 'Thou shalt die the death', we in this our miserable age are bound to admonish the world and the tyrants thereof of their sudden destruction, to assure them and to cry unto them, whether they list to hear or not: 'that the blood of the saints, which by them is shed, continually crieth and craveth vengeance in the presence of the Lord of Hosts'. And further it is our duty to open the truth revealed unto us unto the ignorant and blind world, unless that to our own condemnation we list to wrap up and hide the talent committed to our charge.

The diligence of the old Prophets of God.
1 Kgs. 12. Ezek. 16.
Jer. 29.
Ezek. 7, 8, 9.
God always had his people amongst the wicked, who never lacked their Prophets and teachers. Isa. 13. Jer. 46. Ezek. 36.
[*Ezek.* 33.8.]
Examples what teachers ought to do in this time. Ezek. 2. Rev. 6.

I am assured that God hath revealed to some in this our age that it is more than a monster in nature that a woman shall reign and have empire above man. And yet with us all there is such silence, as if God therewith were nothing offended. The natural man, enemy to God, shall find, I know, many causes why no such doctrine ought to be published in these our dangerous days. First, for that it may seem to tend to sedition; secondarily, it shall be dangerous not only to the

Three chief reasons that do stay man from speaking the truth.

writer or publisher, but also to all such as shall read the writings or favour this truth spoken; and last, it shall not amend the chief offenders, partly because it shall never come to their ears, and partly because they will not be admonished in such cases. I answer, if any of these be a sufficient reason that a truth known shall be concealed, then were the ancient Prophets of God very fools who did not better provide for their own quietness than to hazard their lives for rebuking of vices and for the opening of such crimes as were known to the world. And Christ Jesus did injury to His Apostles, commanding them to preach repentance and remission of sins in His name to every realm and nation. And Paul did not understand his own liberty when he cried: 'Woe be to me, if I preach not the Evangel.'

1 Cor. 9.16.

If fear, I say, of persecution, of slander, or of any inconvenience before named might have excused and discharged the servants of God from plainly rebuking the sins of the world, just cause had every one of them to have ceased from their office. For suddenly their doctrine was accused by terms of sedition, of new learning and of treason; persecution and vehement trouble did shortly come upon the professors with the preachers; kings, princes and worldly rulers did conspire against God and against His anointed Christ Jesus. But what? Did any of these move the Prophets and Apostles to faint in their vocation? No. But by the resistance which the devil made to them by his supposts were they the more inflamed to publish the truth revealed unto them and to witness with their blood that grievous condemnation and God's heavy vengeance should follow the proud contempt of graces offered. The fidelity, bold courage and constancy of those that are passed before us ought to provoke us to follow their footsteps, unless we look for another kingdom than Christ hath promised to such as persevere in profession of His name to the end.

Matt. 26. Acts 18, 21.

Ps. 2. Acts 4.

If any think that the empire of women is not of such importance that for the suppressing of the same any man is bound to hazard his life, I answer that to suppress it is in the hand of God alone. But to utter the impiety and abomination of the same, I say it is the duty of every true messenger of God to whom the truth is revealed in that behalf. For the especial duty of God's messengers is to preach repentance, to admonish the offenders of their offences, and to say to the wicked: 'Thou shalt die the death, except thou repent.' This, I trust, will no man deny to be the proper office of all God's messengers: to preach (as I have said) repentance and remission of sins. But

It is necessary for every man to open the impiety which he knoweth to hurt his commonwealth.

neither of both can be done, except the conscience of the offenders be accused and convicted of transgression. For how shall any man repent not knowing wherein he hath offended? And where no repentance is found, there can be no entry to grace. And therefore I say that of necessity it is that this monstriferous empire of women (which amongst all enormities that this day do abound upon the face of the whole earth is most detestable and damnable) be openly revealed and plainly declared to the world, to the end that some may repent and be saved. And thus far to the first sort.

No man can repent except he know his sin.

To such as think that it will be long before such doctrine come to the ears of the chief offenders, I answer that the verity of God is of that nature that, at one time or at other, it will purchase to itself audience. It is an odour and smell that cannot be suppressed, yea, it is a trumpet that will sound in despite of the adversary. It will compel the very enemies to their own confusion to testify and bear witness of it. For I find that the prophecy and preaching of Elisha was declared in the hall of the king of Syria by the servants and flatterers of the same wicked king, making mention that Elisha declared to the king of Israel whatsoever the said king of Syria spoke in his most secret chamber. And the wondrous works of Jesus Christ were notified to Herod, not in any great praise or commendation of His doctrine, but rather to signify that Christ called that tyrant a fox, and that He did no more regard his authority than did John the Baptist, whom Herod before had beheaded for the liberty of his tongue. But whether the bearers of the rumours and tidings were favourers of Christ or flatterers of the tyrant, certain it is that the same, as well of Christ's doctrines as of His works, came to the ears of Herod. Even so may the sound of our weak trumpet, by the support of some wind (blow it from the south or blow it from the north, it is no matter), come to the ears of the chief offenders. But whether it do or not, yet dare we not cease to blow as God will give strength. For we are debtors to more than to princes: to wit, to the multitude of our brethren, of whom no doubt a great number have heretofore offended by error and ignorance, giving their suffrages, consent and help to establish women in their kingdoms and empires, not understanding how abominable, odious and detestable is all such usurped authority in the presence of God. And therefore must the truth be plainly spoken that the simple and rude multitude may be admonished.

The property of God's truth.

2 Kgs. 6.

Matt. 14. [Luke 13.32.].

Rom. 1.

The ignorant multitude hath set up the authority of women not knowing the danger.

And as concerning the danger which may hereof ensue, I am not altogether so brutish and insensible but that I have laid mine accompt what the finishing of the work may cost me for mine own part. First, I am not ignorant how difficult and dangerous it is to speak against a common error, especially when that the ambitious minds of men and women are called to the obedience of God's simple commandment. For to the most part of men, lawful and godly appeareth whatsoever antiquity hath received. And secondarily, I look to have mine adversaries not only of the ignorant multitude, but also of the wise, politic and quiet spirits of this world, so that as well shall such as ought to maintain the truth and verity of God become enemies to me in this case as shall the princes and ambitious persons who to maintain their unjust tyranny do always study to suppress the same. And thus I am most certainly persuaded that my labour shall not escape reprehension of many. But because I remember that accompts of the talents received must be made to Him who neither respecteth the multitude neither yet approveth the wisdom, policy, peace nor antiquity concluding or determining anything against His eternal will revealed to us in His most blessed Word, I am compelled to cover mine eyes and shut up mine ears that I neither see the multitude that shall withstand me in this matter, neither that I shall hear the opprobries nor consider the dangers which I may incur for uttering the same. I shall be called foolish, curious, despiteful and a sower of sedition. And one day perchance (although now I be nameless) I may be attainted of treason. But seeing that impossible it is but that either I shall offend God, daily calling to my conscience that I ought to manifest the verity known, or else that I shall displease the world for doing the same, I have determined to obey God, notwithstanding that the world shall rage thereat.

A very dangerous thing to speak against old errors.

Accompts will be had of God's gifts.

The cause moving the author to write.

I know that the world offended (by God's permission) may kill the body, but God's majesty offended hath power to punish body and soul forever. His majesty is offended when that His precepts are contemned and His threatenings esteemed to be of none effect. And amongst His manifold precepts given to His Prophets, and amongst His threatenings, none is more vehement than is that which is pronounced to Ezekiel in these words: 'Son of man, I have appointed thee a watchman to the house of Israel that thou shouldst hear from my mouth the word and that thou mayest admonish them plainly when I shall say to the wicked man: O wicked, thou shalt assuredly die. Then if thou shalt not speak that thou mayest plainly admonish

Ezek. 33.7–9.

him that he may leave his wicked way, the wicked man shall die in his iniquity, but his blood will I require of thy hand. But and if thou shalt plainly admonish the wicked man, and yet he shall not turn from his way, such a one shall die in his iniquity, but thou hast delivered thy soul.'

This precept, I say, with the threatening annexed, together with the rest that is spoken in the same chapter, not to Ezekiel only, but to every one whom God placeth watchman over His people and flock (and watchmen are they whose eyes He doth open and whose conscience He pricketh to admonish the ungodly), compelleth me to utter my conscience in this matter notwithstanding that the whole world should be offended with me for so doing. If any wonder why I do conceal my name, let him be assured that the fear of corporal punishment is neither the only neither the chief cause. My purpose is thrice to blow the trumpet in the same matter if God so permit. Twice I intend to do it without name, but at the last blast to take the blame upon myself that all others may be purged.

For the author's name.

THE FIRST BLAST TO AWAKE WOMEN DEGENERATE.

To promote a woman to bear rule, superiority, dominion or empire above any realm, nation or city is repugnant to nature, contumely to God, a thing most contrarious to His revealed will and approved ordinance, and finally it is the subversion of good order, of all equity and justice.

In the probation of this proposition, I will not be so curious as to gather whatsoever may amplify, set forth or decore the same, but I am purposed, even as I have spoken my conscience in most plain and few words, so to stand content with a simple proof of every member, bringing in for my witness God's ordinance in nature, His plain will revealed in His Word, and the minds of such as be most ancient amongst godly writers.

And first, where that I affirm the empire of a woman to be a thing repugnant to nature, I mean not only that God by the order of His creation hath spoiled woman of authority and dominion, but also that man hath seen, proved and pronounced just causes why that it so should be. Man, I say, in many other cases blind, doth in this behalf see very clearly. For the causes be so manifest that they cannot be hid. For who can deny but it repugneth to nature that the blind shall be appointed to lead and conduct such as do see; that the weak, the sick and impotent persons shall nourish and keep the whole and strong; and finally, that the foolish, mad and frenetic shall govern the discreet and give counsel to such as be sober of mind? And such be all women compared unto man in bearing of authority. For their sight in civil regiment is but blindness, their strength weakness, their counsel foolishness, and judgement frenzy, if it be rightly considered.

Causes why women should not have pre-eminence over men.

I except such as God, by singular privilege and for certain causes known only to Himself, hath exempted from the common rank of women, and do speak of women as nature and experience do this day declare them. Nature, I say, doth paint them forth to be weak, frail, impatient, feeble and foolish; and experience hath declared them to be inconstant, variable, cruel and lacking the spirit of counsel and regiment. And these notable faults have men in all ages espied in that kind, for the which not only they have removed women from rule and authority, but also some have thought that men subject to the counsel or empire of their wives were unworthy of all public office. For thus writeth Aristotle in the second [book] of his *Politics*: 'What difference shall we put', saith he, 'whether that women bear authority or the husbands that obey the empire of their wives be appointed to be magistrates? For what ensueth the one must needs follow the other: to wit, injustice, confusion and disorder.' The same author further reasoneth that the policy or regiment of the Lacedemonians (who other ways amongst the Grecians were most excellent) was not worthy to be reputed nor accounted amongst the number of commonwealths that were well governed because the magistrates and rulers of the same were too much given to please and obey their wives. What would this writer (I pray you) have said to that realm or nation where a woman sitteth crowned in parliament amongst the midst of men? O fearful and terrible are thy judgements (O Lord) which thus hast abased man for his iniquity!

Private examples do not break the general ordinance.

Aristotle, Politics, 2.9.9.

[Aristotle, Politics, 2.9.9–13.]

Read Isaiah the third chapter.

I am assuredly persuaded that if any of those men which, illuminated only by the light of nature, did see and pronounce causes sufficient why women ought not to bear rule nor authority, should this day live and see a woman sitting in judgement or riding from parliament in the midst of men, having the royal crown upon her head, the sword and sceptre borne before her in sign that the administration of justice was in her power; I am assuredly persuaded, I say, that

Amazons were monstrous women that could not abide the regiment of men and therefore killed their husbands. Read Justin.[1]

Aristotle, Politics, 2.9.13.

such a sight should so astonish them that they should judge the whole world to be transformed into Amazons, and that such a metamorphosis and change was made of all the men of that country as poets do feign was made of the companions of Ulysses; or at least that, albeit the outward form of men remained, yet should they judge that their hearts were changed from the wisdom, understanding and courage of men to the foolish fondness and cowardice of women. Yea, they further should pronounce that, where women reign or be in authority, that there must needs vanity be preferred to virtue, ambition and pride to temperance and modesty, and finally, that avarice the mother of all mischief must needs devour equity and justice.

Digest, 50.17.2: De diversis regulis iuris antiqui. What women may not be. Digest, 3.1.1–5; De postulando. 16.1.pr.: Ad senatus consultum Velleianum.

But lest that we shall seem to be of this opinion alone, let us hear what others have seen and decreed in this matter. In the rules of the law thus it is written: 'Women are removed from all civil and public office, so that they neither may be judges, neither may they occupy the place of the magistrate, neither yet may they be speakers for others.' The same is repeated in the third and in the sixteenth books of the *Digests* where certain persons are forbidden, *ne pro aliis postulent*; that is, that they be no speakers nor advocates for others. And among the rest are women forbidden; and this cause is added, that they do not against shamefastness intermeddle themselves with the causes of others, neither yet that women presume to use the offices due to men. The law in the same place doth further declare that a natural shamefastness ought to be in womankind which most certainly she loseth whensoever she taketh upon her the office and estate of man. As in Calpurnia was evidently declared, who having licence to speak before the senate, at length became so impudent and importune that by her babbling she troubled the whole assembly, and so gave occasion that this law was established.

Calpurnia. [Digest, 3.1.5.]

De statu hominum. Digest, 1.5.9.[2] *From women power is taken away by the civil law over their own children. Digest, 24.1:*

In the first book of the *Digests*, it is pronounced that the condition of the woman in many cases is worse than of the man. As in jurisdiction (saith the law), in receiving of cure and tuition, in adoption, in public accusation, in delation, in all popular action, and in motherly power which she hath not upon her own sons. The law further will not permit that the woman give anything to her husband because it is against the nature of her kind, being the inferior member, to pre-

[1] Apparently a reference to Justin Martyr's *Discourse to the Greeks*, cap. 1, though Knox is embroidering his source.

[2] The original sidenote refers erroneously to 'Titul. 8'.

sume to give anything to her head. The law doth moreover pronounce womankind to be most avaricious (which is a vice intolerable in those that should rule or minister justice). And Aristotle, as before is touched, doth plainly affirm that, wheresoever women bear dominion, there must needs the people be disordered, living and abounding in all intemperance, given to pride, excess and vanity. And finally, in the end, that they must needs come to confusion and ruin.

De donationibus inter virum & uxorem. Women be covetous, therefore unmeet governors. Digest, 1.3: De legibus senatusque consultis.[3] *Aristotle, Politics, 2.9.13.*

Would to God the examples were not so manifest to the further declaration of the imperfections of women, of their natural weakness and inordinate appetites. I might adduce histories proving some women to have died for sudden joy; some for unpacience to have murdered themselves; some to have burned with such inordinate lust that for the quenching of the same they have betrayed to strangers their country and city; and some to have been so desirous of dominion that for the obtaining of the same they have murdered the children of their own sons. Yea, and some have killed with cruelty their own husbands and children. But to me it is sufficient (because this part of nature is not my most sure foundation) to have proved that men illuminated only by the light of nature have seen and have determined that it is a thing most repugnant to nature that women rule and govern over men. For those that will not permit a woman to have power over her own sons will not permit her (I am assured) to have rule over a realm; and those that will not suffer her to speak in defence of those that be accused, neither that will admit her accusation intended against man, will not approve her that she shall sit in judgement, crowned with the royal crown, usurping authority in the midst of men.

England and Scotland beware. Great imperfections of women. Romilda the wife of Gisulphus betrayed to Cacanus the dukedom of Friuli in Italy. Jane queen of Naples hanged her husband.[4] *Athaliah, 2 Kgs. 11. Irene, Anton. Sabellicus.*[5]

But now to the second part of nature in the which I include the revealed will and perfect ordinance of God. And against this part of nature, I say that it doth manifestly repugn that any woman shall reign or bear dominion over man. For God, first by the order of His creation, and after by the curse and malediction pronounced against

If the less things be denied to women, the greater cannot be granted.

[3] The relevance of this citation is far from clear: there is nothing in *Digest*, 1.3 to support Knox's argument in the text. Likewise, the previous sentences place an interpretation on *Digest*, 24.1 which it cannot bear.

[4] For these references to Romilda, the wife of Gisulf II, duke of Friuli, and Joan I, queen of Naples, see the biographical notes.

[5] The story of the Byzantine empress, Irene, is in Sabellicus, *Opera omnia*, vol. II, pp. 446–7, 451–2. For further details, see the biographical notes. It is possible that Knox drew his references to Romilda and Joan I from the same source; vol. II, pp. 398, 609.

the woman by the reason of her rebellion, hath pronounced the contrary. First, I say that woman in her greatest perfection was made to serve and obey man, not to rule and command him. As St Paul doth reason in these words: 'Man is not of the woman but the woman of the man. And man was not created for the cause of the woman, but the woman for the cause of man, and therefore ought the woman to have a power upon her head' (that is a coverture in sign of subjection). Of the which words it is plain that the Apostle meaneth that woman in her greatest perfection should have known that man was lord above her; and therefore that she should never have pretended any kind of superiority above him, no more than do the angels above God the creator or above Christ Jesus their head. So I say that in her greatest perfection woman was created to be subject to man.

Woman in her greatest perfection was made to serve man. 1 Cor. 11.8–10.

A good comparison.

But after her fall and rebellion committed against God, there was put upon her a new necessity and she was made subject to man by the irrevocable sentence of God pronounced in these words: 'I will greatly multiply thy sorrow and thy conception. With sorrow shalt thou bear thy children, and thy will shall be subject to thy man; and he shall bear dominion over thee.' Hereby may such as altogether be not blinded plainly see that God by His sentence hath dejected all woman from empire and dominion above man. For two punishments are laid upon her: to wit, a dolour, anguish and pain as oft as ever she shall be mother; and a subjection of herself, her appetites and will, to her husband and to his will. From the former part of this malediction can neither art, nobility, policy nor law made by man deliver womankind, but whosoever attaineth to that honour to be mother proveth in experience the effect and strength of God's Word. But (alas) ignorance of God, ambition and tyranny have studied to abolish and destroy the second part of God's punishment. For women are lifted up to be heads over realms and to rule above men at their pleasure and appetites. But horrible is the vengeance which is prepared for the one and for the other, for the promoters and for the persons promoted, except they speedily repent. For they shall be dejected from the glory of the sons of God to the slavery of the devil and to the torment that is prepared for all such as do exalt themselves against God.

A new necessity of woman's subjection.

Woman by the sentence of God subject to man. Gen. 3.16.

The punishment of women unjustly promoted and of their promoters.

Against God can nothing be more manifest than that a woman shall be exalted to reign above man. For the contrary sentence hath He pronounced in these words: 'Thy will shall be subject to thy

Gen. 3.16.

husband, and he shall bear dominion over thee.' As God should say: 'Forasmuch as thou hast abused thy former condition, and because thy free will hath brought thyself and mankind into the bondage of Satan, I therefore will bring thee in bondage to man. For where before thy obedience should have been voluntary, now it shall be by constraint and by necessity; and that because thou hast deceived thy man, thou shalt therefore be no longer mistress over thine own appetites, over thine own will nor desires. For in thee there is neither reason nor discretion which be able to moderate thy affections, and therefore they shall be subject to the desire of thy man. He shall be lord and governor not only over thy body, but even over thy appetites and will.' This sentence, I say, did God pronounce against Eve and her daughters as the rest of the Scriptures doth evidently witness. So that no woman can ever presume to reign above man, but the same she must needs do in despite of God and in contempt of His punishment and malediction.

Let all women take heed.

I am not ignorant that the most part of men do understand this malediction of the subjection of the wife to her husband and of the dominion which he beareth above her. But the Holy Ghost giveth to us another interpretation of this place, taking from all women all kind of superiority, authority and power over man, speaking as followeth by the mouth of St Paul: 'I suffer not a woman to teach neither yet to usurp authority above man.' Here he nameth women in general, excepting none, affirming that she may usurp authority above no man. And that he speaketh more plainly in another place in these words: 'Let women keep silence in the congregation, for it is not permitted to them to speak, but to be subject as the law saith.' These two testimonies of the Holy Ghost be sufficient to prove whatsoever we have affirmed before and to repress the inordinate pride of women as also to correct the foolishness of those that have studied to exalt women in authority above man, against God and against His sentence pronounced.

Answer to an objection.

1 Tim. 2.12.

1 Cor. 14.34.

But that the same two places of the Apostle may the better be understood, it is to be noted that in the latter, which is written in the First Epistle to the Corinthians, the 14th chapter, before the Apostle had permitted that all persons should prophesy one after another, adding this reason: 'That all may learn and all may receive consolation'. And lest that any might have judged that amongst a rude multitude and the plurality of speakers many things little to purpose might

[1 Cor. 14.31]

have been affirmed, or else that some confusion might have arisen, he addeth: 'The spirits of the prophets are subject to the prophets.' As he should say: 'God shall always raise up some to whom the verity shall be revealed and unto such ye shall give place, albeit they sit in the lowest seats.' And thus the Apostle would have prophesying an exercise to be free to the whole church that everyone should communicate with the congregation what God had revealed to them providing that it were orderly done. But from this general privilege he secludeth all woman, saying: 'Let women keep silence in the congregation.' And why I pray you? Was it because that the Apostle thought no woman to have any knowledge? No, he giveth another reason, saying: 'Let her be subject as the law saith.' In which words is first to be noted that the Apostle calleth this former sentence pronounced against woman a law, that is, the immutable decree of God who by His own voice hath subjected her to one member of the congregation, that is, to her husband. Whereupon the Holy Ghost concludeth that she may never rule nor bear empire above man. For she that is made subject to one may never be preferred to many; and that the Holy Ghost doth manifestly express, saying: 'I suffer not that woman usurp the authority above man.' He saith not: 'I will not that woman usurp authority above her husband'; but he nameth man in general, taking from her all power and authority to speak, to reason, to interpret or to teach, but principally to rule or to judge in the assembly of men. So that woman, by the law of God and by the interpretation of the Holy Ghost, is utterly forbidden to occupy the place of God in the offices aforesaid which He hath assigned to man, whom He hath appointed and ordained His lieutenant in earth, secluding from that honour and dignity all woman, as this short argument shall evidently declare.

[*1 Cor. 14.32*]

From a general privilege is woman secluded.

She that is subject to one may not rule many.

The Apostle taketh power from all woman to speak in the assembly; *ergo*, he permitteth no woman to rule above man. The former part is evident, whereupon doth the conclusion of necessity follow. For he that taketh from woman the least part of authority, dominion or rule will not permit unto her that which is greatest. But greater it is to reign above realms and nations, to publish and to make laws and to command men of all estates, and finally to appoint judges and ministers, than to speak in the congregation. For her judgement, sentence or opinion proposed in the congregation may be judged by all, may be corrected by the learned and reformed by the godly. But woman

A strong argument.

NOTE.

being promoted in sovereign authority, her laws must be obeyed, her opinion followed and her tyranny maintained, supposing that it be expressly against God and the profit of the commonwealth, as to manifest experience doth this day witness. And therefore yet again I repeat that which before I have affirmed: to wit, that a woman promoted to sit in the seat of God, that is, to teach, to judge or to reign above man, is a monster in nature, contumely to God, and a thing most repugnant to His will and ordinance. For He hath deprived them as before is proved of speaking in the congregation and hath expressly forbidden them to usurp any kind of authority above man. How then will He suffer them to reign and have empire above realms and nations? He will never, I say, approve it because it is a thing most repugnant to His perfect ordinance, as after shall be declared and as the former Scriptures have plainly given testimony.

To the which to add anything were superfluous were it not that the world is almost now come to that blindness that, whatsoever pleaseth not the princes and the multitude, the same is rejected as doctrine newly forged and is condemned for heresy. I have therefore thought good to recite the minds of some ancient writers in the same matter to the end that such as altogether be not blinded by the devil may consider and understand this my judgement to be no new interpretation of God's Scriptures, but to be the uniform consent of the most part of godly writers since the time of the Apostles.

Tertullian, De habitu muliebri, I.I.2.

Tertullian in his book of women's apparel,[6] after that he hath shown many causes why gorgeous apparel is abominable and odious in a woman, addeth these words, speaking as it were to every woman by name: 'Dost thou not know (saith he) that thou art Eve? The sentence of God liveth and is effectual against this kind, and in this world of necessity it is that the punishment also live. Thou art the port and gate of the devil. Thou art the first transgressor of God's law. Thou didst persuade and easily deceive him whom the devil durst not assault. For thy merit (that is, for thy death) it behooved the Son of God to suffer the death, and doth it yet abide in thy mind to deck thee above thy skin coats?' By these and many other grave sentences and quick interrogations did this godly writer labour to bring every woman in contemplation of herself to the end that, every one deeply weighing what sentence God had pronounced against the

Let women hearken what Tertullian an old doctor saith.

[6] *De habitu muliebri* is the first book of Tertullian's *De cultu feminarum.*

whole race and daughters of Eve, might not only learn daily to humble and subject themselves in the presence of God, but also that they should avoid and abhor whatsoever thing might exalt them or puff them up in pride or that might be occasion that they should forget the curse and malediction of God.

And what, I pray you, is more able to cause woman to forget her own condition than if she be lifted up in authority above man? It is a thing very difficult to a man (be he never so constant), promoted to honours, not to be tickled somewhat with pride (for the wind of vainglory doth easily carry up the dry dust of the earth). But as for woman, it is no more possible that she being set aloft in authority above man shall resist the motions of pride than it is able to the weak reed or to the turning weathercock not to bow or turn at the vehemency of the inconstant wind. And therefore the same writer expressly forbiddeth all woman to intermeddle with the office of man. For thus he writeth in his book *De virginibus velandis*: 'It is not permitted to a woman to speak in the congregation, neither to teach, neither to baptise, neither to vendicate to herself any office of man.' The same he speaketh yet more plainly in the preface of his sixth book written against Marcion where he, recounting certain monstrous things which were to be seen at the sea called *Euxinum*, amongst the rest he reciteth this as a great monster in nature: 'That women in those parts were not tamed nor embased by consideration of their own sex and kind, but that all shame laid apart they made expenses upon weapons and learned the feats of war, having more pleasure to fight than to marry and be subject to man'. Thus far of Tertullian whose words be so plain that they need no explanation. For he that taketh from her all office appertaining to man will not suffer her to reign above man; and he that judgeth it a monster in nature that a woman shall exercise weapons must judge it to be a monster of monsters that a woman shall be exalted above a whole realm and nation. Of the same mind is Origen and diverse others (yea, even till the days of Augustine) whose sentences I omit to avoid prolixity.

Augustine in his 22nd book written against Faustus proveth that a woman ought to serve her husband as unto God, affirming that in

NOTE.

Tertullian, De virginibus velandis, 9.1.[7]

In prooemio 6. lib. Contra Marcionem.[8]

Augustine, Contra Faustum, 22.31.

[7] The original reference to 'Tertull. lib. 8' is clearly erroneous. There is only one book *De virginibus velandis* divided into sixteen chapters.

[8] Again, this is erroneous: Tertullian wrote only five books *Adversus Marcionem*. The passage referred to is from 1.1.3.

nothing hath woman equal power with man, saving that neither of both have power over their own bodies. By which he would plainly conclude that woman ought never to pretend nor thirst for that power and authority which is due to man. For so he doth explain himself in another place, affirming that woman ought to be repressed and bridled betimes if she aspire to any dominion; alleging that dangerous and perilous it is to suffer her to proceed, although it be in temporal and corporal things. And thereto he addeth these words: 'God seeth not for a time, neither is there any new thing in His sight and knowledge'; meaning thereby that what God hath seen in one woman (as concerning dominion and bearing of authority) the same He seeth in all. And what He hath forbidden to one, the same He also forbiddeth to all. And this most evidently yet in another place he writeth, moving this question: 'How can woman be the image of God, seeing (saith he) she is subject to man and hath none authority, neither to teach, neither to be witness, neither to judge, much less to rule or bear empire?' These be the very words of Augustine, of which it is evident that this godly writer doth not only agree with Tertullian before recited, but also with the former sentence of the law which taketh from woman not only all authority amongst men, but also every office appertaining to man.

De Trinitate, 12.7.10.

In quaestiones Veteris Testamenti, quaest. 45.[9]

NOTE.

To the question how she can be the image of God, he answereth as followeth: 'Woman (saith he) compared to other creatures is the image of God for she beareth dominion over them; but compared unto man she may not be called the image of God for she beareth not rule and lordship over man, but ought to obey him', etc. And how that woman ought to obey man, he speaketh yet more clearly in these words: 'The woman shall be subject to man as unto Christ. For woman (saith he) hath not her example from the body and from the flesh, that so she shall be subject to man as the flesh is unto the spirit. Because that the flesh in the weakness and mortality of this life lusteth and striveth against the spirit; and therefore would not the Holy Ghost give example of subjection to the woman of any such thing', etc. This sentence of Augustine ought to be noted of all women, for in it he plainly affirmeth that woman ought to be subject

De continentia, cap. 4.[10]

[9] Not now normally attributed to Augustine, but see *Pseudo-Augustini, quaestiones Veteris et Novi Testamentum CXXVII*, 45.3.

[10] These passages occur in chapter 23 of *De continentia* in the edition of Augustine's *Works* used here.

to man; that she never ought more to desire pre-eminence above him than that she ought to desire above Christ Jesus.

With Augustine agreeth in every point St Ambrose who thus writeth in his *Hexameron*: 'Adam was deceived by Eve and not Eve by Adam, and therefore just it is that woman receive and acknowledge him for governor whom she called to sin lest that again she slide and fall by womanly facility.' And writing upon the Epistle to the Ephesians, he saith: 'Let women be subject to their own husbands as unto the Lord, for the man is head to the woman and Christ is head to the congregation and He is the saviour of the body; but the congregation is subject to Christ, even so ought women to be to their husbands in all things.' He proceedeth further, saying: 'Women are commanded to be subject to men by the law of nature because that man is the author or beginner of the woman; for as Christ is the head of the church, so is man of the woman. From Christ the church took beginning and therefore it is subject unto Him; even so did woman take beginning from man that she should be subject.' Thus we hear the agreeing of these two writers to be such that a man might judge the one to have stolen the words and sentences from the other. And yet plain it is that during the time of their writing the one was far distant from the other. But the Holy Ghost who is the spirit of concord and unity did so illuminate their hearts and direct their tongues and pens that, as they did conceive and understand one truth, so did they pronounce and utter the same, leaving a testimony of their knowledge and concord to us their posterity.

Ambrose, Hexameron, 5.7.18.

Ambrose, Ad Ephesios, 5.22–4.

If any think that all these former sentences be spoken only of the subjection of the married woman to her husband, as before I have proved the contrary by the plain words and reasoning of St Paul, so shall I shortly do the same by other testimonies of the foresaid writers. The same Ambrose writing upon the second chapter of the First Epistle to Timothy, after he hath spoken much of the simple arrayment of women, he addeth these words: 'Woman ought not only to have simple arrayment, but all authority is to be denied unto her; for she must be in subjection to man (of whom she hath taken her original) as well in habit as in service.' And after a few words he saith: 'Because that death did enter into the world by her, there is no boldness that ought to be permitted unto her, but she ought to be in humility.' Hereof it is plain that from all woman, be she married or unmarried, is all authority taken to execute any office that appertai-

Ambrose, Ad Timotheum prima, 2.9–15.

neth to man. Yea, plain it is that all woman is commanded to serve, to be in humility and subjection. Which thing yet speaketh the same writer more plainly in these words: 'It is not permitted to women to speak, but to be in silence, as the law saith. What saith the law? Unto thy husband shall thy conversion be and he shall bear dominion over thee. This is a special law (saith Ambrose) whose sentence, lest it should be violated, infirmed or made weak, women are commanded to be in silence.' Here he includeth all women. And yet he proceedeth further in the same place, saying: 'It is shame for them to presume to speak of the law in the house of the Lord who hath commanded them to be subject to their men.' But most plainly speaketh he writing upon the 16th chapter of the Epistle of St Paul to the Romans, upon these words: 'Salute Rufus and his mother.' 'For this cause (saith Ambrose) did the Apostle place Rufus before his mother, for the election of the administration of the grace of God in the which a woman hath no place. For he was chosen and promoted by the Lord to take care over His business, that is, over the church, to the which officc could not his mother be appointed, albeit she was a woman so holy that the Apostle called her his mother.' Hereof it is plain that the administration of the grace of God is denied to all woman. By the administration of God's grace is understood not only the preaching of the Word and administration of the sacraments, by the which the grace of God is presented and ordinarily distributed unto man, but also the administration of civil justice, by the which virtue ought to be maintained and vices punished. The execution whereof is no less denied to woman than is the preaching of the Evangel or administration of the sacraments, as hereafter shall most plainly appear.

Ambrose, Ad Corinthios prima, 14.34–5. Gen. 3.16.

Whose house I pray you ought the parliament house to be, God's or the devil's?

Rufus is by St Paul saluted before his mother [Ambrose, Ad Romanos, 16.13].

Chrysostom, amongst the Grecian writers of no small credit, speaking in rebuke of men, who in his days were become inferior to some women in wit and in godliness, saith: 'For this cause was woman put under thy power (he speaketh to man in general) and thou was pronounced lord over her, that she should obey thee and that the head should not follow the feet. But often it is that we see the contrary, that he who in his order ought to be the head doth not keep the order of the feet (that is, doth not rule the feet) and that she that is in place of the foot is constitute to be the head.' He speaketh these words as it were in admiration that man was become so brutish that he did not consider it to be a thing most monstrous that woman should be preferred to man in anything whom God had subjected to

Chrysostom, In Gen. 3, Homilia 17.

NOTE.

man in all things. He proceedeth, saying: 'Nevertheless, it is the part of the man with diligent care to repel the woman that giveth him wicked counsel; and woman which gave that pestilent counsel to man ought at all times to have the punishment which was given to Eve sounding in her ears.' And in another place he induceth God speaking to the woman in this sort: 'Because thou left him of whose nature thou was participant and for whom thou was formed and hast had pleasure to have familiarity with that wicked beast and would take his counsel; therefore I subject thee to man and I appoint and affirm him to be thy lord that thou mayest acknowledge his dominion; and because thou couldst not bear rule, learn well to be ruled.'

In Gen. 3, Homilia 15.[11]

Why they should not bear rule, he declareth in other places, saying: 'Womankind is imprudent and soft (or flexible); imprudent because she cannot consider with wisdom and reason the things which she heareth and seeth; and soft she is because she is easily bowed.' I know that Chrysostom bringeth in these words to declare the cause why false prophets do commonly deceive women: because they are easily persuaded to any opinion, especially if it be against God, and because they lack prudence and right reason to judge the things that be spoken. But hereof may their nature be espied, and the vices of the same, which in no wise ought to be in those that are appointed to govern others. For they ought to be constant, stable, prudent and doing everything with discretion and reason, which virtues women cannot have in equality with men. For that he doth witness in another place, saying: 'Women have in themselves a tickling and study of vainglory, and that they may have common with men; they are suddenly moved to anger, and that they have also common with some men; but virtues in which they excel they have not common with man, and therefore hath the Apostle removed them from the office of teaching which is an evident proof that in virtue they far differ from man.' Let the reasons of this writer be marked, for further he yet proceedeth. After that he hath in many words lamented the effeminate manners of men who were so far degenerate to the weakness of women that some might have demanded: 'Why may not women teach amongst such a sort of men who in wisdom and godli-

God grant all women's hearts to understand and follow this sentence. In Matt. cap. 23, Homilia 44.[12]

Woman cannot have virtue in equality with man. Eph. 4.17–19. Homilia 13. NOTE.

[11] In fact, this too is from Homily 17, a few lines prior to the previously quoted passages.

[12] Homily 44 is actually on Matthew 12.46–50 and contains no such quotation. I have been unable to locate the passage either in Homilies 72–4 on Matthew 23 or elsewhere in Chrysostom's commentaries on Matthew.

ness are become inferior unto women?', he finally concludeth that: 'Notwithstanding that men be degenerate, yet may not women usurp any authority above them.' And, in the end, he addeth these words: 'These things do not I speak to extol them (that is, women), but to the confusion and shame of ourselves and to admonish us to take again the dominion that is meet and convenient for us, not only that power which is according to the excellency of dignity, but that which is according to providence and according to help and virtue. For then is the body in best proportion when it hath the best governor.'

The body lacking the head cannot be well governed, neither can commonwealth lacking man.

O, that both man and woman should consider the profound counsel and admonition of this father! He would not that man for appetite of any vainglory should desire pre-eminence above woman. For God hath not made man to be head for any such cause. But having respect to that weakness and imperfection which always letteth woman to govern, He hath ordained man to be superior. And that meaneth Chrysostom, saying: 'Then is the body in best proportion, when it hath the best governor.' But woman can never be the best governor by reason that she being spoiled of the spirit of regiment can never attain to that degree to be called or judged a good governor. Because in the nature of all woman lurketh such vices as in good governors are not tolerable. Which the same writer expresseth in these words: 'Womankind (saith he) is rash and foolhardy and their covetousness is like the gulf of hell, that is, insatiable.' And therefore in another place he will that woman shall have nothing to do in judgement in common affairs or in the regiment of the commonwealth because she is impatient of troubles, but that she shall live in tranquillity and quietness. And if she have occasion to go from the house that yet she shall have no matter of trouble, neither to follow her, neither to be offered unto her, as commonly there must be to such as bear authority. And with Chrysostom fully agreeth Basilius Magnus in a sermon which he maketh upon some places of Scripture wherein he reproveth diverse vices and amongst the rest he affirmeth woman to be a tender creature, flexible, soft and pitiful; which nature God hath

[Eph. 4.17–19. Homilia 13.]

In John 22, Homilia 87.[13]

In John, Homilia 41.[14]

Basilius Magnus, Sermo in aliquot scripturae locos.[15]

[13] This is a loose paraphrase of a passage in Homily 87 where Chrysostom is referring to prostitutes rather than to women in general: '. . . that sort of person is impudent, and Solomon hath compared their love to the grave; and then only do they stop, when they see their lover stripped of all'. The citation of John 22 is clearly an error; the Gospel has only twenty-one chapters.

[14] In fact, Chrysostom makes these remarks in Homily 61.

[15] See his *Opera omnia*, vol. 1, p. 477.

given unto her that she may be apt to nourish children. The which facility of the woman did Satan abuse and thereby brought her from the obedience of God. And therefore in diverse other places doth he conclude that she is not apt to bear rule and that she is forbidden to teach.

Innumerable more testimonies of all sorts of writers may be adduced for the same purpose. But with these I stand content, judging it sufficient to stop the mouth of such as accuse and condemn all doctrine as heretical which displeaseth them in any point that I have proved by the determinations and laws of men illuminated only by the light of nature, by the order of God's creation, by the curse and malediction pronounced against woman, by the mouth of St Paul who is the interpreter of God's sentence and law, and finally by the minds of those writers who in the church of God have been always holden in greatest reverence, that it is a thing most repugnant to nature, to God's will and appointed ordinance (yea, that it cannot be without contumely committed against God), that a woman should be promoted to dominion or empire to reign over man, be it in realm, nation, province or city. Now resteth it in few words to be shown that the same empire of women is the subversion of good order, equity and justice.

De ordine, 1.10.28.

Augustine defineth order to be that thing by the which God hath appointed and ordained all things. Note well, reader, that Augustine will admit no order where God's appointment is absent and lacketh. And in another place he saith that order is a disposition giving their own proper places to things that be unequal, which he termeth in Latin *parium & disparium*, that is, of things equal or like and things unequal or unlike. Of which two places, and of the whole disputation which is contained in his second book *De ordine*, it is evident that whatsoever is done either without the assurance of God's will, or else against His will manifestly revealed in His Word, is done against order. But such is the empire and regiment of all woman (as evidently before is declared); and therefore, I say, it is a thing plainly repugnant to good order, yea, it is the subversion of the same.

De civitas Dei, 19.13.

Whatsoever is done without the appointment of God's will is done without order.

If any list to reject the definition of Augustine, as either not proper to this purpose or else as insufficient to prove mine intent, let the same man understand that in so doing he hath infirmed mine argument nothing. For as I depend not upon the determinations of men, so think I my cause no weaker, albeit their authority be denied unto me, provided that God by His will revealed and manifest Word stand plain and evident on my side. That God hath subjected womankind to man by the order of His creation and by the curse that He hath pronounced against her is before declared. Besides these, He hath set before our eyes two other mirrors and glasses in which He will that we should behold the order which He hath appointed and established in nature: the one is the natural body of man; the other is the politic or civil body of that commonwealth in which God by His own Word hath appointed an order.

Two mirrors in which we may behold the order of nature.

In the natural body of man God hath appointed an order that the head shall occupy the uppermost place. And the head hath He joined with the body that from it doth life and motion flow to the rest of the members. In it hath He placed the eye to see, the ear to hear and the tongue to speak, which offices are appointed to none other member of the body. The rest of the members have every one their own place and office appointed, but none may have neither the place nor office of the head. For who would not judge that body to be a monster where there was no head eminent above the rest, but that the eyes were in the hands, the tongue and mouth beneath in the belly and the ears in the feet? Men, I say, should not only pronounce this body to be a monster, but assuredly they might conclude that such a body could not long endure.

And no less monstrous is the body of that commonwealth where a woman beareth empire. For either doth it lack a lawful head (as in very deed it doth) or else there is an idol exalted in the place of the true head. An idol I call that which hath the form and appearance but lacketh the virtue and strength which the name and proportion do resemble and promise. As images have face, nose, eyes, mouth, hands and feet painted, but the use of the same cannot the craft and art of man give them. As the Holy Ghost by the mouth of David teacheth us, saying: 'They have eyes but they see not, mouth but they speak not, nose but they smell not, hands and feet but they neither touch nor have power to go.' And such, I say, is every realm and nation where a woman beareth dominion. For in despite of God (He of His just judgement so giving them over into a reprobate mind) may a realm, I confess, exalt up a woman to that monstriferous honour, to be esteemed as head. But impossible it is to man and angel to give unto her the properties and perfect offices of a lawful head. For the same God that hath denied power to the hand to speak, to the belly

Commonwealths under the rule of women lack a lawful head.
Idol.

Ps. 115.5–7.

The empire of a woman is an idol.

to hear and to the feet to see, hath denied to woman power to command man and hath taken away wisdom to consider and providence to foresee the things that be profitable to the commonwealth; yea, finally, He hath denied to her in any case to be head to man, but plainly hath pronounced that man is head to woman, even as Christ is head to all man.

1 Cor.11.3.

If men in a blind rage should assemble together and appoint themselves another head than Jesus Christ (as the papists have done their Romish Antichrist), should Christ therefore lose his own dignity or should God give to that counterfeit head power to give life to the body, to see whatsoever might endamage or hurt it, to speak in defence and to hear the request of every subject? It is certain that He would not. For that honour He hath appointed before all times to His only Son, and the same will He give to no creature besides. No more will He admit nor accept woman to be the lawful head over man, although man, devil and angel will conjure in their favour. For seeing He hath subjected her to one (as before is said), He will never permit her to reign over many. Seeing He hath commanded her to hear and obey one, He will not suffer that she speak and with usurped authority command realms and nations.

NOTE.

Chrysostom explaining these words of the Apostle ('the head of the woman is man') compareth God in His universal regiment to a king sitting in his royal majesty to whom all his subjects, commanded to give homage and obedience, appear before him bearing everyone such a badge and cognisance of dignity and honour as he hath given to them; which if they despise and contemn, then do they dishonour their king. 'Even so (saith he) ought man and woman to appear before God bearing the ensigns of the condition which they have received of Him. Man hath received a certain glory and dignity above the woman and therefore ought he to appear before His high majesty bearing the sign of His honour, having no coverture upon his head to witness that in earth man hath no head.' (Beware, Chrysostom, what thou sayest: thou shalt be reputed a traitor if Englishmen hear thee, for they must have my sovereign lady and mistress; and Scotland hath drunken also the enchantment and venom of Circe, let it be so to their own shame and confusion.) He proceedeth in these words: 'But woman ought to be covered to witness that in earth she hath a head, that is, man.' True it is, Chrysostom, woman is covered in both the said realms, but it is not with the sign of subjection, but it is with

1 Cor.11.3.

Mark the similitude of Chrysostom. [*1 Cor.11.7–11. Homilia 26.*]

NOTE.

[*1 Cor.11. Homilia 26.*] *How women be covered in*

England and Scotland.

the sign of superiority, to wit, with the royal crown. To that he answereth in these words: 'What if man neglect his honour? He is no less to be mocked (saith Chrysostom) than if a king should depose himself of his diadem or crown and royal estate and clothe himself in the habit of a slave.' What, I pray you, should this godly father have said if he had seen all the men of a realm or nation fall down before a woman? If he had seen the crown, sceptre and sword which are ensigns of the royal dignity given to her, and a woman, cursed of God and made subject to man, placed in the throne of justice to sit as God's lieutenant? What, I say, in this behalf, should any heart unfeignedly fearing God have judged of such men? I am assured that not only should they have been judged foolish, but also enraged and slaves to Satan, manifestly fighting against God and His appointed order.

Brute beasts to be preferred.

The more that I consider the subversion of God's order, which He hath placed generally in all living things, the more I do wonder at the blindness of man who doth not consider himself in this case so degenerate that the brute beasts are to be preferred unto him in this behalf. For nature hath in all beasts printed a certain mark of dominion in the male and a certain subjection in the female which they keep inviolate. For no man ever saw the lion make obedience and stoop before the lioness, neither yet can it be proved that the hind taketh the conducting of the herd amongst the harts. And yet (alas) man, who by the mouth of God hath dominion appointed to him over woman, doth not only to his own shame stoop under the obedience of women, but also in despite of God and of His appointed order rejoiceth and maintaineth that monstrous authority as a thing lawful and just. The insolent joy, the bonfires and banqueting, which were in London and elsewhere in England when that cursed Jezebel was proclaimed queen did witness to my heart that men were become more than enraged. For else how could they so have rejoiced at their own confusion and certain destruction? For what man was there of so base judgement (supposing that he had any light of God) who did not see the erecting of that monster to be the overthrow of true religion and the assured destruction of England and of the ancient liberties thereof? And yet, nevertheless, all men so triumphed as if God had delivered them from all calamity.

Insolent joy bringeth sudden sorrow.

But just and righteous, terrible and fearful, are thy judgements, O Lord! For as sometimes thou didst so punish men for unthankfulness

Rom. 1.

that man ashamed not to commit villainy with man (and that because that knowing thee to be God, they glorified thee not as God), even so hast thou most justly now punished the proud rebellion and horrible ingratitude of the realms of England and Scotland. For when thou didst offer thyself most mercifully to them both, offering the means by the which they might have been joined together forever in godly concord, then was the one proud and cruel and the other unconstant and fickle of promise.[16] But yet (alas) did miserable England further rebel against thee. For albeit thou didst not cease to heap benefit upon benefit during the reign of an innocent and tender king,[17] yet no man did acknowledge thy potent hand and marvellous working. The stout courage of captains, the wit and policy of counsellors, the learning of bishops, did rob thee of thy glory and honour. For what then was heard, as concerning religion, but the king's proceedings, the king's proceedings must be obeyed? It is enacted by parliament; therefore, it is treason to speak in the contrary. But this was not the end of this miserable tragedy. For thou didst yet proceed to offer thy favours, sending thy prophets and messengers to call for reformation of life in all estates. For even from the highest to the lowest all were declined from thee (yea, even those that should have been the lanterns to others). Some I am assured did quake and tremble, and from the bottom of their hearts thirsted amendment, and for the same purpose did earnestly call for discipline. But then burst forth the venom which before lurked; then might they not contain their despiteful voices, but with open mouths did cry: 'We will not have such a one to reign over us.'

What robbed God of His honour in England in the time of the Gospel.

God's benefits shown to England.

Then, I say, was every man so stout that he would not be brought in bondage; no, not to thee, O Lord, but with disdain did the multitude cast from them the amiable yoke of Christ Jesus. No man would suffer his sin to be rebuked, no man would have his life called to trial. And thus did they refuse thee, O Lord, and thy Son Christ Jesus to be their pastor, protector and prince. And therefore hast thou given them over into a reprobate mind. Thou hast taken from them the spirit of boldness, of wisdom and of righteous judgement. They see their own destruction and yet they have no grace to avoid

Discipline refused in England.

The nobility and the whole

[16] A reference to the 'Rough Wooing' which followed the Scots' rejection in 1543 of the terms of the Treaties of Greenwich by which Mary Stewart was to marry Edward Tudor.

[17] That is, Edward VI.

it. Yea, they are become so blind that, knowing the pit, they headlong cast themselves into the same; as the nobility of England do this day, fighting in the defence of their mortal enemy, the Spaniard. Finally, they are so destitute of understanding and judgement that, although they know that there is a liberty and freedom the which their predecessors have enjoyed, yet are they compelled to bow their necks under the yoke of Satan and of his proud ministers, pestilent papists and proud Spaniards. And yet can they not consider that where a woman reigneth, and papists bear authority, that there must needs Satan be president of the council.

realm of England cast themselves willingly into the pit.

Thus hast thou, O Lord, in thy hot displeasure, revenged the contempt of thy graces offered. But, O Lord, if thou shalt retain wrath to the end, what flesh is able to sustain? We have sinned, O Lord, and are not worthy to be relieved. But worthy art thou, O Lord, to be a true God, and worthy is thy Son Christ Jesus to have His Evangel and glory advanced; which both are trodden underfoot in this cruel murder and persecution which the builders of Babylon commit in their fury, have raised against thy children, for the establishing of their kingdom. Let the sobs therefore of thy prisoners, O Lord, pass up to thine ears, consider their affliction, and let the eyes of thy mercy look down upon the blood of such as die for testimony of thy eternal verity, and let not thine enemies mock thy judgement forever. To thee, O Lord, I turn my wretched and wicked heart; to thee alone I direct my complaint and groans; for in that Isle to thy saints there is left no comfort.

Confession.

Albeit I have thus (talking with my God in the anguish of my heart) somewhat digressed, yet have I not utterly forgotten my former proposition, to wit, that it is a thing repugnant to the order of nature that any woman be exalted to rule over men. For God hath denied unto her the office of a head. And in the entreating of this part, I remember that I have made the nobility both of England and Scotland inferior to brute beasts for that they do to women which no male amongst the common sort of beasts can be proved to do to their females: that is, they reverence them and quake at their presence, they obey their commandments, and that against God. Wherefore I judge them not only subjects to women, but slaves of Satan and servants of iniquity. If any man think these my words sharp or vehement, let him consider that the offence is more heinous than can be expressed by words. For where all things be expressedly concluded against the glory and honour of God, and where the blood of the saints of God is commanded to be shed, whom shall we judge, God or the devil, to be president of that council? Plain it is that God ruleth not by His love, mercy nor grace in the assembly of the ungodly. Then it resteth that the devil, the prince of this world, doth reign over such tyrants. Whose servants, I pray you, shall then be judged such as obey and execute their tyranny? God for His great mercy's sake illuminate the eyes of men that they may perceive into what miserable bondage they be brought by the monstriferous empire of women.

NOTE.

NOTE.

The second glass which God hath set before the eyes of man wherein he may behold the order which pleaseth His wisdom concerning authority and dominion is that commonwealth to the which it pleaseth His majesty to appoint and give laws, statutes, rites and ceremonies, not only concerning religion, but also touching their policy and regiment of the same. And against that order it doth manifestly repugn that any woman shall occupy the throne of God (that is, the royal seat which He by His Word hath appointed to man), as in giving the law to Israel concerning the election of a king is evident. For thus it is written: 'If thou shalt say: I will appoint a king above me as the rest of the nations which are about me, thou shalt make thee a king whom the Lord thy God shall choose, one from amongst the midst of thy brethren thou shalt appoint king above thee. Thou mayest not make a stranger that is not thy brother.' Here expressedly is a man appointed to be chosen king, and a man native amongst themselves; by which precept is all woman and all stranger secluded. What may be objected for the part or election of a stranger shall be, God willing, answered in the *Blast of the Second Trumpet*.[18] For this present, I say that the erecting of a woman to that honour is not only to invert the order which God hath established, but also it is to defile, pollute and profane (so far as in man lieth) the throne and seat of God which He hath sanctified and appointed for man only in the course of this wretched life to occupy and possess as His minister and lieutenant, secluding from the same all woman, as before is expressed.

Deut. 17.14–15.

God hath appointed man His minister and lieutenant.

Answer to an objection.

If any think that the forewritten law did bind the Jews only, let the

[18] *The Second Blast of the Trumpet* was never written in full, but see the notes which Knox appended to the *Letter to the Commonalty*, below pp. 128–9.

same man consider that the election of a king and appointing of judges did neither appertain to the ceremonial law neither yet was it mere judicial, but that it did flow from the moral law as an ordinance, having respect to the conservation of both the Tables. For the office of the magistrate ought to have the first and chief respect to the glory of God commanded and contained in the former Table, as is evident by that which was enjoined to Joshua by God what time he was accepted and admitted ruler and governor over His people, in these words: 'Thou shalt divide the inheritance to this people, the which I have sworn to their fathers to give unto them; so that thou be valiant and strong, that thou mayest keep and do according to that whole law, which my servant Moses hath commanded thee. Thou shalt not decline from it, neither to the right hand neither to the left hand; that thou mayest do prudently in all things that thou takest in hand, let not the book of this law depart from thy mouth, but meditate in it day and night that thou mayest keep and do according to everything that is written in it. For then shall thy ways prosper and then shalt thou do prudently', etc. And the same precept giveth God by the mouth of Moses to kings after they be elected, in these words: 'When he shall sit in the throne or seat of his kingdom, he shall write to himself a copy of this law in a book, and that shall be with him that he may read in it all the days of his life, that he may learn to fear the Lord his God and to keep all the words of this law and all these statutes, that he may do them', etc.

The election of a king floweth from the moral law.

Josh. 1.6–8.

Rulers should take heed to this.

Deut. 17.18–19.

Of these two places it is evident that principally it appertaineth to the king or to the chief magistrate to know the will of God, to be instructed in His law and statutes and to promote His glory with his whole heart and study, which be the chief points of the First Table. No man denieth but that the sword is committed to the magistrate to the end that he should punish vice and maintain virtue. To punish vice, I say, not only that which troubleth the tranquillity and quiet estate of the commonwealth by adultery, theft or murder committed, but also such vices as openly impugn the glory of God as idolatry, blasphemy and manifest heresy taught and obstinately maintained. As the histories and notable acts of Hezekiah, Jehoshaphat and Josiah do plainly teach us, whose study and care was not only to glorify God in their own life and conversation, but also they unfeignedly did travail to bring their subjects to the true worshipping and honouring of God, and did destroy all monuments of idolatry, did punish to

What vices magistrates ought to punish.

death the teachers of it, and removed from office and honours such as were maintainers of those abominations. Whereby I suppose that it be evident that the office of the king or supreme magistrate hath respect to the law moral and to the conservation of both the Tables.

NOTE. *The Gentile no less bound to the law moral than the Jew.*

Now if the law moral be the constant and unchangeable will of God to the which the Gentile is no less bound than was the Jew; and if God will that amongst the Gentiles the ministers and executors of His law be now appointed as sometimes they were appointed amongst the Jews; further, if the execution of justice be no less requisite in the policy of the Gentiles than ever it was amongst the Jews, what man can be so foolish to suppose or believe that God will now admit those persons to sit in judgement or to reign over men in the commonwealth of the Gentiles whom He by His expressed Word and ordinance did before debar and seclude from the same? And that women were secluded from the royal seat, the which ought to be the sanctuary to all poor afflicted, and therefore is justly called the seat of God, besides the place before recited of the election of a king, and besides the places of the New Testament which be most evident, the order and election which was kept in Judah and Israel doth manifestly declare. For when the males of the kingly stock failed, as oft as it chanced in Israel and sometimes in Judah, it never entered into the hearts of the people to choose and promote to honours any of the king's daughters (had he never so many), but knowing God's vengeance to be poured forth upon the father by the away-taking of his sons, they had no further respect to his stock, but elected such one man or other as they judged most apt for that honour and authority. Of which premises, I conclude (as before) that to promote a woman head over men is repugnant to nature and a thing most contrarious to that order which God hath approved in that commonwealth which He did institute and rule by His Word.

NOTE.

But now to the last point, to wit, that the empire of a woman is a thing repugnant to justice and the destruction of every commonwealth where it is received. In probation whereof, because the matter is more than evident, I will use few words. First, I say, if justice be a constant and perpetual will to give to every person their own right (as the most learned in all ages have defined it to be),[19] then to give

The first argument that

[19] This definition derives from the *Digest*, 1.1.9: 'Justice is a steady and enduring will to render unto everyone his right.'

or to will to give to any person that which is not their right must repugn to justice. But to reign above man can never be the right to woman because it is a thing denied unto her by God, as is before declared. Therefore, to promote her to that estate or dignity can be nothing else but repugnancy to justice. If I should speak no more, this were sufficient. For except that either they can improve the definition of justice or else that they can entreat God to revoke and call back His sentence pronounced against woman, they shall be compelled to admit my conclusion. If any find fault with justice as it is defined, he may well accuse others, but me he shall not hurt. For I have the shield, the weapon and the warrant of Him who assuredly will defend this quarrel, and He commandeth me to cry: 'Whatsoever repugneth to the will of God expressed in His most sacred Word repugneth to justice; but that women have authority over men repugneth to the will of God expressed in His Word; and therefore mine author commandeth me to conclude without fear that all such authority repugneth to justice.'

the authority of women repugneth to justice.

The second argument.

The first part of the argument I trust dare neither Jew nor Gentile deny, for it is a principle not only universally confessed, but also so deeply printed in the heart of man, be his nature never so corrupted, that whether he will or no he is compelled at one time or other to acknowledge and confess that justice is violated when things are done against the will of God expressed by His Word. And to this confession are no less the reprobate coacted and constrained than be the chosen children of God, albeit to a diverse end. The elect with displeasure of their fact confess their offence, having access to grace and mercy, as did Adam, David, Peter and all other penitent offenders. But the reprobate, notwithstanding they are compelled to acknowledge the will of God to be just, the which they have offended, yet are they never inwardly displeased with their iniquity, but rage, complain and storm against God whose vengeance they cannot escape, as did Cain, Judas, Herod, Julian called Apostate, yea, Jezebel and Athaliah. For Cain no doubt was convict in conscience that he had done against justice in murdering of his brother. Judas did openly before the high priest confess that he had sinned in betraying innocent blood. Herod being stricken by the angel did mock those his flatterers, saying unto them: 'Behold your God (meaning of himself) cannot now preserve himself from corruption and worms.' Julian was compelled in the end to cry: 'O Galilean (so always in contempt did he name our Saviour

Nature doth confess that repugnancy to God's will is injustice.

How the reprobate confess God's will to be just.

Gen. 4.

Matt. 27.

[Acts 12.]

Jesus Christ) thou hast now overcome.' And who doubteth but Jezebel and Athaliah, before their miserable end, were convicted in their cankered consciences to acknowledge that the murder which they had committed and the empire which the one had six years usurped were repugnant to justice.

Woman's authority bringeth forth monsters.

Even so shall they, I doubt not, which this day do possess and maintain that monstriferous authority of women shortly be compelled to acknowledge that their studies and devices have been bent against God, and that all such authority as women have usurped repugneth to justice because, as I have said, it repugneth to the will of God expressed in His sacred Word. And if any man doubt hereof, let him mark well the words of the Apostle, saying: 'I permit not a woman to teach neither yet to usurp authority above man.' No man, I trust, will deny these words of the Apostle to be the will of God expressed in His Word. And he saith openly 'I permit not', etc. which is as much as 'I will not that a woman have authority, charge or power over man', for so much importeth the Greek word ἀυθεντειν[20] in that place. Now let man and angel conspire against God, let them pronounce their laws, and say: 'We will suffer women to bear authority, who then can depose them?' Yet shall this one word of the eternal God, spoken by the mouth of a weak man, thrust them every one into hell. Jezebel may for a time sleep quietly in the bed of her fornication and whoredom, she may teach and deceive for a season, but neither shall she preserve herself neither yet her adulterous children from great affliction and from the sword of God's vengeance which shall shortly apprehend such works of iniquity.

1 Tim. 2.12.

Rev. 2.

The admonition I defer to the end. Here might I bring in the oppression and injustice which is committed against realms and nations which sometimes lived free and now are brought in bondage of foreign nations by the reason of this monstriferous authority and empire of women. But that I delay till better opportunity. And now I think it expedient to answer such objections as carnal and worldly men, yea, men ignorant of God, use to make for maintenance of this tyranny (authority it is not worthy to be called) and most unjust empire of women. First, they do object the examples of Deborah and of Huldah the Prophetess, of whom the one judged Israel and the other, by all appearance, did teach and exhort. Secondarily, they do

Judg. 4.
2 Chr. 34.
The defences of the adversaries.

20 To have full power or authority over.

object the law made by Moses for the daughters of Zelophehad. *Num. 27.* Thirdly, the consent of the estates of such realms as have approved the empire and regiment of women. And last, the long custom which hath received the regiment of women, their valiant acts and prosperity, together with some papistical laws which have confirmed the same.

Answer to the first objection.

To the first, I answer that particular examples do establish no common law. The causes were known to God alone why He took the spirit of wisdom and force from all men of those ages and did so mightily assist women against nature and against His ordinary course that the one He made a deliverer to His afflicted people Israel and to the other He gave not only perseverance in the true religion, when the most part of men had declined from the same, but also to her He gave the spirit of prophecy to assure King Josiah of the things which were to come. With these women, I say, did God work potently and miraculously, yea, to them He gave most singular grace and privilege. But who hath commanded that a public, yea, a tyrannical and most wicked law be established upon these examples?

Examples against law have no strength when the question is of law.

The men that object the same are not altogether ignorant that examples have no strength when the question is of law. As if I should ask: 'What marriage is lawful?', and it should be answered that: 'Lawful it is to man not only to have many wives at once, but also it is lawful to marry two sisters and to enjoy them both living at once, because that David, Jacob and Solomon, servants of God, did the same.' I trust that no man would justify the vanity of this reason. Or if the question were demanded if a Christian with good conscience may defraud, steal or deceive, and answer were made that so he might by the example of the Israelites who at God's commandment deceived the Egyptians and spoiled them of their garments, gold and silver, I think likewise this reason should be mocked. And what greater force, I pray you, hath the former argument? Deborah did rule in Israel and Huldah spoke prophecy in Judah; *ergo*, it is lawful for women to reign above realms and nations or to teach in the presence of men. The consequent is vain and of none effect. For of examples, as is before declared, we may establish no law, but we are always bound to the law written and to the commandment expressed in the same. And the law written and pronounced by God forbiddeth no less that any woman reign over man than it forbiddeth man to take plurality of wives, to marry two sisters living at once, to steal, to

NOTE.

rob, to murder or to lie. If any of these hath been transgressed, and yet God hath not imputed the same, it maketh not the like fact or deed lawful unto us. For God being free may for such causes as be approved by His inscrutable wisdom dispense with the rigour of His law and may use His creatures at His pleasure. But the same power is not permitted to man whom He hath made subject to His law and not to the examples of his fathers.

And this I think sufficient to the reasonable and moderate spirits. But to repress the raging of woman's madness, I will descend somewhat deeper into the matter and not fear to affirm that as we find a contrary spirit in all these most wicked women that this day be exalted into this tyrannous authority to the spirit that was in those godly matrons, so I fear not, I say, to affirm that their condition is unlike and that their end shall be diverse. In those matrons we find that the spirit of mercy, truth, justice and of humility did reign. Under them we find that God did show mercy to His people, delivering them from the tyranny of strangers and from the venom of idolatry by the hands and counsel of those women. But in these of our ages, we find cruelty, falsehood, pride, covetousness, deceit and oppression. In them we also find the spirit of Jezebel and Athaliah, under them we find the simple people oppressed, the true religion extinguished and the blood of Christ's members most cruelly shed. And finally, by their practices and deceit, we find ancient realms and nations given and betrayed into the hands of strangers, the titles and liberties of them taken from the just possessors. Which one thing is an evident testimony how unlike our mischievous Marys be unto Deborah, under whom were strangers chased out of Israel, God so raising her up to be a mother and deliverer to His oppressed people. But (alas) He hath raised up these Jezebels to be the uttermost of His plagues, the which man's unthankfulness hath long deserved. But His secret and most just judgement shall neither excuse them neither their maintainers because their counsels be diverse.

Antithesis betwixt the former matrons and our Jezebels.

NOTE.

But to prosecute my purpose, let such as list to defend these monsters in their tyranny prove first that their sovereign mistresses be like to Deborah in godliness and pity; and secondarily, that the same success doth follow their tyranny which did follow the extraordinary regiment of that godly matron. Which thing, although they were able to do (as they never shall be, let them blow till they burst), yet shall her example profit them nothing at all. For they are never able to

NOTE.

prove that either Deborah or any other godly woman (having the commendation of the Holy Ghost within the Scriptures) hath usurped authority above any realm or nation by reason of their birth and blood. Neither yet did they claim it by right or inheritance. But God, by His singular privilege, favour and grace, exempted Deborah from the common malediction given to women in that behalf; and against nature He made her prudent in counsel, strong in courage, happy in regiment and a blessed mother and deliverer to His people. The which He did partly to advance and notify the power of His majesty, as well to His enemies as to His own people, in that He declared Himself able to give salvation and deliverance by means of the most weak vessels; and partly He did it to confound and ashame all man of that age because they had for the most part declined from His true obedience. And therefore was the spirit of courage, regiment and boldness taken from them for a time to their confusion and further humiliation.

No godly woman did ever claim authority over man by reason of her birth and blood.

Why God sometimes worketh by extraordinary means.

But what maketh this for Mary and her match Philip? One thing I would ask of such as depend upon the example of Deborah: whether she was widow or wife when she judged Israel and when that God gave that notable victory to His people under her? If they answer she was widow, I would lay against them the testimony of the Holy Ghost witnessing that she was wife to Lapidoth. And if they will shift and allege that so she might be called notwithstanding that her husband was dead, I urge them further that they are not able to prove it to be any common phrase and manner of speech in the Scriptures that a woman shall be called the wife of a dead man except that there be some note added whereby it may be known that her husband is departed, as is witnessed of Anna. But in this place of the Judges, there is no note added that her husband should be dead, but rather the expressed contrary. For the text saith: 'In that time a woman named Deborah, a Prophetess, wife to Lapidoth, judged Israel.' The Holy Ghost plainly speaketh that what time she judged Israel she was wife to Lapidoth. If she was wife, and if she ruled all alone in Israel, then I ask why did she not prefer her husband to that honour to be captain and to be leader to the host of the Lord? If any think that it was her husband, the text proveth the contrary. For it affirmeth that Barak of the tribe of Naphtali was appointed to that office. If Barak had been her husband, to what purpose should the Holy Ghost so diligently have noted the tribe and another name than was before

Judg. 4.

Luke 2.36–7.

Judg. 4.4.

NOTE.

expressed? Yea, to what purpose should it be noted that she sent and called him? Whereof I doubt not but that every reasonable man doth consider that this Barak was not her husband, and thereof likewise it is evident that her judgement or government in Israel was no such usurped power as our queens unjustly possess this day, but that it was the spirit of prophecy which rested upon her what time the multitude of the people had wrought wickedly in the eyes of the Lord; by the which spirit she did rebuke the idolatry and iniquity of the people, exhort them to repentance and, in the end, did bring them this comfort: that God should deliver them from the bondage and thraldom of their enemies. And this she might do notwithstanding that another did occupy the place of the supreme magistrate (if any was in those days in Israel). For so I find did Huldah, the wife of Shallum, in the days of Josiah, king of Judah, speak prophecy and comfort the king, and yet he resigned to her neither the sceptre nor the sword.

NOTE.

2 Kgs. 22.

That this our interpretation, how that Deborah did judge in Israel, is the true meaning of the Holy Ghost, the pondering and weighing of the history shall manifestly prove. When she sendeth for Barak, I pray you, in whose name giveth she him his charge? Doth she speak to him as kings and princes use to speak to their subjects in such cases? No, but she speaketh as she that had a special revelation from God which neither was known to Barak nor to the people, saying: 'Hath not the Lord God of Israel commanded thee?' This is her preface by the which she would stir up the dull senses of Barak and of the people, willing to persuade unto them that the time was come when God would show Himself their protector and deliverer, in which preface she usurpeth to herself neither power nor authority. For she saith not: 'I being thy princess, thy mistress, thy sovereign lady and queen, command thee upon thine allegiance and under pain of treason to go and gather an army.' No, she spoileth herself of all power to command, attributing that authority to God, of whom she had her revelation and certitude to appoint Barak captain, which after appeareth more plainly. For when she had declared to him the whole counsel of God, appointing unto him as well the number of his soldiers as the tribes out of which they should be gathered; and when she had appointed the place of the battle (which she could not have done but by especial revelation of God) and had assured him of victory in the name of God; and yet that he fainted and openly refused

Deborah commanded not as princes use to command.

[Judg. 4.6.]

to enter into that journey except that the Prophetess would accompany him, she did use against him no external power, she did not threaten him with rebellion and death, but for assurance of his faint heart and weak conscience, being content to go with him, she pronounceth that the glory should not be his in that journey, but that 'the Lord should sell Sisera into the hand of a woman'. [*Judg.* 4.9.]

Such as have more pleasure in light than in darkness may clearly perceive that Deborah did usurp no such power nor authority as our queens do this day claim, but that she was endued with the spirit of wisdom, of knowledge and of the true fear of God, and by the same she judged the facts of the rest of the people. She rebuked their defection and idolatry, yea, and also did redress to her power the injuries that were done by man to man. But all this, I say, she did by the spiritual sword, that is, by the Word of God, and not by any temporal regiment or authority which she did usurp over Israel. In which, I suppose, at that time there was no lawful magistrate by the reason of their great affliction. For so witnesseth the history, saying: [*Judg.*4.1–2.] 'And Ehud being dead, the Lord sold Israel into the hand of Jabin, King of Canaan.' And he by Sisera his captain afflicted Israel greatly the space of twenty years. And Deborah herself in her song of thanksgiving confesseth that before she did arise mother in Israel, and in [*Judg.*5.3–7.] the days of Jael, there was nothing but confusion and trouble.

If any stick to the term, alleging that the Holy Ghost saith that she judged Israel, let them understand that neither doth the Hebrew word neither yet the Latin always signify civil judgement or the execution of the temporal sword, but most commonly is taken in the sense which we have before expressed. For of Christ it is said: 'He shall judge many nations', and that: 'He shall pronounce judgement to the Gentiles'. And yet it is evident that He was no minister of the temporal sword. God commandeth Jerusalem and Judah to judge betwixt Him and His vineyard, and yet He appointed not them all to be civil magistrates. To Ezekiel it is said: 'Shalt thou not judge them, son of man?'; and after: 'Thou, son of man, shalt thou not judge? Shalt thou not judge, I say, the city of blood?'; and also: 'Behold, I shall judge betwixt beast and beast.' And such places in great number are to be found throughout the whole Scriptures, and yet I trust no man will be so foolish as to think that any of the Prophets were appointed by God to be politic judges or to punish the sins of man by corporal punishment. No, the manner of their judgement is expressed in these

To judge is not always understood of the civil regiment.
Isa. 2.4.
Isa. 42.1.
Mic. 4.3.
Isa. 5.3.
Ezek. 20.4.
Ezek. 22.2.
Ezek. 34.17.

Ezek. 22.2–4. words: 'Declare to them all their abominations; and thou shalt say to them: Thus saith the Lord God: a city shedding blood in the midst of her, that her time may approach, and which hath made idols against herself, that she might be polluted. Thou hast transgressed in the blood which thou hast shed and thou art polluted in the idols which thou hast made.' Thus, I say, do the Prophets of God judge, pronouncing the sentence of God against malefactors. And so I doubt not but Deborah judged what time Israel had declined from God, rebuking their defection and exhorting them to repentance without usurpation of any civil authority. And if the people gave unto her for a time any reverence or honour, as her godliness and happy counsel did well deserve, yet was it no such empire as our monsters claim. For which of her sons or nearest kinsmen left she ruler and judge in Israel after her? The Holy Ghost expresseth no such thing. Whereof it is evident that by her example God offereth no occasion to establish any regiment of women above men, realms and nations.

NOTE.

An answer to the second objection.

But now to the second objection, in which women require (as to them appeareth) nothing but equity and justice, whilst they and their patrons for them require dominion and empire above men. For this is their question: 'Is it not lawful that women have their right and inheritance like as the daughters of Zelophehad were commanded by the mouth of Moses to have their portion of ground in their tribe?' [*Num. 36.*]

What woman would not gladly hear.

I answer it is not only lawful that women possess their inheritance, but I affirm also that justice and equity require that so they do. But therewith I add that which gladly they list not understand: that to bear rule or authority over man can never be right nor inheritance to woman. For that can never be just inheritance to any person which God by His Word hath plainly denied unto them; but to all women hath God denied authority above man, as most manifestly is before declared; therefore to her it can never be inheritance. And thus must the advocates of our ladies provide some better example and stronger argument. For the law made in favour of the daughters of Zelophehad will serve them nothing. And assuredly great wonder it is that in so great light of God's truth men list to grope and wander in darkness. For let them speak of conscience if the petition of any of these forenamed women was to reign over any one tribe, yea, or yet over any one man within Israel. Plain it is they did not, but only required that they might have a portion of ground among the men of their tribe lest that the name of their father should be abolished. And this was

The daughters of Zelophehad desired to reign over no man in Israel.

granted unto them without respect had to any civil regiment. And what maketh this, I pray you, for the establishing of this monstrous empire of women? The question is not if women may not succeed to possession, substance, patrimony or inheritance, such as fathers may leave to their children, for that I willingly grant. But the question is if women may succeed to their fathers in offices, and chiefly to that office the executor whereof doth occupy the place and throne of God. And that I absolutely deny, and fear not to say that to place a woman in authority above a realm is to pollute and profane the royal seat, the throne of justice which ought to be the throne of God; and that to maintain them in the same is nothing else but continually to rebel against God.

Women may succeed to inheritance but not to office.

One thing there is yet to be noted and observed in the law made concerning the inheritance of the daughters of Zelophehad, to wit, that it was forbidden unto them to marry without their own tribe lest that such portion as fell to their lot should be transferred from one tribe to another and so should the tribe of Manasseh be defrauded and spoiled of their just inheritance by their occasion. For avoiding of which it was commanded by Moses that they should marry in the family or household of the tribe and kindred of their father. Wonder it is that the advocates and patrons of the right of our ladies did not consider and ponder this law before that they counselled the blind princes and unworthy nobles of their countries to betray the liberties thereof into the hands of strangers. England, for satisfying of the inordinate appetites of that cruel monster Mary (unworthy by reason of her bloody tyranny of the name of a woman), betrayed (alas) to the proud Spaniard; and Scotland, by the rash madness of foolish governors, and by the practices of a crafty dame, resigned likewise under title of marriage into the power of France.[21]

Num.36.6–9.

Our patrons for women do not mark this caution.

Mary Guise

Doth such translation of realms and nations please the justice of God, or is the possession by such means obtained lawful in His sight? Assured I am that it is not. No otherwise, I say, than is that possession whereunto thieves, murderers, tyrants and oppressors do attain by theft, murder, tyranny, violence, deceit and oppression, which God of His secret (but yet most just) judgement doth often permit for

Realms gotten by practices are no just possession.

[21] Mary Tudor married Philip II of Spain in July 1554; Mary Stewart was pledged to the French royal house by the terms of the Treaty of Haddington of July 1548, negotiated by the then regent or governor, Arran, and the queen mother, Mary of Guise.

punishment as well of the sufferers as of the violent oppressors, but doth never approve the same as lawful and godly. For if He would not permit that the inheritance of the children of Israel should pass from one tribe to another by the marriage of any daughter, notwithstanding that they were all one people, all spoke one tongue, all were descended of one father, and all did profess one God and one religion; if yet, I say, God would not suffer that the commodity and usual fruit which might be gathered of the portion of ground limited and assigned to one tribe should pass to another, will He suffer that the liberties, laws, commodities and fruits of whole realms and nations be given into the power and distribution of others by the reason of marriage; and in the powers of such as, besides that they be of a strange tongue, of strange manners and laws, they are also ignorant of God, enemies to His truth, deniers of Christ Jesus, persecutors of His true members, and haters of all virtue? As the odious nation of Spaniards doth manifestly declare, who for very despite which they do bear against Christ Jesus, whom their forefathers did crucify (for Jews they are, as histories do witness and they themselves confess),[22] do this day make plain war against all true professors of His Holy Gospel. And how blindly and outrageously the French king and his pestilent prelates do fight against the verity of God, the flaming fires which lick up the innocent blood of Christ's members do witness and by his cruel edicts is notified and proclaimed.[23] And yet

NOTE.

The Spaniards are Jews and they brag that Mary of England is of the root of Jesse.

Note the law which he hath proclaimed in France against

[22] Knox's source for these specific assertions remains unclear, though see S. R. Maitland, *Essays on the Reformation in England* (London, 1849), pp. 150–76, for other examples of anti-Spanish invective during Mary Tudor's reign. In the dynastic wars of the fourteenth and fifteenth centuries, a good deal of the propaganda aimed against monarchs like Peter IV of Aragon (1336–87) and Henry IV of Castile (1454–74) was virulently anti-semitic and could have given rise to the perception of the Spanish monarchy as Jewish to which Knox is referring. It is possible in addition that Knox was aware of Spanish anti-semitic literature such as Alonso de Espina's *Fortalitium fidei contra Judeos, Sarracenos aliosque Christiane fidei inimicos* (Lyon, 1511) and was drawing his own conclusions regarding Mary Tudor's Spanish mother. I am grateful to Professor Angus MacKay for his help with this point.

[23] Henry II, king of France (1547–59), was strongly opposed to the rising tide of Protestant dissent within his realm. Knox may have had in mind the decree of July 1557 confirming a papal bull establishing the Inquisition in France and the accompanying Edict of Compiegne which increased the penalties that the secular courts could impose on heretics. During his stay in Dieppe, following the arrest in Paris of over 100 Protestants who had been celebrating the Lord's Supper in the rue St-Jacques and the subsequent execution of three of their number on 27 September 1557, Knox translated with additions of his own *An Apology for the Protestants who are holden in Prison at Paris* (Laing, vol. IV, pp. 287–347).

to these two cruel tyrants (to France and Spain, I mean) is the right and possession of England and Scotland appointed. *such as he termeth Lutherians.*

But just or lawful shall that possession never be till God do change the statute of His former law, which He will not do for the pleasure of man. For He hath not created the earth to satisfy the ambition of two or three tyrants, but for the universal seed of Adam; and hath appointed and defined the bounds of their habitation to diverse nations, assigning diverse countries, as He Himself confesseth speaking to Israel in these words: 'You shall pass by the bounds and limits of your brethren, the sons of Esau, who dwell in Mount Seir. They shall fear you. But take diligent heed that ye show not yourselves cruel against them. For I will give you no part of their land. No, not the breadth of a foot. For Mount Seir I have given to Esau to be possessed.' And the same He doth witness of the sons of Lot to whom He had given Ar to be possessed. And Moses plainly affirmeth that when the Almighty did distribute and divide possessions to the Gentiles, and when He did disperse and scatter the sons of men, that then He did appoint the limits and bounds of peoples for the number of the sons of Israel. Whereof it is plain that God hath not exposed the earth in prey to tyrants, making all thing lawful which by violence and murder they may possess, but that He hath appointed to every several nation a several possession, willing them to stand content (as nature did teach an Ethnic to affirm) with that portion which by lot and just means they had enjoyed.

Acts 17.

Deut. 2.4–5.

[*Deut. 2.18–19.*]

Deut. 32.8.

NOTE.

Cicero, De officiis, 1.21.

For what causes God permitteth this His distribution to be troubled, and the realms of ancient nations to be possessed of strangers, I delay at this time to entreat. Only this I have recited to give the world to understand that the reign, empire and authority of women hath no ground within God's Scriptures. Yea, that realms or provinces possessed by their marriage is nothing but unjust conquest. For so little doth the law made for the daughters of Zelophehad help the cause of your queens that utterly it fighteth against them, both damning their authority and fact. But now to the third objection.

Realms gotten by marriage is unjust conquest.

The consent, say they, of realms, and laws pronounced and admitted in this behalf, long consuetude and custom, together with the felicity of some women in their empires, have established their authority. To whom I answer that neither may the tyranny of princes, neither the foolishness of people, neither wicked laws made against God, neither yet the felicity that in this earth may hereof ensue, make

Answer to the third objection.

that thing lawful which He by His Word hath manifestly condemned. For if the approbation of princes and people, laws made by men or the consent of realms, may establish anything against God and His Word, then should idolatry be preferred to the true religion. For more realms and nations, more laws and decrees published by emperors with common consent of their councils, have established the one than have approved the other. And yet I think that no man of sound judgement will therefore justify and defend idolatry. No more ought any man to maintain this odious empire of women, although that it were approved of all men by their laws. For the same God that in plain words forbiddeth idolatry doth also forbid the authority of women over man, as the words of St Paul before rehearsed do plainly teach us. And therefore whether women be deposed from that unjust authority (have they never usurped it so long) or if all such honour be denied unto them, I fear not to affirm that they are neither defrauded of right nor inheritance. For to women can that honour never be due nor lawful (much less inheritance) which God hath manifestly denied unto them.

Women may and ought to be deposed from authority.

I am not ignorant that the subtle wits of carnal men (which can never be brought under the obedience of God's simple precepts) to maintain this monstrous empire have yet two vain shifts. First, they allege that, albeit women may not absolutely reign by themselves because they may neither sit in judgement, neither pronounce sentence, neither execute any public office, yet may they do all such things by their lieutenants, deputies and judges substitute. Secondarily, say they, a woman born to rule over any realm may choose her a husband and to him she may transfer and give her authority and right. To both I answer in few words: first, that from a corrupt and venomed fountain can spring no wholesome water; secondarily, that no person hath power to give the thing which doth not justly appertain to themselves. But the authority of a woman is a corrupted fountain and therefore from her can never spring any lawful officer. She is not born to rule over men, and therefore she can appoint none by her gift nor by her power (which she hath not) to the place of a lawful magistrate. And therefore whosoever receiveth of a woman office or authority are adulterous and bastard officers before God.

The fourth objection.

Woman can make no lawful officer.

Let England and Scotand take heed.

This may appear strange at the first affirmation, but if we will be as indifferent and equal in the cause of God as that we can be in the cause of man, the reason shall suddenly appear. The case supposed that a tyrant by conspiracy usurped the royal seat and dignity of a king and in the same did so establish himself that he appointed officers and did what him list for a time, and in this meantime the native king made strait inhibition to all his subjects that none should adhere to this traitor, neither yet receive any dignity of him, yet nevertheless they would honour the same traitor as king and become his officers in all affairs of the realm; if, after, the native prince did recover his just honour and possession, should he repute or esteem any man of the traitor's appointment for a lawful magistrate or for his friend and true subject? Or should he not rather with one sentence condemn the head with the members? And if so he should do, who were able to accuse him of rigour much less to condemn his sentence of injustice? And dare we deny the same power to God in the like case? For that woman reigneth above man, she hath obtained it by treason and conspiracy committed against God. How can it be then that she, being criminal and guilty of treason against God committed, can appoint any officer pleasing in His sight? It is a thing impossible. Wherefore let men that receive of women authority, honour or office, be most assuredly persuaded that in so maintaining that usurped power, they declare themselves enemies to God.

Woman in authority is rebel against God.

If any think that because the realm and estates thereof have given their consents to a woman, and have established her and her authority, that therefore it is lawful and acceptable before God, let the same men remember what I have said before, to wit, that God cannot approve the doing nor consent of any multitude concluding anything against His Word and ordinance; and therefore they must have a more assured defence against the wrath of God than the approbation and consent of a blinded multitude or else they shall not be able to stand in the presence of the consuming fire. That is, they must acknowledge that the regiment of a woman is a thing most odious in the presence of God. They must refuse to be her officers because she is a traitress and rebel against God. And finally they must study to repress her inordinate pride and tyranny to the uttermost of their power.

What the nobility ought to do in this behalf.

The same is the duty of the nobility and estates by whose blindness a woman is promoted. First, in so far as they have most heinously offended against God, placing in authority such as God by His Word hath removed from the same, unfeignedly they ought to call for mercy and, being admonished of their error and damnable fact, in sign and token of true repentance, with common consent they ought to retreat that which unadvisedly and by ignorance they have pronounced, and ought without further delay to remove from authority all such persons as by usurpation, violence or tyranny do possess the same. For so did Israel and Judah after they had revolted from David, and Judah alone in the days of Athaliah. For after that she, by murdering her son's children, had obtained the empire over the land and had most unhappily reigned in Judah six years, Jehoiada the high priest called together the captains and chief rulers of the people, and showing to them the king's son Joash, did bind them by an oath to depose that wicked woman and to promote the king to his royal seat, which they faithfully did, killing at his commandment not only that cruel and mischievous woman, but also the people did destroy the temple of Baal, break his altars and images, and kill Mattan, Baal's high priest, before his altars. The same is the duty as well of the estates as of the people that hath been blinded. First, they ought to remove from honour and authority that monster in nature (so call I a woman clad in the habit of man, yea, a woman against nature reigning above man). Secondarily, if any presume to defend that impiety, they ought not to fear first to pronounce and then after to execute against them the sentence of death. If any man be afraid to violate the oath of obedience which they have made to such monsters, let them be most assuredly persuaded that as the beginning of their oaths, proceeding from ignorance, was sin, so is the obstinate purpose to keep the same nothing but plain rebellion against God. But of this matter in the *Second Blast*, God willing, we shall speak more at large.

2 Kgs. 11.

Mark this fact, for it agreeth with God's law pronounced.

And now to put an end to the *First Blast*: seeing that by the order of nature, by the malediction and curse pronounced against woman by the mouth of St Paul, the interpreter of God's sentence, by the example of that commonwealth in which God by His Word planted order and policy, and finally, by the judgement of the most godly writers, God hath dejected woman from rule, dominion, empire and authority above man; moreover, seeing that neither the example of Deborah, neither the law made for the daughters of Zelophehad, neither yet the foolish consent of an ignorant multitude, be able to justify that which God so plainly hath condemned, let all men take heed what quarrel and cause from henceforth they do defend. If God raise up any noble heart to vindicate the liberty of his country and

An admonition.

to suppress the monstrous empire of women, let all such as shall presume to defend them in the same most certainly know that in so doing they lift their hand against God and that one day they shall find His power to fight against their foolishness. Let not the faithful, godly and valiant hearts of Christ's soldiers be utterly discouraged, neither yet let the tyrants rejoice, albeit for a time they triumph against such as study to repress their tyranny and to remove them from unjust authority. For the causes [are known to God] alone why He suffereth the soldiers to fail in battle whom nevertheless He commandeth to fight, as sometimes did Israel fighting against Benjamin. The cause of the Israelites was most just, for it was to punish that horrible abomination of those sons of Belial, abusing the Levite's wife, whom the Benjamites did defend. And they had God' s precept to assure them of well-doing. For He did not only command them to fight, but also appointed Judah to be their leader and captain, and yet fell they twice in plain battle against those most wicked adulterers.

Judg. 20.

The secret cause of this, I say, is known to God alone. But by His evident Scriptures we may assuredly gather that by such means doth His wisdom sometimes beat down the pride of the flesh (for the Israelites at the first trusted in their multitude, power and strength), and sometimes by such overthrows He will punish the offences of His own children and bring them to the unfeigned knowledge of the same before He will give them victory against the manifest contemners, whom He hath appointed nevertheless to uttermost perdition, as the end of that battle did witness. For although with great murder the children of Israel did twice fall before the Benjamites, yet after they had wept before the Lord, after they had fasted and made sacrifice in sign of their unfeigned repentance, they so prevailed against that proud tribe of Benjamin that, after 25 thousand strong men of war were killed in battle, they destroyed man, woman, child and beast, as well in the fields as in the cities, which all were burned with fire, so that only of that whole tribe remained six hundred men who fled to the wilderness where they remained four months and so were saved.

Why God permitteth sometimes His own soldiers to fall in battle.

Judg. 20.

The same God who did execute this grievous punishment, even by the hands of those whom He suffered twice to be overcome in battle, doth this day retain His power and justice. Cursed Jezebel of England, with the pestilent and detestable generation of papists, make

NOTE.

no little brag and boast that they have triumphed not only against Wyatt,[24] but also against all such as have enterprised anything against them or their proceedings. But let her and them consider that yet they have not prevailed against God; His throne is more high than that the length of their horns be able to reach. And let them further consider that in the beginning of this their bloody reign the harvest of their iniquity was not come to full maturity and ripeness. No, it was so green, so secret I mean, so covered and so hid with hypocrisy that some men (even the servants of God) thought it not impossible but that wolves might be changed into lambs and also that the viper might remove her natural venom. But God who doth reveal in His time appointed the secrets of hearts, and that will have His judgements justified even by the very wicked, hath now given open testimony of her and their beastly cruelty. For man and woman, learned and unlearned, nobles and men of baser sort, aged fathers and tender damsels, and finally the bones of the dead, as well women as men, have tasted of their tyranny; so that now not only the blood of father Latimer, of the mild man of God the bishop of Canterbury, of learned and discreet Ridley, of innocent Lady Jane Dudley,[25] and many godly and worthy preachers that cannot be forgotten, such as fire hath consumed and the sword of tyranny most unjustly hath shed, doth call for vengeance in the ears of the Lord God of Hosts; but also the sobs and tears of the poor oppressed, the groanings of the angels, the watchmen of the Lord, yea, and every earthly creature abused by their tyranny, do continually cry and call for the hasty execution of the same.

I fear not to say that the day of vengeance which shall apprehend that horrible monster Jezebel of England and such as maintain her monstrous cruelty is already appointed in the counsel of the Eternal; and I verily believe that it is so nigh that she shall not reign so long in tyranny as hitherto she hath done, when God shall declare Himself to be her enemy, when He shall pour forth contempt upon her according to her cruelty, and shall kindle the hearts of such as some-

[24] Sir Thomas Wyatt, leader of an unsuccessful rebellion against Mary Tudor's regime in 1554 which resulted in his execution.

[25] Hugh Latimer, bishop of Winchester, Nicholas Ridley, bishop of London, and Thomas Cranmer, archbishop of Canterbury, were burned at the stake in 1555–6. Lady Jane Grey, wife of Guildford Dudley, was proclaimed queen in 1553 and executed after the failure of Wyatt's rebellion in 1554.

times did favour her with deadly hatred against her that they may execute His judgements. And therefore let such as assist her take heed what they do. For assuredly her empire and reign is a wall without foundation. I mean the same of the authority of all women. It hath been underpropped this blind time that is past with the foolishness of people and with the wicked laws of ignorant and tyrannous princes. But the fire of God's Word is already laid to those rotten props (I include the pope's law with the rest) and presently they burn, albeit we espy not the flame. When they are consumed (as shortly they will be, for stubble and dry timber cannot long endure the fire), that rotten wall, the usurped and unjust empire of women, shall fall by itself in despite of all man, to the destruction of so many as shall labour to uphold it. And therefore let all man be advertised, for the trumpet hath once blown.

The authority of all women is a wall without foundation.

Praise God ye that fear Him.

THE COPY OF A LETTER

delivered to the Lady Mary, Regent of Scotland, from John Knox, minister of God's Word, in the year of our Lord 1556, and now augmented and explained by the Author, in the year of our Lord 1558.

'Enter in at the strait gate; for wide
is the gate, and broad is the way,
that leadeth to destruction.'
Matthew 7.13

Printed at Geneva,
by James Poullain and Antony Reboul

M.D.LVIII

TO THE EXCELLENT LADY MARY, Dowager Regent of Scotland.

The cause moving me, Right Honourable, to present this my supplication unto your Grace, enlarged and in some places explained (which being in the realm of Scotland in the month of May 1556, I caused to be presented to your Grace), is the incredible rage of such as bear the title of bishops who against all justice and equity have pronounced against me a most cruel sentence, condemning my body to fire, my soul to damnation and all doctrine taught by me to be false, deceivable and heretical. If this injury did tend to me alone, having the testimony of a good conscience, with silence I could pass the matter, being assured that such as they curse and expel their synagogues for such causes shall God bless and Christ Jesus receive in His eternal society. But considering that this their blasphemy is vomited forth against the eternal truth of Christ's Evangel (whereof it hath pleased the great mercy of God to make me a minister), I cannot cease to notify, as well to your Grace as unto them, that so little I am afraid of their tyrannical and surmised sentence that in place of the picture (if God impede not my purpose) they shall have the body to justify that doctrine which they (members of Satan) blasphemously do condemn.[1] Advertising your Grace in the meantime that from them, their sentence and tyranny, and from all those that list maintain them in the same, I do appeal to a lawful and general council; beseeching your Grace to take in good part that I call you for witness that I have required the liberty of tongue, and my cause to be heard before your Grace and the body of that realm, before that any such process was laid against me. As this my letter directed to your Grace doth testify.

The Beginning of the Letter

The eternal providence of the same God who hath appointed His chosen children to fight in this transitory and wretched life a battle strong and difficult hath also appointed their final victory by a marvellous fashion and the manner of their preservation in their battle more marvellous. Their victory standeth not in resisting, but in suffering, as our Sovereign Master pronounceth to His disciples, that in their patience should they possess their souls. And the same foresaw the Prophet Isaiah when that he painteth forth all other battle to be with violence, tumult and bloodshedding, but the victory of God's people to be in quietness, silence and hope, meaning that all others that obtain victory do enforce themselves to resist their adversaries, to shed blood and to murder. But so do not the elect of God, but all things they sustain at the commandment of Him who hath appointed them to suffer, being most assuredly persuaded that then only they triumph when all men judge them oppressed. For in the cross of Christ always is included a secret and hid victory, never well known till the sufferer appear altogether to be (as it were) exterminate. For

Gen. 3. Matt. 10. Acts 14.

Matt. 5.

John 14, 16.

Isa. 9.

In the cross of Christ is victory hid.

[1] A reference to the bishops' condemnation of Knox in 1556 as a heretic and the subsequent public burning of his effigy.

[*Gen. 4.*] then only did the blood of Abel cry to God when proud Cain judged all memory of his brother to have been extinguished.

And so, I say, their victory is marvellous. And how that they can be preserved and not brought to utter confusion, the eye of man perceiveth not. But He whose power is infinite, by secret and hid motions, toucheth the hearts of such as to man's judgement have power to destroy them of very pity and compassion to save His people. As that He did the hearts of the Egyptian midwives to preserve the men children of the Israelites when precept was given by Pharaoh of their destruction; the heart of Pharaoh's daughter likewise to pity Moses in his young infancy exposed to the danger of the waters; the heart of Nebuchadnezzar to preserve the captives alive and liberally to nourish the children that were found apt to letters; and finally the heart of Cyrus to set at liberty the people of God after long bondage and thraldom.

Isa. 40, 41, 51.

Exod. 2.

2 Kgs. 25. Jer. 52.

Ezra 1.

And thus doth the invisible power and love of God manifest itself towards His elect from time to time for two causes specially. First, to comfort His weak warriors in their manifold temptations, letting them understand that He is able to compel such as sometimes were enemies to His people to fight in their cause and to promote their deliverance. And secondarily, to give a testimony of His favour to them that by all appearance did live before (as St Paul speaketh) wanting God in the world, as strangers from the commonwealth of Israel, and without the league of His merciful promise and free grace made to His church. For who could have affirmed that any of these persons aforenamed had been of that nature and clemency before occasions were offered unto them? But the works of mercy shown to the afflicted have left to us assurance that God used them as vessels of His honour. For pity and mercy shown to Christ's afflicted flock, as they never lacked reward temporal, so if they be continued and be not changed into cruelty, are assured signs and seals of everlasting mercy to be received from God, who by His Holy Spirit moveth their hearts to show mercy to the people of God oppressed and afflicted.

NOTE.

Eph. 2.

Addition

This preface I used to give your Grace occasion more deeply to consider what hath been the condition of Christ's members from the beginning, that in so doing ye might see that it is no new thing that the saints of God be oppressed in the world; that ye, moved by earnest contemplation of the same, might also study rather to save them from murder (although by the wicked counsels of many ye were provoked to the contrary) than to be a slave to Satan, obeying his servants, your clergy, whose fury is bent against God and His verity. But this will after follow in our letter, which thus proceedeth.

Letter

Your Grace perchance doth wonder to what purpose these things be recited, and I in very deed cannot wonder enough that occasion is offered to me (a worm most wretched) to recite the same at this present. For I have looked rather for the sentence of death than to have written to your Grace in these last and most wicked days in which Satan so blindeth the hearts of many that innocents are damned, their cause never tried.

Addition

Hereof ye cannot be ignorant. For besides these whom ye hear from time to time most cruelly to be murdered in France, Italy, Spain, Flanders, and now of late years besides you in England, for no cause but that they profess Christ Jesus to be the only saviour of the world, the only mediator betwixt God and man, the only sacrifice acceptable for the sins of all faithful, and finally the only head to His church; besides these, I say (of whom ye hear the bruit), ye have been witness that some within the realm of Scotland for the same cause most cruelly have been murdered, whose cause was never heard with indifferency. But murderers occupying the seat of justice have shed the blood of Christ's true witnesses, which albeit did then appear to be consumed away with fire, yet is it recent in the presence of Him for whose cause they did suffer, and ceaseth not to call for vengeance, with the blood of Abel, to fall not only upon such as were authors of that murder, but also upon all those that maintain those tyrants in their tyranny or that do consent to their beastly cruelty.

The causes why the saints of God be this day persecuted. 1 John 1, 2. Heb. 6, 10. Eph. 5.

Take not this as the affirmation of any man, but hear and consider the voice of the Son of God: 'Fulfil (saith He) the measure of your fathers, that all the blood which hath been shed since the blood of Abel the just till the blood of Zechariah', etc. 'may come upon this generation.' Hereby it is evident that the murderers of our time, as well as in the time of Christ, are guilty of all blood that hath been

Matt. 23.32–6.

shed from the beginning. Fearful I grant is the sentence, yet is it most equal and just. For whosoever sheddeth the blood of any one of Christ Jesus His members for professing of His truth, consenteth to all the murder which hath been made since the beginning of the world for that cause. So that as there is one communion of all God's elect, of whom every member is participant of the whole justice of Christ, so is there a communion among the reprobate, by which every one of the serpent's seed are criminal and guilty of all iniquity which the whole body committeth, for because they are all together conjured against Christ Jesus and against His eternal verity, every one serving Satan, the prince of this world, in their rank, age, degree and estate. The murderers of their brethren which this day live are guilty with Cain of the blood of Abel. The kings and princes which by power oppress the people of God and will not suffer that the people truly worship God as He hath commanded, but will retain them in Egypt, are brethren and companions to Pharaoh. The prelates and priests, whose horrible iniquities and insolent life have infected all realms where they reign, have with their fathers, the old Pharisees, taken away the key of knowledge and have shut up the kingdom of heaven before men, so that neither they themselves will enter, neither yet will they suffer others to enter in the same. And the multitude blinded, some by ignorance, some by fear and by insatiable appetite of their part of the spoil (for Christ being crucified, the soldiers parted amongst them His garments), are conjured to defend those murderers, proud pestilent prelates, against Christ Jesus and against His poor flock. And therefore, because of one crime they are all guilty (which is of treason and rebellion against Christ), of one torment they shall all taste, which is of the fire that never shall be quenched.

Whosoever sheddeth the blood of one of Christ's members for His name's sake, consenteth to the blood of all that have suffered since the beginning.

NOTE. *Gen. 4.*

Matt. 23.

And herein ought you, Madam, be circumspect and careful, if that ye have any hope of the life to come. For if the consent which proceedeth of ignorance and blindness bringeth destruction and death (as Christ our Master doth witness, saying: 'If the blind lead the blind, they shall both fall in the ditch'), what shall become of the proud and malicious contemner of God's verity offered? But our doctrine perchance shall be denied to be the verity. Whereunto I answer that so was the doctrine of Noah, of Moses, of the Prophets, of Christ Jesus and of His Apostles; and yet the original world perished by

Matt. 15.14.

Answer to an objection.

water, Sodom and Gomorrah by fire descending from heaven, Pharaoh and his adherents in the Red Sea, [and] the city of Jerusalem, the whole nation of the Jews, by punishments and plagues, notwithstanding that the whole multitude cried: 'This is a new doctrine, this his heresy, and tendeth to sedition.' Our petition is that our doctrine may be tried by the plain Word of God, that liberty be granted to us to utter and declare our minds at large in every article and point which now are in controversy, which if ye deny, giving ear to Christ's enemies (who condemn His doctrine for heresy), ye shall drink the cup of God's vengeance with them. But now to the former letter.

Gen. 19. Exod. 14. Josephus.[2]

The petition of such as be persecuted.

Letter

I doubt not but the rumours which have come to your Grace's ears of me have been such that, if all reports were true, I were unworthy to live in the earth; and wonder it is that the voices of the multitude should not so have inflamed your Grace's heart with just hatred of such a one as I am accused to be that all access to pity should have been shut up. I am traduced as a heretic, accused as a false teacher and seducer of the people, besides other opprobries which (affirmed by men of worldly honour and estimation) may easily kindle the wrath of magistrates where innocency is not known. But blessed be God, the Father of our Lord Jesus Christ, who by the dew of His heavenly grace hath so quenched the fire of displeasure as yet in your Grace's heart (which of late days I have understood) that Satan is frustrate of his enterprise and purpose. Which is to my heart no small comfort, not so much (God is witness) for any benefit that I can receive in this miserable life by protection of any earthly creature (for the cup which it behooveth me to drink is appointed by the wisdom of Him whose counsels are not changeable), as that I am for that benefit which I am assured your Grace shall receive if that ye continue in like moderation and clemency towards others that most unjustly are and shall be accused as that your Grace hath begun towards me and my most desperate cause. That is, if that by godly wisdom ye shall study to bridle the fury and rage of them who, for the maintenance

[2] Like a similar sidenote in the *Letter to the Commonalty*, this probably refers to the destruction of Jerusalem in AD 70 described in Josephus, *Jewish War*, 7.1.

of their worldly pomp, regard nothing the cruel murdering of simple innocents, then shall He who doth pronounce mercy to appertain to the merciful, and promiseth that a cup of cold water given for His name's sake shall not lack reward, first cause your happy government to be praised in this present age, and in posterity's to come, and last recompense your godly pains and study with that joy and glory which the eye hath not seen nor yet can enter into the heart of mortal creature.

Matt. 5.
Matt. 10.
1 Cor. 2.

Addition

Matt. 10.

If Christ's words were esteemed true, that of every idle word an accompt shall be given, and that nothing is so secretly done which shall not come to knowledge and light, I suppose that the tongues of men should be better bridled than impudently to speak their pleasure in matters unknown. For albeit that the true fear of God should not move them to speak truth, yet would I think (if any spark of humanity remained) that worldly shame should impede them to lie. When reasoning was before your Grace what man it was that preached in Ayr, and diverse men were of diverse opinion, some affirming that it was an Englishman, and some supposing the contrary, a prelate, not of the least pride, said: 'Nay, no Englishman, but it is Knox that knave.'[3] It was my lord's pleasure so to baptise a poor man. The reason whereof, if it should be required, his rochet and mitre must stand for authority. What further liberty he used in defining things like uncertain to him, to wit, of my learning and doctrine, at this present I omit. Lamenting more that such pestilent tongues have liberty to speak in the presence of princes than that I am sorry for any hurt that their venom can do to me in body or fame. For what hath my life and conversation been since it hath pleased God to call me from the puddle of papistry, let my very enemies speak. And what learning I have, they may prove when they please. The report of your Grace's moderation, as well at that time as after when suit was made for my apprehension, moved me to write this my other letter. In which, albeit I have not played the orator, dilating and decking the matter for the pleasure of itching and delicate ears, yet doth my conscience bear me record that with simplicity I have advertised you of a mortal danger. As this portion subsequent shall prove.

[3] The passage refers to Knox's mission in Scotland in 1555–6 when he spent some months in Ayrshire (Laing, vol. 1, pp. 249–51). The proud prelate remains unidentified.

Letter

Superfluous and foolish it shall appear to many that I, a man of base estate and condition, dare enterprise to admonish a princess so honourable, endued with wisdom and graces singular. But when I consider the honour which God commandeth to be given to magistrates, which no doubt (if it be true honour) containeth in itself in lawful things obedience and in all things love and reverence; when further I consider the troublesome estate of Christ's true religion this day oppressed by blindness of men; and last, the great multitude of flatterers and the rare number of them that boldly and plainly dare speak the naked verity in presence of their princes, and principally in the cause of Christ Jesus; these things, I say, considered, whatsoever any man shall judge of my enterprise, I am compelled to say that, unless in your regiment and in using of power, your Grace be found different from the multitude of princes and head rulers, that this pre-eminence wherein ye are placed shall be your dejection to torment and pain everlasting.

Exod. 20. Rom. 13. 1 Pet. 2.

The first proposition.

This proposition is sore, but, alas, it is so true that, if I should conceal and hide it from your Grace, I committed no less treason against your Grace than if I did see you by imprudency take a cup which I knew to be poisoned or envenomed and yet would not admonish you to abstain from drinking of the same. The religion which this day men defend by fire and sword is a cup envenomed of which whosoever drinketh (except that by true repentance he after drink of the water of life) drinketh therewith damnation and death. How and by whom it hath been envenomed, if it were no more tedious to your Grace to read or hear than it is painful to me to write or rehearse, I would not spare the labour. But for this present I have thought it some discharge of one part of my duty if I, of very love, admonish your Grace of the danger. Which I do, as God one day shall declare, preferring your Grace's salvation and the salvation of the people (now committed to your charge) to any corporal benefit that can redound to myself.

The second proposition.

John 4. Rev. 14, 17.

Addition

As Satan by craft hath corrupted the most holy ordinances of God's precepts, I mean of the First Table, in the place of the spiritual honouring of God introducing men's dreams, inventions and fantasies, so hath he, abusing the weakness of man, corrupted this precept of the Second Table, touching the honour which is due to parents under whom are comprehended princes and teachers. For now the devil hath so blinded the senses of many that they cannot or, at the least, will not learn what appertaineth to God and what to Caesar. But because the spirit of God hath said 'honour the king', therefore whatsoever they command, be it right or wrong, must be obeyed. But heavy shall the judgement be which shall apprehend such blasphemers of God's majesty who dare be so bold as to affirm that God hath commanded any creature to be obeyed against Himself. Against God it is that for the commandment of any prince, be he never so potent, men shall commit idolatry, embrace a religion which God hath not approved by His Word, or confirm by their silence wicked and blasphemous laws made against the honour of His majesty. Men, I say, that so do give no true obedience, but as they are apostates from God, so are they traitors to their princes whom by flattery they confirm in rebelling against God. Only they which to the death resist such wicked laws and decrees are acceptable to God and faithful to their princes. As were the three children in the presence of Nebuchadnezzar, and Daniel, in the days of Darius (the Persian emperor), whose constant and free confession, as it glorified God, so did it notify, as well to those tyrants as to all ages following, the great blasphemy which in their rage and fury they committed against God. From the which (by all appearance) neither of both so suddenly should have been called if the three children had bowed among the rest and Daniel had not declared the confession of his faith, which was with windows open to pray towards Jerusalem, manifestly thereby declaring that he did not consent to the blasphemous law and decree which was established by the king and his council.

Take heed of unlawful obedience.

Dan. 3.

Dan. 6.

Experience hath taught us what surmises and blasphemies the adversaries of Christ Jesus, of His eternal verity, do invent and devise against such as begin to detect their impiety. They are accused to be authors of sedition, raisers of tumults, violators of common orders, etc. I answer with the Prophet Isaiah: 'that all is not reputed before God sedition and conjuration which the foolish multitude so esteemeth'.[4] Neither yet is every tumult and breach of public order contrary

Answer to an objection.

[4] I have been unable to identify this alleged quotation. Isaiah 8.12 bears some resemblance, but is hardly convincing.

to God's commandment. For Christ Jesus Himself, coming to rive the spoil from the strong armed, who before did keep His house in quietness, is not come to send peace but a sword and to make a man disassent from his father, etc. His Prophets before Him and Apostles after Him feared not to break public orders established against God, and in so doing to move, as it were, the one half of peoples, nations and cities against the other. And yet I trust that none, except the hired servant of Satan, will accuse Christ of sedition, nor His Apostles of the troubling of commonwealths. True it is that the most wholesome medicine most troubleth for a time the body replenished with wicked and corrupted humours. But the cause hereof is known to be not in the medicine, but in the body subject to malady. Even so the true Word of God, when it entereth to fight where Satan hath borne dominion (as he still doth in the whole papistry), cannot but appear to be occasion of great trouble. But Madam, more profitable it is that the pestilent humours be expelled with pain than that they be nourished to the destruction of the body. The papistical religion is a mortal pestilence which shall assuredly bring to death eternal the bodies and souls from the which it is not purged in this life.

Matt. 10.34–7.

Acts 14.

The papistical religion a mortal pestilence.

And therefore, take heed betimes, God calleth upon you; beware that ye shut not up your ears. Judge not the matter after the vility of my body, whom God hath appointed ambassador and messenger unto you, but with reverence and fear consider Him whose message I bear. I come to you in the name of the eternal God, and of Christ Jesus His Son, to whom the Father hath committed all power, whom He hath established sovereign judge over all flesh, before whose throne ye must make accompts with what reverence ye hear such as He sendeth. It shall not excuse you to say or think that ye doubt whether I be sent of God or no. I cry unto you that the religion which the princes and blinded papists maintain with fire and sword is not the religion of Christ, that your proud prelates are none of Christ's bishops. I admonish you that Christ's flock is oppressed by them, and therefore I require, and that yet again in the name of the Lord Jesus, that with indifferency I may be heard to preach, to reason and to dispute in that cause, which if ye deny, ye declare yourself to bear no reverence to Christ nor love to His true religion.

The admonition.

Letter

Answer to an objection.

But ye think peradventure that the care of religion is not committed to magistrates, but to the bishops and estate ecclesiastical, as they term it. But deceive not yourself. For the negligence of bishops shall no less be required of the hands of magistrates than shall the oppression of false judges. For they unjustly promote, foster and maintain the one and the other. The false and corrupt judge to spoil the goods and to oppress the bodies of the simple, but the proud prelates do kings maintain to murder the souls for the which the blood of Christ Jesus was shed. And that they do either by withholding from them the true Word of life or else by causing teach unto them a pestilent doctrine such as now is taught in the papistical churches.

I know that ye wonder how that the religion which is universally received can be so damnable and corrupted. But if your Grace shall consider that ever from the beginning the multitude hath declined from God (yea, even in the people to whom He spoke by His Law and Prophets); if ye shall consider the complaint of the Holy Ghost, complaining that nations, people, princes and kings of the earth have raged, made conspiracies and holden councils against the Lord and against His anointed Christ Jesus; further, if he shall consider the question which Jesus Himself doth move in these words: 'When the son of man shall come, shall he find faith in the earth?'; and last, if your Grace shall consider the manifest contempt of God and of all His holy precepts which this day reign without punishment upon the face of the whole earth, for as Hosea complaineth: 'There is no verity, there is no mercy, there is no truth this day among men, but lies, perjury and oppression overflow all, and blood toucheth blood', that is, every iniquity is joined to another; if deeply, I say, your Grace shall contemplate the universal corruption that this day reigneth in all estates, then shall your Grace cease to wonder that 'many are called and few chosen'. And ye shall begin to tremble and fear to follow the multitude to perdition. The universal defection whereof St Paul did prophesy is easy to be espied as well in religion as in manners. The corruption of life is evident, and religion is not judged nor measured by the plain Word of God, but by custom, consuetude, will, consent and determinations of men.

Gen. 6. *Ps. 14.* *Ps. 2.* *Acts 4.* *Luke 18.8.* *Hos. 4.1–2.* *Matt. 20.16.* *Matt. 7.* *2 Thess. 2.*

But shall He who hath pronounced all cogitations of man's heart to be vain at all times accept the counsels and consents of men for a religion pleasing and acceptable before Him? Let not your Grace be deceived. God cannot lie; God cannot deny Himself. He hath witnessed from the beginning that no religion pleaseth Him except that which He by His own Word hath commanded and established. The verity itself pronounceth this sentence: 'In vain do they worship me, teaching doctrines the precepts of men'; and also: 'All plantation which my heavenly father hath not planted shall be rooted out.' Before the coming of his well-beloved Son in flesh, severely He punished all such as durst enterprise to alter or change His ceremonies and statutes, as in Saul, Uzziah, Nadab, Abihu, is to be read. And will He now, after that He hath opened His counsel to the world by His only Son, whom He commandeth to be heard, and after that by His Holy Spirit speaking in His Apostles He hath established the religion in which He will His true worshippers abide to the end; will He now, I say, admit men's inventions in the matter of religion which He reputed for damnable idolatry? If man and angels would affirm that He will or may do it, His own verity shall convict them of a lie. For this sentence He pronounceth: 'Not that which seemeth good in thy eyes shalt thou do to the Lord thy God, but that which the Lord thy God hath commanded thee, that do thou; add nothing unto it, diminish nothing from it.' Which, sealing up His New Testament, He repeateth in these words: 'That which ye have, hold till I come', etc. And therefore yet again it repenteth me not to say that in this point, which is chief and principal, your Grace must disassent from the multitude of rulers, or else ye can possess no portion with Christ Jesus in His kingdom and glory.

Deut. 4, 12.

Matt. 15.9,13.

1 Kgs. 13,15.
2 Chr. 26.
Lev. 10.

Matt. 17.

Acts 1, 2, 3.
1 Cor. 11.

Col. 2.

Deut. 4.2, 12.32.

Rev. 2.25.

Addition

Knowing by what craft Satan laboureth continually to keep the world in blindness, I added these two former points, to wit, that ye should not think yourself free from the reformation of religion because ye have bishops within your realm, neither yet that ye should judge that religion most perfect which the multitude by wrong custom hath embraced. In these two points doth Satan busily travail. First, that no civil magistrate presume to take cognition in the cause of religion, for that must be deferred to the determinations of the church. Secondarily, that impossible it is that that religion should be false which so long time, so many councils, and so great a multitude of men, so

The craft of Satan.

The ground of papistical religion.

diverse nations and realms have allowed, authorised and confirmed.

What is the duty of magistrates, and what power the people hath in such cases granted by God, my purpose is to write in a several letter to the nobility and estates of the realm,[5] and therefore to avoid tediousness and repetition of one thing I now supersede. And as touching the second, if ye rightly consider the testimonies of Scriptures which I have before adduced, I trust ye shall find that objection sufficiently answered. For if the opinion of the multitude ought always to be preferred, then did God injury to the original world. For they were all of one mind, to wit, conjured against God (except Noah and his family). And if antiquity of time shall be considered in such cases, then shall not only the idolatry of the Gentiles, but also the false religion of Mahomet be preferred to the papistry. For both the one and the other is more ancient than is the papistical religion; yea, Mahomet had established his Alcoran before any pope in Rome was crowned with a triple crown. But as touching antiquity, I am content with Tertullian to say: 'Let that be the most pure and perfect religion, which shall be proved most ancient.'[6] For this is a chief point wherein I will join with all the papists in the earth: that their religion (such as it is this day) is not of such antiquity as is that which we contend to be the true and only religion acceptable before God, neither yet that their church is the Catholic church, but that it is of late days in respect of Christ's institution crept in and devised by man, and therefore am bold to affirm it odious and abominable.

NOTE.

Tertullian Apologeticum.

For this is our chief proposition: that in the religion of God only ought His own Word to be considered. That no authority of man nor angel ought in that case to be respected. And as for their councils, when the matter shall come to trial, it shall be easily seen for whom the most godly and most ancient councils shall most plainly speak. I will prove by a council that of more authority is the sentence of one man (founded upon the simple truth of God) than is the determination of the whole council without the assurance of God's Word. But that all their determinations which we impugn are not only maintained without any assurance of Scriptures, but also are established

The chief proposition.

Nicen. 1.[7]

[5] That is, the *Appellation*.

[6] There is no exact equivalent of this in Tertullian's *Apology*. However, there are a number of passages (e.g. 19.1–8; 47.1–14) which might conceivably be taken to imply the sentiment Knox attributes to him.

[7] That is, the First Council of Nicaea convened by the Emperor Constantine in 325.

against the truth of the same, yea, and for the most part against the decrees of the former councils, I offer myself evidently to prove. But now shortly to the rest of the former letter.

Letter

An orator, and God's messenger also, justly might require of you (now by God's hand promoted to high dignity) a motherly pity upon your subjects; a justice inflexible to be used against murderers and common oppressors; a heart void of avarice and partiality; a mind studious and careful for maintenance of that realm and commonwealth (above whom God hath placed you and by it hath made you honourable); with the rest of [those] virtues which not only God's Scriptures, but also writers illuminated only with the light of nature require in godly rulers. But vain it is to crave reformation of manners where religion is corrupted. For like as a man cannot do the office of a man till first he have a being and life, so to work works pleasant in the sight of God the Father can no man do without the spirit of the Lord Jesus which doth not abide in the hearts of idolaters. And therefore the most godly princes Josiah, Hezekiah and Jehoshaphat, seeking God's favour to rest upon them, and upon their people, before all things began to reform the religion. For it is as the stomach within the body which, if it be corrupted, of necessity it infecteth the whole mass. And therefore (often I repeat that which to be done is most necessary), if your Grace pretend to reign with Christ Jesus, then it behooveth you to take care of His true religion, which this day within your realm is so deformed that no part of Christ's ordinances remain in their first strength and original purity. Which, I praise God, to me is less difficult to prove than dangerous to speak. And yet neither the one nor the other I fear, partly because the love of life eternal quencheth the terror of temporal death, and partly because I would with St Paul wish myself accursed from Christ (as touching earthly pleasure) for the salvation of my brethren and illumination of your Grace; which thing, work and very deed, and not bare word or writing, shall witness and declare, if I may purchase the liberty of tongue but forty days only.

The duty of magistrates.

The spirit of God abideth not with idolaters.

1 Kgs. 15. 2 Chr. 17. 2 Kgs. 22. 2 Chr. 34. 2 Kgs. 18. 2 Chr. 29, 30, 31.

The second proposition.

Addition

Stobaeus Sermo 14.[8]

The wise and facund Democritus had sometimes a familiar sentence that: 'Honest it was to commend such works as were worthy of praise, but to praise things that were wicked could not proceed but from a deceivable mind.' And Themistius, a philosopher of great fame, seeing the hall of Jovinian the Roman emperor replenished with flatterers, said: 'Of their manners it may be espied that more they worship the sceptre and the purple than God' – signifying that they little regarded whether the emperor was godly or ungodly, so that they might retain themselves in favour with him. Albeit that those were Ethnics and neither had knowledge of God, as we pretend, neither had given so plain a confession to declare themselves enemies to all iniquity (as we have done by baptism and by our whole profession of Christianity), yet do their words damn no small number of us, and chiefly of such as be conversant with princes. For who in these miserable days judgeth himself to have offended, albeit he praise, allow and maintain whatsoever the princes and upper powers devise? Yea, although it be to oppress and to spoil the poor, to pull from them their skins and, as the Prophet saith: 'To break their bones and to cut them in pieces as flesh for the cauldron or pot'? Yet, I say, that the princes shall not lack judges to cry: 'It is right, it is for the commonwealth, for defence of the realm and ease of the subjects.' So that the estate of times is even now such as when the Prophet complained, saying: 'The princes ask, and the judge is ready to give, not his own, but the life and blood of the poor.'

Nicephorus, Historia Ecclesiasticae, lib. 10, cap. 42.

Mic. 3.3.

[*Mic. 7.3.*]

How soon a great man hath spoken the corruption of his mind, he hath his flatterers ready to applaud and confirm whatsoever he speaketh. And let the princes be of what religion they please, that is all one to the most part of men, so that with abnegation of God, of His honour and religion, they may retain the friendship of the court. But, alas, how miserable be princes that so are abused, and how contagious a pestilence be such flatterers to commonwealths, empires and realms, God hath declared even from the beginning to paint out the mischief which from them proceedeth to such as give ear unto them. The ancient writers compare them to harlots, to ravens and to more ravenous beasts, and not without cause. For as harlots can never

Flatterers are a contagious pestilence.

[8] The sidenote in the original – *Stob. ser. 12* – is either a mistake or refers to an edition of Stobaeus which is arranged differently from those I have been able to consult.

abide that their lovers should return to repentance and soberness of mind, so cannot flatterers sustain that such as they deceive shall come to right judgement. And as ravens pick out the eyes of dead carrions, and as ravenous beasts devour the same, so do flatterers (being more cruel) pick at the eyes of living men and, blinding the eyes of their understanding and judgement, do expone them to be devoured in body and soul to Satan.

This we have by profane writers only, but the Holy Spirit taught us this infallible truth: that where iniquity reigneth in a commonwealth and none is found boldly and openly to reprehend the same, that there shall sudden vengeance and destruction follow. For thus is it written and pronounced by the Prophet Ezekiel: 'Shalt thou not judge the city of blood which hath made idols? Whose rulers shed blood to the uttermost of their power? They have despised my holy things, they have devised iniquity, and have performed the same. The conjuration of prophets hath gathered up the riches and whatsoever is precious within the same. The priests violently have torn and rent my law. The people of the land hath wrought deceitfully. They have oppressed the poor and have done violence to the stranger without judgement. And I have sought of them a man to repair the hedge and to stand in the gap before me, but I have found none. Therefore have I poured forth my wrath upon them, and in the fire of my hot displeasure I have consumed them.' Advert, Madam, for these are not the words of mortal man, but of the eternal God, and were not spoken against Jerusalem only, but against every realm and nation that so offendeth. The sins that here be named are idolatry in all; avarice and cruelty in the princes and rulers; conjuration of the prophets to defend the wicked; deceit, fraud and violence in the common people; and finally, a universal silence of all man, none being found to reprehend these enormities.

Ezek. 22.2–3 25–31.

NOTE.

Would to God that I might with safety of conscience excuse you, your council, and the idolaters of that realm from any of these crimes aforenamed. The idolatry which is committed is more evident than that it can be denied. The avarice and cruelty as well of yourself as of such as be in authority may be known by the facts. For fame carrieth the voices of the poor (oppressed by intolerable taxes) not only to us here in a strange country, but I am assured to the ears of the God of Hosts. The conspiracy and conjuration of your false prophets is known to the world, and yet is none found so faithful to

God nor merciful to your Grace that freely will and dare admonish you to repent before that God rise Himself in judgement.

When I name repentance, I mean no outward show of holiness, which commonly is found in hypocrites, but I mean a true conversion to the Lord God from your whole heart, with a damning of all superstition and idolatry, in which ye have been nourished, which with your presence ye have decored, and to your power maintained and defended. Unless, I say, that this poison be purged from your heart (be your outward life never so glistering before the world), yet in the presence of God it is but abominable. Yea, further I say, that where this venom of the serpent (idolatry I mean) lurketh in the heart, it is impossible but that at one time or other it shall produce pestilent fruits, albeit peradventure not openly before men, yet before God no less odious than the facts of murderers, publicans and harlots. And therefore in my former letter I said that superfluous it was to require reformation of manners where the religion is corrupted. Which yet again I repeat to the end that your Grace more deeply may weigh the matter. But now to the rest of the same my former letter.

Idolatry is mother to all vice.

Letter

I am not ignorant how dangerous a thing it appeareth to the natural man to innovate anything in matters of religion, and partly I consider that your Grace's power is not so free as a public reformation perchance would require. But if your Grace shall consider the danger and damnation perpetual which inevitably hangeth upon all maintainers of a false religion, then shall the greatest danger easily devour and swallow up the smaller. If your Grace shall consider that either ye must serve God to life everlasting or else serve the world to death and damnation, then albeit that man and angel should dissuade you, ye will choose life and refuse death. And if further ye shall consider that the very life consisteth in the knowledge of the only true God and of His Son Christ Jesus, and that true knowledge hath annexed with it God's true worship and honour, which requireth a testimony of His own will expressed by His Word that such honour doth please Him; if these things aforesaid your Grace do earnestly meditate, then albeit ye may not do suddenly what ye would, yet shall ye not cease to do what ye may. Your Grace cannot hastily abolish superstition and remove from offices unprofitable pastors, of whom speaketh

Matt. 6. Rom. 8. 1 Kgs. 18. John 17.

Ezekiel the Prophet, which to a public reformation is requisite and necessary. But if the zeal of God's glory be fervent in your Grace's heart, ye will not by wicked laws maintain idolatry, neither will ye suffer the fury of bishops to murder and devour the poor members of Christ's body as in times bypast they have been accustomed. Which thing if either by blind ignorance ye do or yet for pleasure of others within this realm permit to be done, then except you speedily repent, ye and your posterity shall suddenly feel the depressing hand of Him who hath exalted you. Ye shall be compelled, will ye or not, to know that He is eternal against whom ye address the battle, and that it is He that moderateth the times and disposeth kingdoms, ejecting from authority such as be inobedient and placing others according to His good pleasure; that it is He that glorifieth them that do glorify Him, and poureth forth contempt upon princes that rebel against His graces offered.

Ezek. 34.

NOTE.

Dan. 2.

1 Kgs. 2. Job 12. Ps. 107. Dan. 2.

Addition

In writing of this parcel, as I remembered the impediments which might call you back from God and from His true obedience, so did I consider what occasion ye had to tremble and to fear before His majesty and to enterprise the loss of all worldly glory for the promoting of the glory of God. I do consider that your power is but borrowed, extraordinary and unstable, for ye have it but by permission of others. And seldom it is that women do long reign with felicity and joy. For as nature hath denied to them a constant spirit of good government, so hath God pronounced that they are never given to reign over men but in His wrath and indignation.[9] Your most especial friends, moreover, blinded by the vanity of this world, yea, being drunken with the cup of that Roman harlot, are mortal enemies to Christ Jesus and to His true religion. These things may easily abash the mind of a woman not confirmed by grace. But yet, if ye shall a little consider with me the causes why that ye ought to hazard all for the glory of God in this behalf, the former terrors shall suddenly vanish.

NOTE.

Isa. 3.

I do not esteem that thing greatest which peradventure some other do: to wit, that if ye shall enterprise to innovate anything in matters

[9] These themes are explored much more fully in the *First Blast*.

of religion, that then ye shall lose your authority and also the favours of your carnal friends. I look further, to wit, to the judgements of God, who hath begun already to declare Himself angry with you, with your seed and posterity, yea, with the whole realm above which it should have ruled. Impute not to fortune that first your two sons were suddenly taken from you within the space of six hours, and after your husband reft, as it were, by violence from life and honour, the memorial of his name, succession and royal dignity perishing with himself.[10] For albeit the usurped abuse or rather tyranny of some realms have permitted women to succeed to the honour of their fathers, yet must their glory be transferred to the house of a stranger. And so I say that with himself was buried his name, succession and royal dignity. And in this, if ye espy not the anger and hot displeasure of God (threatening you and the rest of your posterity with the same plague), ye are more obstinate than I would wish you to be. I would ye should ponder and consider deeply with yourself that God useth not to punish realms and nations with such rare plagues without great cause, neither useth He to restore to honours and glory the house which He beginneth once to deject till repentance of the former crimes be found.

NOTE.

NOTE.

Ye may perchance doubt what crimes should have been in your husband, you or the realm for the which God should so grievously have punished you. I answer: the maintenance and defence of most horrible idolatry with the shedding of the blood of the saints of God who laboured to notify and rebuke the same. This, I say (other iniquities omitted), is such a crime before the eyes of His majesty that for the same He hath poured forth His extreme vengeance upon kings and upon their posterity, depriving them from honours and dignity forever. As by the histories of the Books of the Kings is most evident. To Jeroboam it is said: 'Because I have exalted thee from the midst of the people and have made thee prince over my people Israel, I have rent the kingdom from the house of David for idolatry also and have given it unto thee; but thou hast not been as David my servant', etc. 'But thou hast done wickedly, above all that have gone before thee. For thou hast made to thee other gods and molten images to provoke me and hast cast me behind thy back. Therefore shall I bring affliction upon the house of Jeroboam and I shall destroy

1 Kgs. 14.7–10.

[10] Mary of Guise's two sons died within hours of each other in April 1541 and her husband, James V, in December 1542. Her sole surviving child, Mary Stewart, thus succeeded to the throne when only six days old.

to Jeroboam all that pisseth against the wall (signifying thereby the male children) and shall cast forth the posterity of Jeroboam as dung is cast forth till it be consumed.' This sentence was not only executed against this idolater, but also against the rest of idolaters in that realm as they succeeded one after another. For to Baasha, whom God used as instrument to root out the seed of Jeroboam, it is said: 'Because thou hast walked in the way of Jeroboam, and hast caused my people Israel sin, that thou shouldst provoke me in their sins, therefore shall I cut down the posterity of Baasha and the posterity of his house and shall make thy house as the house of Jeroboam. He that shall die to Baasha in the city, him shall dogs eat, and he that shall die in the field, him shall the fowls devour.' Of the same cup, and for the same cause, drank Elah and Ahab, yea, and the posterity of Jehu, following the footsteps of their forefathers.

1 Kgs. 16.2–4.

1 Kgs. 16.
2 Kgs. 10
2 Kgs. 17.

By these examples you may evidently espy that idolatry is the cause why God destroyeth the posterity of princes. Not only of those that first invent abominations, but also of such as follow and defend the same. Consider, Madam, that God hath begun very sharply with you, taking from you, as it were together, two children and a husband. He hath begun, I say, to declare Himself angry; beware that ye provoke not the eyes of His majesty. It will not be the haughty looks of the proud, the strength of your friends, nor multitude of men that can justify your cause in His presence. If ye presume to rebel against Him (and against Him ye rebel if ye deny my most humble request which I make in His name, and it is this: with the hazard of mine own life I offer to prove that religion which now ye maintain to be false, deceivable and abomination before God, and that I shall do by most evident testimonies of His blessed, holy and infallible Word); if this, I say, ye deny (rebelling against God), the favour of your friends shall little avail you when He shall declare Himself enemy to you and to your posterity. Which assure yourself He shall shortly do if ye begin to display the banner of your malice against Him. Let not the prosperity of others, be they princes, queens, kings or emperors, bolden you to contemn God and His loving admonition. They shall drink the cup of His wrath, everyone in their rank, as He hath appointed them. No realm in these quarters (except it that next lieth to you) hath He so manifestly stricken with His terrible rod as He hath done you and your realm. And therefore it becometh you first to stoop, except that ye will have the threatenings pronounced by Isaiah the Prophet ratified upon you. To wit: 'that your sudden

The offer of John Knox.

Advert.

Prosperity for a time proveth not religion good.

No realm, England except, so grievously plagued as Scotland.

destruction be as the rotten wall, and your breaking as the breaking of a potsherd which is broken without pity, so that no portion of it can be found able either to carry fire or water'. Whereby the Prophet doth signify that the proud contemners of God and of His admonitions shall so perish from all honours that they shall have nothing worthy of memorial behind them in the earth. Yea, if they do leave anything, as it shall be unprofitable, so shall it be in execration and hatred to the elect of God. And therefore thus proceedeth my former letter.

Isa. 30.13–14.

Isa. 14.

Isa. 6.

Letter

How dangerous that ever it shall appear to the flesh to obey God and to make war against the devil, the prince of darkness, pride and superstition, yet if your Grace look to have yourself and seed to continue in honour worldly and everlasting, subject yourself by times under the hand of Him that is omnipotent. Embrace His will, despise not His Testament, refuse not His graces offered. When He calleth upon you, withdraw not your ear. Be not led away with the vain opinion that your church cannot err. Be ye most assuredly persuaded that so far as in life ye see them degenerate from Christ's true Apostles, so in religion are they further corrupted. Lay the book of God before your eyes and let it be judge to that which I say. Which if ye with fear and reverence obey, as did Josiah the admonitions of the Prophetess, then shall He (by whom kings do reign) crown your battle with double benediction and reward you with wisdom, riches, glory, honour and long life in this your regiment temporal, and with life everlasting when the king of all kings (whose members now do cry for your help) the Lord Jesus shall appear to judgement accompanied with His angels, before whom ye shall make accompt of your present regiment, when the proud and disobedient shall cry: 'Mountains fall upon us and hide us from the face of the Lord.' But then it shall be too late because they contemned His voice when He lovingly called.

Exhortation.

Josh. 1.

2 Chr. 34.

2 Chr. 1.

Rev. 6.16.

God the Father of our Lord Jesus Christ, by the power of His Holy Spirit, move your heart so to consider and accept the things that be said that they be not a testimony of your just condemnation in that great day of the Lord Jesus to whose omnipotent Spirit I unfeignedly commit your Grace.

Addition

When Jeremiah the Prophet, at the commandment of God, had written the sermons, threatenings and plagues which he had spoken against Israel and Judah, and had commanded them to be read by Baruch his scribe, because himself was excommunicated and forbidden to enter into the temple, by the providence of God it came to pass that Michaiah, the son of Gamariah, hearing the said sermons, passed to the king's house and did communicate the matter with the rest of the princes, who also, after they had read the same volume of Jeremiah's preachings, did not conceal the truth from King Jehoiakim who then did reign in Jerusalem. But the proud and desperate prince, commanding the book to be read in his presence, before he had heard three or four leaves of the same, did cut it and cast it into the fire, notwithstanding that some of the princes (I think not all) made request in the contrary. But the Prophet was charged by God to write again and to say to Jehoiakim the King: 'Thus saith the Lord: thou hast burnt this book, saying, why hast thou written in it according to this sentence? Assuredly the king of Babylon shall come and shall destroy this land and shall make it void of men and beasts. Therefore thus saith the Lord of Jehoiakim the King: there shall not be one left alive to sit in the seat of David. Their carcasses shall be cast to the heat of the day and to the frost of the night (whereby the Prophet did signify the most vile contempt and most cruel torment) and I shall visit the iniquity of himself, of his seed and servants, and I shall bring upon them, and upon the inhabiters of Jerusalem, and upon all Judah, all the calamities which I have spoken against them. Albeit they would not hear.'

Jer. 36.

[*Jer. 36.29–31.*]

This is not written, Madam, for that time only, but to assure us that the like punishment abideth the like contemners of what estate, condition or degree that ever they be. I did write unto you before, having testimony of a good conscience, that I did it in the fear of my God and by the motion of His Holy Spirit (for the request of faithful brethren in things lawful and appertaining to God's glory I cannot but judge to be the voice of the Holy Ghost). But how ye did accept the same my former writing, I do not otherwise than by conjectures understand; whether ye did read it to the end or not I am uncertain. One thing I know, that ye did deliver it to one of your prelates, saying: 'My lord, will ye read a pasquil?'[11] As charity persuadeth me to interpret things (doubtfully spoken) in the best sense, so my duty to God (who hath commanded me to flatter no prince in the earth) compelleth me to say that, if no more ye esteem the admonition of God nor the cardinals do the scoffing of pasquils, that then He shall shortly send you messengers with whom ye shall not be able on that manner to jest. If my person be considered, I grant my threatenings are no more to be feared than be the merry sports which fearful men do father upon Pasquillus in Rome. But, Madam, if ye shall deeply consider that God useth men (yea, and most commonly those that be of lowest degree and most abject before the world) to be His messengers and ambassadors, not only to notify His will to the simple people, but also to rebuke the most proud tyrants and potent princes, then will ye not judge the liquor by the outward appearance and nature of the vessel. For ye are not ignorant that the most noble wine is enclosed within the tun made of frail wood and that the precious ointment is often kept within the pot made of clay. If further ye shall consider that God will do nothing touching the punishment of realms and nations which He will not reveal to His servants, the Prophets, whose tongues He will compel to speak sometimes contrary to the appetites and desires of their own hearts and whose words He will perform be they never so unapparent to the judgement of men; if these ye do deeply weigh, then will ye fear the thing which presently is not seen.

Amos 3.7.

Zech. 1.

Elijah was but a man, as St James doth witness, like to his brethren, and yet at his prayer was Ahab the idolater and all Israel with him punished three years and six months, God shutting up the heaven that neither rain nor dew fell upon the earth the space aforewritten. And in the end God so wrought by him that Baal's priests were first confounded and after justly punished. And albeit that Jezebel sought his blood, and by oath had determined his death, yet as she was frustrate of her intent, so could she not keep her own bones from the dogs, which punishment the Prophet (God so ruling his tongue) had before appointed to that wicked woman. Albeit, Madam, that the messengers of God are not sent this day with visible miracles, because they teach none other doctrine than that which is confirmed with

Jas. 5.
1 Kgs. 17.
1 Kgs. 18.
1 Kgs. 19.
2 Kgs. 9.
1 Kgs. 19.

[11] In his *History*, Knox identifies the prelate as James Beaton, archbishop of Glasgow (Laing, vol. I, p. 252).

miracles from the beginning of the world, yet will not He (who hath promised to take charge over His poor and little flock to the end) suffer the contempt of their embassade escape punishment and vengeance. For the truth itself hath said: 'He that heareth you, heareth me, and he that contemneth you, contemneth me.' I did not speak unto you, Madam, by my former letter, neither yet do I now, as Pasquillus doth to the pope and his carnal cardinals in the behalf of such as dare not utter their names. But I come in the name of Christ Jesus, affirming that the religion which ye maintain is damnable idolatry, the which I offer myself to prove by the most evident testimonies of God's Scriptures. And in this quarrel I present myself against all the papists within the realm, desiring none other armour but God's Holy Word and the liberty of my tongue. God move your heart to understand my petition, to know the truth and unfeignedly to follow the same.

Matt. 10.
[*Luke* 10.16.]

AMEN.

Rev. 21.6–8.

I am the beginning and the end. I will give to him that is athirst of the well of the water of life freely. He that overcometh shall inherit all things and I will be his God and he shall be my son. But the fearful and unbelieving, and the abominable and murderers, and whoremongers and sorcerers, and idolaters and all liars, shall have their part in the lake which burneth with fire and brimstone, which is the second death.

THE APPELLATION OF JOHN KNOX

from the cruel and most injust sentence pronounced against him by the false bishops and clergy of Scotland, with his supplication and exhortation to the nobility, estates and commonalty of the same realm.

*

Printed at GENEVA

M.D.LVIII

TO THE NOBILITY AND ESTATES of Scotland John Knox wisheth grace, mercy and peace from God the Father of our Lord Jesus Christ with the spirit of righteous judgement.

*

It is not only the love of life temporal (Right Honourable), neither yet the fear of corporal death, that moveth me at this present to expone unto you the injuries done against me and to crave of you, as of lawful powers by God appointed, redress of the same. But partly it proceedeth from that reverence which every man oweth to God's eternal truth, and partly from a love which I bear to your salvation, and to the salvation of my brethren abused in that realm by such as have no fear of God before their eyes.

Every man ought to confess and reverence God's truth.

It hath pleased God of His infinite mercy not only so to illuminate the eyes of my mind and so to touch my dull heart that clearly I see, and by His grace unfeignedly believe, that 'there is no other name given to men under the heaven in which salvation consisteth save the name of Jesus alone', 'who by that sacrifice which he did once offer upon the cross hath sanctified forever those that shall inherit the kingdom promised'. But also it hath pleased Him of His superabundant grace to make and appoint me, most wretched of many thousands, a witness, minister and preacher of the same doctrine. The sum whereof I did not spare to communicate with my brethren, being with them in the realm of Scotland in the year 1556,[1] because I know myself to be a steward and that accompts of the talent committed to my charge shall be required by Him who will admit no vain excuse which fearful men pretend. I did therefore (as God did minister), during the time I was conversant with them (God is record and witness), truly and sincerely, according to the gift granted unto me, divide the Word of salvation, teaching all men to hate sin, which before God was and is so odious that none other sacrifice could satisfy His justice except the death of His only Son, and to magnify the great mercies of our heavenly Father, who did not spare the substance of His own glory but did give Him to the world to suffer the ignominious and cruel death of the cross, by that means to reconcile His chosen children to Himself; teaching further what is the duty of such as do believe themselves purged by such a price from their former filthiness: to wit, that they are bound to walk in the newness of life, fighting against the lusts of the flesh, and studying at all times to glorify God by such good works as He hath prepared His children to walk in. In doctrine I did further affirm, so taught by my Master Christ Jesus, that 'whosoever denieth Him, yea, or is ashamed of Him before this wicked generation, him shall Christ Jesus deny, and of him shall He be ashamed when He shall appear in His majesty'. And therefore I feared not to affirm that of necessity it is that such as hope for life everlasting avoid all superstition, vain religion and idolatry.

Acts 4.12. *Heb. 10.10.* *1 Cor. 3.* *Matt. 25.* *John 3.* *Rom. 5, 8.* *2 Cor. 5.* *Rom. 6.* *Eph. 4, 5.* *Eph. 2.* *Matt. 10.33.*

Vain religion and idolatry I call whatsoever is done in God's service or honour without the express commandment of His own Word. This doctrine did I believe to be so conformable to God's Holy Scriptures

Vain religion or idolatry.

[1] For Knox's own account of his mission to Scotland in 1555–6, see Laing, vol. 1, pp. 245–54.

that I thought no creature could have been so impudent as to have damned any point or article of the same. Yet nevertheless, me as an heretic and this doctrine as heretical have your false bishops and ungodly clergy damned, pronouncing against me a sentence of death, in testification whereof they have burned a picture.[2] From which false and cruel sentence, and from all judgement of that wicked generation, I make it known to your Honours that I appeal to a lawful and general council, to such I mean as the most ancient laws and canons do approve to be holden by such as whose manifest impiety is not to be reformed in the same; most humbly requiring of your Honours that, as God hath appointed you princes in that people, and by reason thereof requireth of your hands the defence of innocents troubled in your dominion, in the meantime, and till the controversies that this day be in religion be lawfully decided, ye receive me and such others as most unjustly by those cruel beasts are persecuted in your defence and protection.

A sentence pronounced. Appellation from the same.

The request of John Knox.

Your Honours are not ignorant that it is not I alone who doth sustain this cause against the pestilent generation of papists, but that the most part of Germany, the country of Helvetia, the king of Denmark, the nobility of Polonia, together with many other cities and churches reformed, appeal from the tyranny of that Antichrist, and most earnestly do call for a lawful and general council wherein may all controversies in religion be decided by the authority of God's most sacred Word. And unto this same, as said is, do I appeal yet once again, requiring of your Honours to hold my simple and plain appellation of no less value nor effect than if it had been made with greater circumstance, solemnity and ceremony, and that ye receive me, calling unto you as to the powers of God ordained, in your protection and defence against the rage of tyrants, not to maintain me in any iniquity, error or false opinion, but to let me have such equity as God by His Word, ancient laws and determinations of most godly councils grant to men accused or infamed. The Word of God will that no man shall die except he be found criminal and worthy of death for offence committed, of the which he must be manifestly convicted by two or three witnesses; ancient laws do permit just defences to such as be accused (be their crimes never so horrible); and godly councils will that neither bishop nor person ecclesiastical

The petition of Protestants.

Deut. 17.6.

[2] Knox is referring here to the bishops' burning of his effigy in 1556.

whatsoever, accused of any crime, shall sit in judgement, consultation or council where the cause of such men as do accuse them is to be tried.

The petitions of John Knox.

These things require I of your Honours to be granted unto me: to wit, that the doctrine which our adversaries condemn for heresy may be tried by the simple and plain Word of God, that just defences be admitted to us that sustain the battle against this pestilent generation of Antichrist, and that they be removed from judgement in our cause, seeing that our accusation is not intended against any one particular person, but against that whole kingdom, which we doubt not to prove to be a power usurped against God, against His commandment and against the ordinance of Christ Jesus established in His church by His chief Apostles. Yea, we doubt not to prove the kingdom of the pope to be the kingdom and power of Antichrist. And therefore, my Lords, I cannot cease in the name of Christ Jesus to require of you that the matter may come in examination, and that ye, the estates of the realm, by your authority compel such as will be called bishops not only to desist from their cruel murdering of such as do study to promote God's glory in detecting and disclosing the damnable impiety of that man of sin, the Roman Antichrist, but also that ye compel them to answer to such crimes as shall be laid to their charge for not righteously instructing the flock committed to their cares.

Note well.

Answer to objections.

But here I know two things shall be doubted. The former, whether that my appellation is lawful and to be admitted, seeing that I am damned as an heretic; and secondarily, whether your Honours be bound to defend such as call for your support in that case, seeing that your bishops (who in matters of religion claim all authority to appertain to them) have by their sentence already condemned me. The one and the other I nothing doubt most clearly to prove. First, that my appellation is most lawful and just; and secondarily, that your Honours cannot refuse to defend me, thus calling for your aid, but that in so doing ye declare yourselves rebellious to God, maintainers of murderers and shedders of innocent blood.

1\.
2.

NOTE.

The appellation is just and lawful.

How just cause I have by the civil law (as for their canon it is accursed of God) to appeal from their unjust sentence my purpose is not to make long discourse. Only I will touch the points which all men confess to be just causes of appellation. First, lawfully could I not be summoned by them being for that time absent from their jurisdiction, charged with the preaching of Christ's Evangel in a free city not subject to their tyranny.[3] Secondarily, to me was no intimation made of their summons, but so secret was their surmised malice that the copy of the summons being required was denied. Thirdly, to the realm of Scotland could I have had no free nor sure access being before exiled from the same by their unjust tyranny. And last, to me they neither could nor can be competent and indifferent judges, for that before any summons were raised against me I had accused them by my letters published to the queen dowager,[4] and had intended against them all crimes, offering myself with hazard of life to prove the same, for the which they are not only unworthy of ecclesiastical authority, but also of any sufferance within a commonwealth professing Christ. This my accusation preceding their summons, neither by the law of God neither yet by the law of man can they be to me competent judges till place be granted unto me openly to prove my accusation intended against them and they be compelled to make answer as criminals. For I will plainly prove that not only bishops but also popes have been removed from all authority and pronouncing of judgement till they have purged themselves of accusations laid against them. Yea, further I will prove that bishops and popes most justly have been deprived from all honours and administration for smaller crimes than I have to charge the whole rabble of your bishops.

God's messengers may appeal from unjust sentences, and civil powers are bound to admit them. Jer. 26.

But because this is not my chief ground, I will stand content for this present to show that lawful it is to God's prophets and to preachers of Christ Jesus to appeal from the sentence and judgement of the visible church to the knowledge of the temporal magistrate, who by God's law is bound to hear their causes and to defend them from tyranny.

The prophet Jeremiah was commanded by God to stand in the court of the house of the Lord and to preach this sermon in effect: that Jerusalem should be destroyed and be exponed in opprobry to all nations of the earth, and that also that famous temple of God should be made desolate, like unto Shiloh, because the priests, the prophets and the people did not walk in the law which God had proposed unto them, neither would they obey the voices of the prophets whom God sent to call them to repentance. For this sermon

[3] That is, Geneva, whither Knox had returned in July 1556.

[4] In other words, the *Letter to the Regent*, first published in 1556, and reprinted with additions in 1558.

was Jeremiah apprehended and a sentence of death was pronounced against him, and that by the priests, by the prophets and by the people. Which things being bruited in the ears of the princes of Judah, they passed up from the king's house to the temple of the Lord and sat down in judgement for further knowledge of the cause. But the priests and prophets continued in their cruel sentence which before they had pronounced, saying: 'This man is worthy of the death, for he hath prophesied against this city as your ears have heard.' But Jeremiah, so moved by the Holy Ghost, began his defence against that their tyrannous sentence in these words: 'The Lord (saith he) hath sent me to prophesy against this house and against this city all the words which you have heard. Now therefore make good your ways and hear the voice of the Lord your God, and then shall He repent of the evil which He hath spoken against you. As for me, behold, I am in your hands (so doth he speak to the princes), do to me as you think good and righteous. Nevertheless, know you this most assuredly, that if ye murder or slay me, ye shall make yourselves, this city and the inhabitants of the same criminal and guilty of innocent blood. For of a truth the Lord hath sent me to speak in your ears all those words.' Then the princes and the people (saith the text) said: 'This man is not worthy of death for he hath spoken to us in the name of the Lord our God.' And so after some contention was the Prophet delivered from that danger.

[*Jer.* 26.11.]

[*Jer.* 26.12–16.]

Advert.

The princes did absolve the Prophet whom the priests had condemned.

This fact and history manifestly proveth whatsoever before I have affirmed. To wit, that it is lawful for the servants of God to call for the help of the civil magistrate against the sentence of death if it be unjust, by whomsoever it be pronounced, and also that the civil sword hath power to repress the fury of the priests and to absolve whom they have condemned. For the Prophet of God was damned by those who then only in earth were known to be the visible church, to wit, priests and prophets, who then were in Jerusalem the successors of Aaron, to whom was given a charge to speak to the people in the name of God, and a precept given to the people to hear the law from their mouths, to the which if any should be rebellious or inobedient he should die the death without mercy. These men, I say, thus authorised by God, first did excommunicate Jeremiah for that he did preach otherwise than did the common sort of prophets in Jerusalem, and last apprehended him, as you have heard, pronouncing against

Deut. 17.

him this sentence aforewritten, from the which nevertheless the Prophet appealed, that is, sought help and defence against the same, and that most earnestly did he crave of the princes.

[*Jer.* 26.14.] For albeit he saith: 'I am in your hands: do with me as ye think righteous', he doth not contemn nor neglect his life as though he regarded not what should become of him, but in those his words most vehemently did he admonish the princes and rulers of the people, giving them to understand what God should require of them.

The meaning of these words 'I am in your hands', etc.

As he should say: 'You princes of Judah and rulers of the people to whom appertaineth indifferently to judge betwixt party and party, to justify the just man and to condemn the malefactor, you have heard a sentence of death pronounced against me by those whose lips ought to speak no decept because they are sanctified and appointed by God Himself to speak His law and to pronounce judgement with equity.

Deut. 17. *Jer.* 1. *Deut.* 1, 10.

But as they have left the living God and have taught the people to follow vanity, so are they become mortal enemies to all God's true servants, of whom I am one, rebuking their iniquity, apostasy and defection from God, which is the only cause they seek my life. But a thing most contrary to all equity, law and justice it is that I, a man sent of God to call them, this people, and you again to the true service of God from the which you are all declined, shall suffer the death because that my enemies do so pronounce sentence. I stand in your presence whom God hath made princes, your power is above their tyranny, before you do I expone my cause. I am in your hands and cannot resist to suffer what ye think just. But lest that my lenity and patience should either make you negligent in the defence of me in my just cause appealing to your judgement, either yet encourage my enemies in seeking my blood, this one thing I dare not conceal: that if you murder me (which thing ye do if ye defend me not), ye make not only my enemies guilty of my blood, but also yourselves and this whole city.'

By these words, I say, it is evident that the Prophet of God, being damned to death by the priests and by the prophets of the visible church, did seek aid, support and defence at the princes and temporal magistrates, threatening his blood to be required of their hands if they by their authority did not defend him from the fury of his enemies. Alleging also just causes of his appellation and why he ought to have been defended: to wit, that he was sent of God to rebuke their vices and defection from God; that he taught no doctrine which God

The causes of his appellation

before had not pronounced in His law; that he desired their conversion to God, continually calling upon them to walk in the ways which God had approved; and therefore doth he boldly crave of the princes, as of God's lieutenants, to be defended from the blind rage and tyranny of the priests, notwithstanding that they claimed to themselves authority to judge in all matters of religion. And the same did he what time he was cast in prison and thereafter was brought to the presence of King Zedekiah. After, I say, that he had defended his innocency, affirming that he neither had offended against the king, against his servants nor against the people, at last he made intercession to the king for his life, saying: 'But now, my lord the king, take heed, I beseech thee, let my prayer fall into thy presence, command me not to be carried again into the house of Jonathan the scribe, that I die not there.' And the text witnesseth that the king commanded the place of his imprisonment to be changed. Whereof it is evident that the Prophet did oftener than once seek help at the civil power and that first the princes and thereafter the king did acknowledge that it appertained to their office to deliver him from the injust sentence which was pronounced against him.

and why he ought to have been defended.

Jer. 38.

[*Jer.* 37.20.]

If any think that Jeremiah did not appeal because he only declared the wrong done unto him, and did but crave defence according to his innocency, let the same man understand that none otherwise do I appeal from that false and cruel sentence which your bishops have pronounced against me. Neither yet can there be any other just cause of appellation but innocency hurt or suspected to be hurt, whether it be by ignorance of a judge or by malice and corruption of those who under the title of justice do exercise tyranny. If I were a thief, murderer, blasphemer, open adulterer, or any offender whom God's word commandeth to suffer for a crime committed, my appellation were vain and to be rejected. But I being innocent, yea, the doctrine which your bishops have condemned in me being God's eternal verity, have no less liberty to crave your defence against that cruelty than had the Prophet Jeremiah to seek the aid of the princes and king of Judah. But this shall more plainly appear in the fact of St Paul who, after that he was apprehended in Jerusalem, did first claim to the liberty of Roman citizens for avoiding torment what time that the captain would have examined him by questions. Thereafter in the council, where no righteous judgement was to be hoped for, he affirmed that he was a Pharisee and that he was accused of the

Just cause of appellation.

Acts 22, 23, 24, 25.

resurrection of the dead. And last, in the presence of Festus, he appealed from all knowledge and judgement of the priests at Jerusalem to the emperor. Of which last point, because it doth chiefly appertain to this my cause, I will somewhat speak.

After that Paul had diverse times been accused, as in the Acts of the Apostles is manifest, at the last the chief priests and their faction came to Caesarea with Festus the president, who presented to them Paul in judgement, whom they accused of horrible crimes. Which nevertheless they could not prove, the Apostle defending that he had not offended neither against the law, neither against the temple, neither yet against the emperor. But Festus, willing to gratify the Jews, said to Paul: 'Wilt thou go up to Jerusalem and there be judged of these things in my presence?' But Paul said: 'I stand at the justice seat of the emperor where it behooveth me to be judged. I have done no injury to the Jews as thou better knowest. If I have done anything injustly or yet committed crime worthy of death, I refuse not to die. But if there be nothing of these things true whereof they accuse me, no man may give me to them. I appeal to Caesar.'

Acts 25.9–11.

It may appear at the first sight that Paul did great injury to Festus the judge, and to the whole order of the priesthood, who did hope greater equity in a cruel tyrant than in all that session and learned company. Which thing no doubt Festus did understand, pronouncing these words: 'Hast thou appealed to Caesar? Thou shalt go to Caesar.' As he would say: 'I, as a man willing to understand the truth before I pronounce sentence, have required of thee to go to Jerusalem where the learned of thine own nation may hear thy cause and discern in the same. The controversy standeth in matters of religion. Thou art accused as an apostate from the law, as a violator of the temple and transgressor of the traditions of their fathers; in which matters I am ignorant, and therefore desire information by those that be learned in the same religion whereof the question is. And yet dost thou refuse so many godly fathers to hear thy cause, and dost appeal to the emperor, preferring him to all our judgements, of no purpose belike, but to delay time.'

[*Acts 25.12.*]

Thus, I say, it might have appeared that Paul did not only injury to the judge and to the priests, but also that his cause was greatly to be suspected, partly for that he did refuse the judgement of those that had most knowledge (as all men supposed) of God's will and religion, and partly because he appealed to the emperor who then was at Rome far absent from Jerusalem, a man also ignorant of God and enemy to all virtue. But the Apostle, considering the nature of his enemies and what things they had intended against him even from the first day that he began freely to speak in the name of Christ, did not fear to appeal from them and from the judge that would have gratified them. They had professed themselves plain enemies to Christ Jesus and to His blessed Evangel and had sought the death of Paul, yea, even by factions and treasonable conspiracy. And therefore by no means would he admit them either judges in his cause, either auditors of the same as Festus required, but grounding himself upon strong reasons, to wit, that he had not offended the Jews, neither yet the law, but that he was innocent, and therefore that no judge ought to give him in the hands of his enemies; grounding, I say, his appellation upon these reasons, he neither regarded the displeasure of Festus, neither yet the bruit of the ignorant multitude, but boldly did appeal from all cognition of them to the judgement of the emperor, as said is.

Why Paul would admit none of the Levitical order to judge in his cause.

Upon what reasons the appellation of Paul was grounded.

By these two examples I doubt not but your Honours do understand that lawful it is to the servants of God oppressed by tyranny to seek remedy against the same, be it by appellation from their sentence or by imploring the help of civil magistrates. For what God hath approved in Jeremiah and Paul, He can condemn in none that likewise be entreated. I might allege some histories of the primitive church serving to the same purpose: as of Ambrose and Athanasius, of whom the one would not be judged but at Milan, where that [h]is doctrine was heard of all his church and received and approved by many; and the other would in no wise give place to those councils where he knew that men conspired against the truth of God should sit in judgement and consultation. But because the Scriptures of God are my only foundation and assurance in all matters of weight and importance, I have thought the two former testimonies sufficient as well to prove my appellation reasonable and just as to declare to your Honours that with safe conscience ye cannot refuse to admit the same.

If any think it arrogance or foolishness in me to compare myself with Jeremiah and Paul, let the same man understand that as God is immutable so is the verity of His glorious Evangel of equal dignity whensoever it is impugned, be the members suffering never so weak. What I think touching mine own person, God shall reveal when the secrets of all hearts shall be disclosed, and such as with whom I have

The cause is to be regarded and not the person.

been conversant can partly witness what arrogance or pride they espy in me. But touching the doctrine and cause which that adulterous and pestilent generation of Antichrist's servants (who will be called bishops amongst you) have condemned in me, I neither fear nor shame to confess and avow before man and angel to be the eternal truth of the eternal God. And in that case I doubt not to compare myself with any member in whom the truth hath been impugned since the beginning. For as it was the truth which Jeremiah did preach in these words: 'The priests have not known me (saith the Lord) but the pastors have traitorously declined and fallen back from me. The prophets have prophesied in Baal and have gone after those things which cannot help. My people have left the fountain of living waters and have digged to themselves pits which can contain no water'; as it was a truth that the pastors and watchmen in the days of Isaiah were become dumb dogs, blind, ignorant, proud and avaricious; and finally as it was a truth that the princes and the priests were murderers of Christ Jesus and cruel persecutors of His Apostles, so likewise it is a truth (and that most infallible) that those that have condemned me (the whole rabble of the papistical clergy) have declined from the true faith, have given ear to deceivable spirits and to doctrine of devils, are the stars fallen from the heaven to the earth, are fountains without water, and finally are enemies to Christ Jesus, deniers of His virtue and horrible blasphemers of His death and passion.

Jer. 2.8, 13.

Jer. 1.

Isa. 56.10–11.

Acts 3, 4.

1 Tim. 4.1.

Jude 1.13.

2. Pet. 2.17.

And further, as that visible church had no crime whereof justly they could accuse either the Prophets either the Apostles, except their doctrine only, so have not such as seek my blood other crime to lay to my charge except that I affirm, as always I offer to prove, that the religion which now is maintained by fire and sword is no less contrarious to the true religion taught and established by the Apostles than is darkness to light or the devil to God; and also that such as now do claim the title and name of the church are no more the elect spouse of Christ Jesus than was the synagogue of the Jews the true church of God what time it crucified Christ Jesus, damned His doctrine and persecuted His Apostles. And therefore, seeing that my battle is against the proud and cruel hypocrites of this age, as that battle of those most excellent instruments was against the false prophets and malignant church of their ages, neither ought any man think it strange that I compare myself with them with whom I sustain a common cause; neither ought you, my Lords, judge yourselves less

Let the cause be noted.

addebted and bound to me, calling for your support, than did the princes of Judah think themselves bound to Jeremiah whom for that time they delivered notwithstanding the sentence of death pronounced against him by the visible church.

And thus much for the right of my appellation which, in the bowels of Christ Jesus, I require your Honours not to esteem as a thing superfluous and vain, but that ye admit it, and also accept me in your protection and defence, that by you assured I may have access to my native country which I never offended, to the end that freely and openly in the presence of the whole realm I may give my confession of all such points as this day be in controversy. And also that you, by your authority, which ye have of God, compel such as of long time have blinded and deceived both yourselves and the people to answer to such things as shall be laid to their charge. But lest that some doubt remain that I require more of you than you of conscience are bound to grant, in few words I hope to prove my petition to be such as without God's heavy displeasure ye cannot deny. My petition is that ye, whom God hath appointed heads in your commonwealth, with single eye do study to promote the glory of God, to provide that your subjects be rightly instructed in His true religion, that they be defended from all oppression and tyranny, that true teachers may be maintained and such as blind and deceive the people, together also with all idle bellies which do rob and oppress the flock, may be removed and punished as God's law prescribeth. And to the performance of every one of these do your offices and names, the honours and benefits which ye receive, the law of God universally given to all men, and the example of most godly princes, bind and oblige you.

Answer to an objection or doubt.
The petition of John Knox.

My purpose is not greatly to labour to prove that your whole study ought to be to promote the glory of God, neither yet will I study to allege all reasons that justly may be brought to prove that ye are not exalted to reign above your brethren as men without care and solicitude. For these be principles so grafted in nature that very Ethnics have confessed the same. For seeing that God only hath placed you in His chair, hath appointed you to be His lieutenants, and by His own seal hath marked you to be magistrates and to rule above your brethren, to whom nature nevertheless hath made you like in all points (for in conception, birth, life and death ye differ nothing from the common sort of men, but God only, as said is, hath promoted you and of His especial favour hath given unto you this prerogative

The singular honours which magistrates receive of God ought to move them with all diligence to promote His religion.

to be called gods); how horrible ingratitude were it then that you should be found unfaithful to Him that thus hath honoured you? And further, what a monster were it that you should be proved unmerciful to them above whom ye are appointed to reign as fathers above their children?

Because, I say, that very Ethnics have granted that the chief and first care of princes, and of such as be appointed to rule above others, ought to be to promote the glory and honour of their gods and to maintain that religion which they supposed to have been true, and that their second care was to maintain and defend the subjects committed to their charge in all equity and justice, I will not labour to show unto you what ought to be your study in maintaining God's true honour lest that in so doing I should seem to make you less careful over God's true religion than were the Ethnics over their idolatry. But because other petitions may appear more hard and difficult to be granted, I purpose briefly, but yet freely, to speak what God by His Word doth assure me to be true. To wit, first, that in conscience you are bound to punish malefactors and to defend innocents imploring your help; secondarily, that God requireth of you to provide that your subjects be rightly instructed in His true religion and that the same by you be reformed whensoever abuses do creep in by malice of Satan and negligence of men; and last, that ye are bound to remove from honour and to punish with death (if the crime so require) such as deceive the people or defraud them of that food of their souls, I mean God's lively Word.

The duties of magistrates.

Rom. 13.1–4.

The first and second are most plain by the words of St Paul, thus speaking of lawful powers: 'Let every soul (saith he) submit himself unto the higher powers. For there is no power but of God. The powers that be are ordained of God. Whosoever therefore resisteth power, resisteth the ordinance of God, and they that resist shall receive to themselves damnation. For rulers are not to be feared of those that do well, but of those that do evil. Wilt thou then be without fear of the power? Do that which is good and so shalt thou be praised of the same. For he is the minister of God for thy wealth. But if thou do that which is evil, fear. For he beareth not the sword for nought, for he is the minister of God to take vengeance on them that do evil.' As the Apostle in these words most straitly commandeth obedience to be given to lawful powers, pronouncing God's wrath and vengeance against such as shall resist the ordinance of God, so doth he assign to the powers their offices, which be to take vengeance upon evil doers, to maintain the well doers, and so to minister and rule in their office that the subjects by them may have a benefit and be praised in well doing. Now if you be powers ordained by God (and that I hope all men will grant), then by the plain words of the Apostle is the sword given unto you by God for maintenance of the innocent and for punishment of malefactors. But I, and my brethren with me accused, do offer not only to prove ourselves innocents in all things laid to our charge, but also we offer most evidently to prove your bishops to be the very pestilence who have infected all Christianity. And therefore by the plain doctrine of the Apostle you are bound to maintain us and to punish the other being evidently convict and proved criminal.

In what points be powers bound to their subjects.

Rom. 13.6.

Moreover, the former words of the Apostle do teach how far high powers be bound to their subjects: to wit, that because they are God's ministers by Him ordained for the profit and utility of others, most diligently ought they to intend upon the same. For that cause assigneth the Holy Ghost, commanding subjects to obey and to pay tribute, saying: 'For this do you pay tribute and toll.' That is, because they are God's ministers, bearing the sword for your utility. Whereof it is plain that there is no honour without a charge annexed. And this one point I wish your wisdoms deeply to consider: that God hath not placed you above your brethren to reign as tyrants without respect of their profit and commodity. You hear the Holy Ghost witness the contrary, affirming that all lawful powers be God's ministers ordained for the wealth, profit and salvation of their subjects and not for their destruction. Could it be said (I beseech you) that magistrates, enclosing their subjects in a city without all victuals, or giving unto them no other victuals but such as were poisoned, did rule for the profit of their subjects? I trust that none would be so foolish as so to affirm. But that rather every discreet person would boldly affirm that such as so did were tyrants unworthy of all regiment. If we will not deny that which Christ Jesus affirmeth to be a truth infallible, to wit, that the soul is greater and more precious than is the body, then shall we easily espy how unworthy of authority be those that this day debar their subjects from the hearing of God's Word and by fire and sword compel them to feed upon the very poison of their souls, the damnable doctrine of Antichrist.

Let the similitude be noted.

And therefore in this point, I say, I cannot cease to admonish your

Honours diligently to take heed over your charge which is greater than the most part of men suppose. It is not enough that you abstain from violent wrong and oppression which ungodly men exercise against their subjects, but ye are further bound, to wit, that ye rule above them for their wealth. Which ye cannot do if that ye, either by negligence not providing true pastors, or yet by your maintenance of such as be ravening wolves, suffer their souls to starve and perish for lack of the true food which is Christ's Evangel sincerely preached. It will not excuse you in His presence, who will require accompt of every talent committed to your charge, to say that ye supposed that the charge of the souls had been committed to your bishops. No no, my Lords, so ye cannot escape God's judgement. For if your bishops be proved to be no bishops, but deceivable thieves and ravening wolves (which I offer myself to prove by God's Word, by law and councils, yea, by the judgement of all the godly learned from the primitive church to this day), then shall your permission and defence of them be reputed before God a participation with their theft and murder. For thus accused the Prophet Isaiah the princes of Jerusalem: 'Thy princes (saith he) are apostates (that is, obstinate refusers of God), and they are companions of thieves.' This grievous accusation was laid against them, albeit that they ruled in that city, which sometime was called holy, where then were the temple, rites and ordinances of God, because that not only they were wicked themselves, but chiefly because they maintained wicked men, their priests and false prophets, in honours and authority. If they did not escape this accusation of the Holy Ghost in that age, look ye neither to escape the accusation nor the judgement which is pronounced against the maintainers of wicked men: to wit, that the one and the other shall drink the cup of God's wrath and vengeance together.

It is not enough that rulers oppress not their subjects.

The offer of John Knox and his accusation intended against the papistical bishops.

Isa. 1.23.

Jer. 23, 27. Ezek. 13. Hos. 4.

And lest ye should deceive yourselves, esteeming your bishops to be virtuous and godly, this do I affirm and offer myself to prove the same: that more wicked men than be the whole rabble of your clergy were never from the beginning universally known in any age. Yea, Sodom and Gomorrah may be justified in their respect, for they permitted just Lot to dwell amongst them without any violence done to his body, which that pestilent generation of your shaven sort doth not, but most cruelly persecute by fire and sword the true members of Christ's body for no other cause but for the true service and honouring of God. And therefore I fear not to affirm that which God

[*Gen. 19.*]

shall one day justify: that by your offices ye be bound not only to repress their tyranny, but also to punish them as thieves and murderers, as idolaters and blasphemers of God, and in their rooms ye are bound to place true preachers of Christ's Evangel for the instruction, comfort and salvation of your subjects, above whom else shall never the Holy Ghost acknowledge that you rule in justice for their profit. If ye pretend to possess the kingdom with Christ Jesus, ye may not take example neither by the ignorant multitude of princes, neither by the ungodly and cruel rulers of the earth, of whom some pass their time in sloth, insolence and riot without respect had to God's honour or to the salvation of their brethren, and other most cruelly oppress with proud Nimrod such as be subject to them. But your pattern and example must be the practice of those whom God hath approved by the testimony of His Word, as after shall be declared.

NOTE. *If powers provide not for instruction of their subjects, they do never rule above them for their profit.*

Of the premises it is evident that to lawful powers is given the sword for punishment of malefactors, for maintenance of innocents and for the profit and utility of their subjects. Now let us consider whether the reformation of religion fallen in decay and punishment of false teachers do appertain to the civil magistrate and nobility of any realm. I am not ignorant that Satan of old time, for maintenance of his darkness, hath obtained of the blind world two chief points. Former, he hath persuaded to princes, rulers and magistrates that the feeding of Christ's flock appertaineth nothing to their charge, but that it is rejected upon the bishops and estate ecclesiastical; and secondarily, that the reformation of religion, be it never so corrupt, and the punishment of such as be sworn soldiers in their kingdom, are exempted from all civil power and are reserved to themselves and to their own cognition. But that no offender can justly be exempted from punishment, and that the ordering and reformation of religion with the instruction of subjects doth especially appertain to the civil magistrate, shall God's perfect ordinance, His plain Word, and the facts and examples of those that of God are highly praised, most evidently declare.

What Satan hath obtained of the blind world.

When God did establish His law, statutes and ceremonies in the midst of Israel, He did not exempt the matters of religion from the power of Moses, but as He gave him charge over the civil polity, so He put in his mouth and in his hand: that is, He first revealed to him and thereafter commanded to put in practice whatsoever was to

The matters and reformation of religion appertain to the care of the

civil power. Exod. 21, 24, 25, etc.

be taught or done in matters of religion. Nothing did God reveal particularly to Aaron, but altogether was he commanded to depend from the mouth of Moses. Yea, nothing was he permitted to do to himself or to his children either in his or their inauguration and sanctification to the priesthood, but all was committed to the care of Moses. And therefore were these words so frequently repeated to Moses: 'Thou shalt separate Aaron and his sons from the midst of the people of Israel that they may execute the office of the priesthood. Thou shalt make unto them garments, thou shalt anoint them, thou shalt wash them, thou shalt fill their hands with the sacrifice.' And so forth of every rite and ceremony that was to be done unto them, especial commandment was given unto Moses that he should do it. Now if Aaron and his sons were so subject to Moses that they did nothing but at his commandment, who dare be so bold as to affirm that the civil magistrate hath nothing to do in matters of religion? For seeing that then God did so straitly require that even those who did bear the figure of Christ should receive from the civil power, as it were, their sanctification and entrance to their office, and seeing also that Moses was so far preferred to Aaron that the one commanded and the other did obey, who dare esteem that the civil power is now become so profane in God's eyes that it is sequestered from all intromission with the matters of religion?

Note.

Exod. 28.1–4.

The Holy Ghost in diverse places declareth the contrary. For one of the chief precepts commanded to the king when that he should be placed in his throne was to write the example of the book of the Lord's law, that it should be with him, that he might read in it all the days of his life, that he might learn to fear the Lord his God and to keep all the words of His law, and His statutes to do them. This precept requireth not only that the king should himself fear God, keep His law and statutes, but that also he as the chief ruler should provide that God's true religion should be kept inviolated of the people and flock which by God was committed to his charge. And this did not only David and Solomon perfectly understand. But also some godly kings in Judah, after the apostasy and idolatry that infected Israel by the means of Jeroboam, did practise their understanding and execute their power in some notable reformations. For Asa and Jehoshaphat, kings in Judah, finding the religion altogether corrupt, did apply their hearts (saith the Holy Ghost) to serve the Lord and to walk in His ways. And thereafter doth witness that Asa

[*Josh. 1.7–8.*]

The facts of godly kings are an interpretation of the law and declaration of their power.

removed from honours his mother, some say grandmother, because she had committed and laboured to maintain horrible idolatry. And Jehoshaphat did not only refuse strange gods himself, but also, destroying the chief monuments of idolatry, did send forth the Levites to instruct the people. Whereof it is plain that the one and the other did understand such reformations to appertain to their duties.

2 Chr. 14–17.

Note.

But the facts of Hezekiah and of Josiah do more clearly prove the power and duty of the civil magistrate in the reformation of religion. Before the reign of Hezekiah, so corrupt was the religion that the doors of the house of the Lord were shut up, the lamps were extinguished, no sacrifice was orderly made. But in the first year of his reign, the first month of the same, did the king open the doors of the temple, bring in the priests and Levites and, assembling them together, did speak unto them as followeth: 'Hear me, O ye Levites, and be sanctified now, and sanctify also the house of the Lord God of your fathers and carry forth from the sanctuary all filthiness (he meaneth all monuments and vessels of idolatry). For our fathers have transgressed and have committed wickedness in the eyes of the eternal our God, they have left Him and have turned their faces from the tabernacle of the Lord, and therefore is the wrath of the Lord come upon Judah and Jerusalem. Behold our fathers have fallen by the sword, our sons, daughters and wives are led in captivity. But now have I purposed in my heart to make a covenant with the Lord God of Israel that He may turn the wrath of His fury from us. And therefore my sons (he sweetly exhorteth) be not faint, for the Lord hath chosen you to stand in His presence and to serve Him.'

2 Chr. 29.

Advert that the king taketh upon him to command the priests.

[*2 Chr. 29.5–11.*]

Such as be not more than blind clearly may perceive that the king doth acknowledge that it appertained to his charge to reform the religion, to appoint the Levites to their charges and to admonish them of their duty and office. Which thing he more evidently declareth, writing his letters to all Israel, to Ephraim and Manasseh, and sent the same by the hands of messengers having this tenor: 'You sons of Israel, return to the Lord God of Abraham, Isaac and Israel, and He shall return to the residue that resteth from the hands of Assyria. Be not as your fathers and as your brethren were who have transgressed against the Lord God of their fathers, who hath made them desolate as you see. Hold not your heart, therefore, but give your hand unto the Lord, return unto His sanctuary, serve Him and He shall show mercy unto you, to your sons and daughters that

2 Chr. 30.6–9.

be in bondage, for He is pitiful and easy to be entreated.' Thus far did Hezekiah by letters and messengers provoke the people, declined from God, to repentance not only in Judah where he reigned lawful king, but also in Israel subject then to another king. And albeit that by some wicked men his messengers were mocked, yet as they lacked not their just punishment (for within six years after Samaria was destroyed and Israel led captive by Shalmaneser), so did not the zealous King Hezekiah desist to prosecute his duty in restoring the religion to God's perfect ordinance, removing all abominations.

NOTE.

[2 *Kgs.* 17.]

The same is to be read of Josiah who did not only restore the religion, but did further destroy all monuments of idolatry which of long time had remained. For it is written of him that, after that the book of the law was found, and that he had asked counsel at the Prophetess Huldah, he sent and gathered all the elders of Judah and Jerusalem and, standing in the temple of the Lord, he made a covenant that all the people from the great to the small should walk after the Lord, should observe His law, statutes and testimonies with all their heart and all their soul, and that they should ratify and confirm whatsoever was written in the book of God. He further commanded Hilkiah the high priest and the priests of the inferior order that they should carry forth of the temple of the Lord all the vessels that were made to Baal, which he burnt and did carry their powder to Bethel. He did further destroy all monuments of idolatry, yea, even those that had remained from the days of Solomon. He did burn them, stamp them to powder, whereof one part he scattered in the brook Kidron and the other upon the sepulchres and graves of the idolaters, whose bones he did burn upon the altars where before they made sacrifice, not only in Judah, but also in Bethel where Jeroboam had erected his idolatry. Yea, he further proceeded and did kill the priests of the high places who were idolaters and had deceived the people; he did kill them, I say, and did burn their bones upon their own altars, and so returned to Jerusalem. This reformation made Josiah, and for the same obtained this testimony of the Holy Ghost, that neither before him neither after him was there any such king who returned to God with his whole soul and with all his strength according to all the law of Moses.

2 Chr. 34.

2 Kgs. 23.

The king commanded the priests.

Of which histories it is evident that the reformation of religion in all points, together with the punishment of false teachers, doth appertain to the power of the civil magistrate. For what God required of them, His justice must require of others having the like charge and authority; what He did approve in them, He cannot but approve in all others who with like zeal and sincerity do enterprise to purge the Lord's temple and sanctuary. What God required of them, it is before declared, to wit, that most diligently they should observe His law, statutes and ceremonies. And how acceptable were their facts to God doth He Himself witness. For to some He gave most notable victories without the hand of man, and in their most desperate dangers did declare His especial favours towards them by signs supernatural; to other He so established the kingdom that their enemies were compelled to stoop under their feet. And the names of all He hath registered not only in the book of life, but also in the blessed remembrance of all posterities since their days. Which also shall continue till the coming of the Lord Jesus who shall reward with the crown of immortality not only them, but also such as unfeignedly study to do the will and to promote the glory of His heavenly Father in the midst of this corrupted generation. In consideration whereof, ought you, my Lords, all delay set apart, to provide for the reformation of religion in your dominions and bounds, which now is so corrupt that no part of Christ's institution remaineth in the original purity. And therefore of necessity it is that speedily ye provide for reformation or else ye declare yourselves not only void of love towards your subjects, but also to live without care of your own salvation, yea, without all fear and true reverence of God.

2 Chr. 32.

Two things perchance may move you to esteem these histories before briefly touched to appertain nothing to you. First, because you are no Jews but Gentiles, and secondarily, because you are no kings but nobles in your realm. But be not deceived. For neither of both can excuse you in God's presence from doing your duty. For it is a thing more than certain that whatsoever God required of the civil magistrate in Israel or Judah concerning the observation of true religion during the time of the Law, the same doth he require of lawful magistrates professing Christ Jesus in the time of the Gospel, as the Holy Ghost hath taught us by the mouth of David, saying (Psalm 2): 'Be learned, you that judge the earth, kiss the Son, lest that the Lord wax angry and that ye perish from the way.' This admonition did not extend to the judges under the Law only, but doth also include all such as be promoted to honours in the time of the Gospel, when Christ Jesus doth reign and fight in His spiritual kingdom, whose

The facts of the godly kings in Judah do appertain to the powers among the Gentiles professing Christ.
[Ps. 2.10–12.]

enemies in that Psalm be first most sharply taxed, their fury expressed and vanity mocked. And then are kings and judges, who think themselves free from all law and obedience, commanded to repent their former blind rage, and judges are charged to be learned. And last are all commanded to serve the Eternal in fear, to rejoice before Him in trembling, to kiss the Son, that is, to give unto Him most humble obedience. Whereof it is evident that the rulers, magistrates and judges now in Christ's kingdom are no less bound to obedience unto God than were those under the Law.

And how is it possible that any shall be obedient who despise His religion in which standeth the chief glory that man can give to God and is a service which God especially requireth of kings and rulers? Which thing St Augustine plainly did note, writing to one Bonifacius, a man of war, according to the same argument and purpose which I labour to persuade your Honours. For after that he hath in that his epistle declared the difference betwixt the heresy of the Donatists and Arians, and hath somewhat spoken of their cruelty, he showeth the way how their fury should and ought to be repressed and that it is lawful for the injustly afflicted to seek support and defence at godly magistrates. For thus he writeth: 'Either must the verity be kept close or else must their cruelty be sustained. But if the verity should be concealed not only should none be saved nor delivered by such silence, but also should many be lost through their decept. But if by preaching of the verity their fury should be provoked more to rage, and by that means yet some were delivered and made strong, yet should fear hinder many weaklings to follow the verity if their rage be not stayed.' In these first words Augustine showeth three reasons why the afflicted church in those days called for the help of the emperor and of godly magistrates against the fury of the persecutors. The first, 'The verity must be spoken or else mankind shall perish in error.' The second, the verity being plainly spoken provoketh the adversaries to rage. And because that some did allege that rather we ought to suffer all injury than to seek support by man, he addeth the third reason: to wit, that many weak ones be not able to suffer persecution and death for the truth's sake, to whom not the less respect ought to be had that they may be won from error and so be brought to greater strength.

Epist. 50.[5]

Advert. [*Epist. 185.18.*]

Note well.

O, that the rulers of this age should ponder and weigh the reasons

[5] In the modern edition used here, the following quotations are in fact from Epistle 185.

of this godly writer and provide the remedy which he requireth in these words following: 'Now when the church was thus afflicted, if any think that rather they should have sustained all calamity than that the help of God should have been asked by Christian emperors, he doth not well advert that of such negligence no good compts or reason could be given. For where such, as would that no just laws should be made against their impiety, allege that the Apostles sought no such things of the kings of the earth, they do not consider that then the time was other than it is now and that all things are done in their own time. What emperor then believed in Christ that should serve Him in making laws for godliness against impiety, while yet that saying of the Prophet was complete: "Why hath nations raged and people have imagined vanity? The kings of the earth have stand up and princes have convented together against the Lord and against His anointed"? That which is after said in the same Psalm was not yet come to pass: "And now understand, O, you kings, be learned you that judge the earth, serve the Lord in fear and rejoice to Him with trembling." How do kings serve the Lord in fear but in punishing and by a godly severity forbidding those things which are done against the commandment of the Lord? For otherwise doth he serve in so far as he is man, otherwise in so far as he is king. In so far as he is man he serveth Him by living faithfully, but because he is also king he serveth establishing laws that command the things that be just and that with a convenient rigour forbid things contrary. As Hezekiah served destroying the groves, the temples of idols and the places which were builded against God's commandment; so served also Josiah doing the same; so served the king of Ninevites compelling the whole city to mitigate the Lord; so served Darius giving in the power of Daniel the idol to be broken and his enemies to be cast to the lions; so served Nebuchadnezzar by a terrible law forbidding all that were in his realm to blaspheme God. Herein therefore do kings serve the Lord in so far as they are kings: when they do those things to serve Him which none except kings be able to do.' He further proceedeth and concludeth that as when wicked kings do reign impiety cannot be bridled by laws, but rather is tyranny exercised under the title of the same, so is it a thing without all reason that kings professing the knowledge and honour of God should not regard nor care who did defend nor who did oppugn the church of God in their dominions.

Augustine's words. [*Epist.* 185.18–19.]

[*Ps.* 2.1–2.]

[*Ps.* 2.10–11.]

Advert the mind of Augustine.

In two sorts ought kings to serve God.

O, that the world should understand.

By these words of this ancient and godly writer, your Honours may perceive what I require of you, to wit, to repress the tyranny of your bishops and to defend the innocents professing the truth. He did require [the same] of the emperor and kings of his days professing Christ, and manifestly concludeth that they cannot serve Christ except that so they do. Let not your bishops think that Augustine speaketh for them because he nameth the church. Let them read and understand that Augustine writeth for that church which professeth the truth and doth suffer persecution for the defence of the same, which your bishops do not, but rather with the Donatists and Arians do cruelly persecute all such as boldly speak Christ's eternal verity to manifest their impiety and abomination. But thus much we have of Augustine: that it appertaineth to the obedience and service which kings owe to God, as well now in the time of the Gospel as before under the Law, to defend the afflicted for matters of religion and to repress the fury of the persecutors by the rigour and severity of godly laws. For which cause no doubt doth Isaiah the Prophet say that 'kings should be nourishers to the church of God, that they should abase their heads and lovingly embrace the children of God'. And thus, I say, your Honours may evidently see that the same obedience doth God require of rulers and princes in the time of the Gospel that He required in the time of the Law.

NOTE.

Isa. 49.23.

An answer to the second objection.

[Ps. 2.10–11.]

If you do think that the reformation of religion and defence of the afflicted doth not appertain to you because you are no kings but nobles and estates of a realm, in two things you are deceived. Former, in that you do not advert that David requireth as well that the princes and judges of the earth be learned and that they serve and fear God as that he requireth that the kings repent. If you therefore be judges and princes, as no man can deny you to be, then by the plain words of David you are charged to be learned, to serve and fear God, which ye cannot do if you despise the reformation of His religion. And this is your first error. The second is that ye neither know your duty which ye owe to God neither yet your authority which of Him ye have received if ye for pleasure or fear of any earthly man despise God's true religion and contemn your brethren that in His name call for your support. Your duty is to hear the voice of the Eternal your God and unfeignedly to study to follow His precepts who, as is before said, of especial mercy hath promoted you to honours and dignity. His chief and principal precept is that with reverence ye receive and embrace His only beloved Son Jesus, that ye promote to the uttermost of your powers His true religion, and that ye defend your brethren and subjects whom He hath put under your charge and care.

Now if your king be a man ignorant of God, enemy to His true religion, blinded by superstition and a persecutor of Christ's members, shall ye be excused if with silence ye pass over his iniquity? Be not deceived, my Lords, ye are placed in authority for another purpose than to flatter your king in his folly and blind rage: to wit, that as with your bodies, strength, riches and wisdom ye are bound to assist and defend him in all things which by your advice he shall take in hand for God's glory and for the preservation of his commonwealth and subjects, so by your gravities, counsel and admonition ye are bound to correct and repress whatsoever ye know him to attempt expressedly repugning to God's Word, honour and glory, or what ye shall espy him to do, be it by ignorance or be it by malice, against his subjects great or small. Of which last part of your obedience, if ye defraud your king, ye commit against him no less treason than if ye did extract from him your due and promised support what time by his enemies injustly he were pursued.

But this part of their duty I fear do a small number of the nobility of this age rightly consider. Neither yet will they understand that for that purpose hath God promoted them. For now the common song of all men is: 'We must obey our kings be they good or be they bad, for God hath so commanded.' But horrible shall the vengeance be that shall be poured forth upon such blasphemers of God, His holy name and ordinance. For it is no less blasphemy to say that God hath commanded kings to be obeyed when they command impiety than to say that God by His precept is author and maintainer of all iniquity. True it is, God hath commanded kings to be obeyed, but like true it is that in things which they commit against His glory, or when cruelly without cause they rage against their brethren, the members of Christ's body, He hath commanded no obedience, but rather He hath approved, yea, and greatly rewarded, such as have opponed themselves to their ungodly commandments and blind rage. As in the examples of the three children, of Daniel and Ebedmelech it is evident. The three children would neither bow nor stoop before the golden image at the commandment of the great king Nebuchadnezzar. Daniel did openly pray, his windows being open, against the established law of Darius and of his council. And Ebedmelech feared not to enter in before the presence of Zedekiah and boldly to defend

[*Dan. 3.*]

[*Dan. 6.*]

Jer. 38. the cause and innocency of Jeremiah the Prophet whom the king and his council had condemned to death.

Every one of these facts should this day be judged foolish by such as will not understand what confession God doth require of His children when His verity is oppugned or His glory called in doubt. Such men, I say, as prefer man to God and things present to the heavenly inheritance should have judged every one of these facts stubborn inobedience, foolish presumption and singularity or else bold controlling of the king and his wise council. But how acceptable in God's presence was this resistance to the ungodly commandments and determinations of their king the end did witness. For the three children were delivered from the furnace of fire and Daniel from the den of lions to the confusion of their enemies, to the better instruction of the ignorant kings and to the perpetual comfort of God's afflicted children. And Ebedmelech, in the day of the Lord's visitation, when *Jer. 39.* the king and his council did drink the bitter cup of God's vengeance, did find his life for a prey and did not fall in the edge of the sword when many thousands did perish. And this was signified unto him by the Prophet himself at the commandment of God before that Jerusalem was destroyed. The promise and cause were recited unto *[Jer. 39.16–18.]* him in these words: 'I will bring my words upon this city unto evil and not unto good, but most assuredly I shall deliver thee because thou hast trusted in me, saith the Lord.' The trust and hope which Ebedmelech had in God made him bold to oppone himself, being but a man, to the king and to his whole council who had condemned to death the Prophet whom his conscience did acknowledge to be innocent. For this did he speak in the presence of the king sitting in *[Jer. 38.9.]* the port of Benjamin: 'My Lord the king (saith Ebedmelech) these men do wickedly in all things that they have done to Jeremiah the Prophet.' Advert and take heed, my Lords, that the men who had condemned the Prophet were the king, his princes and council, and yet did one man accuse them all of iniquity and did boldly speak in the defence of him of whose innocency he was persuaded. And the same, I say, is the duty of every man in his vocation, but chiefly of the nobility which is joined with their kings to bridle and repress that folly and blind rage. Which thing if the nobility do not, neither yet labour to do, as they are traitors to their kings, so do they provoke the wrath of God against themselves and against the realm in which they abuse the authority which they have received of God to maintain virtue and to repress vice.

For hereof I would your Honours were most certainly persuaded: that God will neither excuse nobility nor people, but the nobility least of all, that obey and follow their kings in manifest iniquity. But with the same vengeance will God punish the prince, people and nobility conspiring together against Him and His holy ordinances. As in the punishment taken upon Pharaoh, Israel, Judah and Babylon is evidently to be seen. For Pharaoh was not drowned alone, but his captains, chariots and great army drank the same cup with him. The kings of Israel and Judah were not punished without company, but with them were murdered the councillors, their princes imprisoned and their people led captive. And why? Because none was found so faithful to God that he durst enterprise to resist nor againstand the manifest impiety of their princes. And therefore was God's wrath poured forth upon the one and the other. But the more ample discourse of this argument I defer to better opportunity. Only at this time I thought expedient to admonish you that before God it shall not excuse you to allege: 'We are no kings and therefore neither can we reform religion nor yet defend such as be persecuted.' Consider, my Lords, that ye are powers ordained by God (as before is declared) and therefore doth the reformation of religion and the defence of such as injustly are oppressed appertain to your charge and care, which thing shall the law of God, universally given to be kept of all men, most evidently declare. Which is my last and most assured reason why I say ye ought to remove from honours and to punish with death such as God hath condemned by His own mouth.

After that Moses had declared what was true religion, to wit, to honour God as He commanded, adding nothing to His Word, neither yet diminishing anything from it, and after also that vehemently he had exhorted the same law to be observed, he denounceth the punishment against the transgressors in these words: 'If thy brother, son, daughter, wife or neighbour, whom thou lovest as thine own life, solicitate thee secretly, saying: Let us go serve other gods whom neither thou nor thy fathers have known, consent not to him, hear him not, let not thine eye spare him, show him no indulgence or favour, hide him not, but utterly kill him; let thy hand be the first upon him that he may be slain, and after the hand of the whole

Deut. 12.

[*Deut. 13.6–9.*]

Deut. 23, 27.

people.' Of these words of Moses are two things appertaining to our purpose to be noted. Former, that such as solicitate only to idolatry ought to be punished to death without favour or respect of person. For He that will not suffer man to spare his son, his daughter nor his wife, but straitly commandeth punishment to be taken upon the idolaters (have they never so nigh conjunction with us), will not wink at the idolatry of others of what estate or condition soever they be.

Idolatry ought to be punished without respect of person.

If any estate might have claimed privilege, it was the Prophets.

1 Sam. 3, 9, 15.

1 Kgs. 22.

1 Kgs. 21.

2 Kgs. 8.

It is not unknown that the Prophets had revelations of God which were not common to the people, as Samuel had the revelation that Eli and his posterity should be destroyed, that Saul should first be king and thereafter that he should be rejected, [and] that David should reign for him; Micaiah understood by vision that Ahab should be killed in battle against the Syrians; Elijah saw that dogs should eat Jezebel in the fortress of Jezreel; Elisha did see hunger come upon Israel by the space of seven years; Jeremiah did foresee the destruction of Jerusalem and the time of their captivity; and so diverse other Prophets had diverse revelations of God which the people did not otherwise understand but by their affirmation. And therefore in those days were the Prophets named seers because that God did open unto them that which was hid from the multitude. Now if any man might have claimed any privilege from the rigour of the law or might have justified his fact, it should have been the Prophet. For he might have alleged for himself his singular prerogative that he had above other men to have God's will revealed unto him by vision or by dream, or that God had declared particularly unto him that His pleasure was to be honoured in that manner, in such a place and by such means. But all such excuses doth God remove, commanding that the Prophet that shall solicitate the people to serve strange gods shall die the death notwithstanding that he allege for himself dream, vision or revelation. Yea, although he promise miracles, and also that such things as he promiseth come to pass, yet, I say, commandeth God that no credit be given to him, but that he die the death because he teacheth apostasy and defection from God.

[Deut. 13.].

Hereof your Honours may easily espy that none provoking the people to idolatry ought to be exempted from the punishment of death. For if neither that inseparable conjunction which God Himself hath sanctified betwixt man and wife, neither that unspeakable love grafted in nature which is betwixt the father and the son, neither yet that reverence which God's people ought to bear to the Prophets, can excuse any man to spare the offender or to conceal his offence, what excuse can man pretend which God will accept? Evident it is that no estate, condition nor honour can exempt the idolater from the hands of God when He shall call him to accompts or shall inflict punishment upon him for his offence. How shall it then excuse the people that they, according to God's commandment, punish not to death such as shall solicitate or violently draw the people to idolatry? And this is the first which I would your Honours should note of the former words: to wit, that no person is exempted from punishment if he can be manifestly convicted to have provoked or led the people to idolatry. And this is most evidently declared in that solemn oath and covenant which Asa made with the people to serve God and to maintain His religion, adding this penalty to the transgressors of it: to wit, that 'Whosoever should not seek the Lord God of Israel should be killed, were he great or were he small, were it man or were it woman.' And of this oath was the Lord compleased. He was fond of them and gave them rest on every part because they sought Him with their whole heart and did swear to punish the offenders according to the precept of His law without respect of persons. And this is it which, I say, I would your Honours should note for the first: that no idolater can be exempted from punishment by God's law.

2 Chr. 15.13.

The second is that the punishment of such crimes as are idolatry, blasphemy and others that touch the majesty of God doth not appertain to kings and chief rulers only, but also to the whole body of that people and to every member of the same, according to the vocation of every man, and according to that possibility and occasion which God doth minister to revenge the injury done against His glory, what time that impiety is manifestly known. And that doth Moses more plainly speak in these words: 'If in any of thy cities (saith he) which the Lord thy God giveth unto thee to dwell in them, thou shalt hear this bruit: there are some men, the sons of Belial, passed forth from thee and have solicited the citizens of their cities by these words: Let us go and serve strange gods which you have not known; search and inquire diligently and, if it be true that such abomination is done in the midst of thee, thou shalt utterly strike the inhabitants of that city with the sword, thou shalt destroy it and whatsoever is within it, thou shalt gather the spoil of it in the midst of the marketplace, thou shalt burn that city with fire, and the spoil of it to the Lord thy God, that it may be a heap of stones forever, neither shall it be any more

Deut. 13.12–17.

builded. Let nothing of that execration cleave to thy hand, that the Lord may turn from the fury of His wrath and be moved towards thee with inward affection.'

Why every man in Israel was bound to obey God's commandment.

Plain it is that Moses speaketh nor giveth not charge to kings, rulers and judges only, but he commandeth the whole body of the people, yea, and every member of the same according to their possibility. And who dare be so impudent as to deny this to be most reasonable and just? For seeing that God had delivered the whole body from bondage, and to the whole multitude had given His law, and to the twelve tribes had He so distributed the inheritance of the land of Canaan that no family could complain that it was neglected, was not the whole and every member addebted to confess and acknowledge the benefits of God? Yea, had it not been the part of every man to have studied to keep the possession which he had received? Which thing God did plainly pronounce they should not do, except that in their hearts they did sanctify the Lord God, that they embraced and inviolably kept His religion established, and finally, except they did cut out iniquity from amongst them, declaring themselves earnest enemies to those abominations which God declared Himself so vehemently to hate that first He commanded the whole inhabitants of that country to be destroyed and all monuments of their idolatry to be broken down, and thereafter He also straitly commandeth that a city declining to idolatry should fall in the edge of the sword and that the whole spoil of the same should be burned, no portion of it reserved.

Deut. 28, 30.

Deut. 7.

God's judgements to the carnal man appear rigorous.

To the carnal man this may appear a rigorous and severe judgement, yea, it may rather seem to be pronounced in a rage than in wisdom. For what city was ever yet in which, to man's judgement, were not to be found many innocent persons, as infants, children and some simple and ignorant souls, who neither did nor could consent to such impiety? And yet we find no exception, but all are appointed to the cruel death. And as concerning the city and the spoil of the same, man's reason cannot think but that it might have been better bestowed than to be consumed with fire and so to profit no man. But in such cases will God that all creatures stoop, cover their faces and desist from reasoning when commandment is given to execute His judgement. Albeit I could adduce diverse causes of such severity, yet will I search none other than the Holy Ghost hath assigned. First, that all Israel hearing the judgement should fear to commit the like abomination; and secondarily, that the Lord might turn from the fury of His anger, might be moved towards the people with inward affection, be merciful unto them, and multiply them according to His oath made unto their fathers. Which reasons, as they are sufficient in God's children to correct the murmuring of the grudging flesh, so ought they to provoke every man, as before I have said, to declare himself enemy to that which so highly provoketh the wrath of God against the whole people. For where Moses saith: 'Let the city be burned and let no part of the spoil cleave to thy hand that the Lord may return from the fury of his wrath', etc., he plainly doth signify that by the defection and idolatry of a few, God's wrath is kindled against the whole, which is never quenched till such punishment be taken upon the offenders that whatsoever served them in their idolatry be brought to destruction because that it is execrable and accursed before God. And therefore He will not that it be reserved for any use of His people.

[Deut. 13.17.]

For the idolatry of a small number is God's wrath kindled against the multitude not punishing the offenders.

I am not ignorant that this law was not put in execution as God commanded. But what did thereof ensue and follow histories declare: to wit, plague after plague till Israel and Judah were led in captivity, as the Books of Kings do witness. The consideration whereof maketh me more bold to affirm that it is the duty of every man that list to escape the plague and punishment of God to declare himself enemy to idolatry, not only in heart, hating the same, but also in external gesture, declaring that he lamenteth, if he can do no more, for such abominations. Which thing was showed to the Prophet Ezekiel what time He gave him to understand why He would destroy Judah with Israel, and that He would remove His glory from the temple and place that He had chosen, and so pour forth His wrath and indignation upon the city that was full of blood and apostasy, which became so impudent that it durst be bold to say: 'The Lord hath left the earth and seeth not.' At this time, I say, the Lord revealed in vision to His Prophet who they were that should find favour in that miserable destruction: to wit, 'those that did mourn and lament for all the abominations done in the city, in whose foreheads did God command to print and seal Tau',[6] to the end that the destroyer, who was commanded to strike the rest without mercy, should not hurt them in whom that sign was found.

Ezek. 9.

Ezek. 8, 9.

[Ezek. 9.9]

[Ezek. 9.4.]

[6] This specific reference to Tau (as opposed simply to a 'mark') occurs in the Latin Vulgate but in no English version of the Bible except Tyndale's.

Of these premises I suppose it be evident that the punishment of idolatry doth not appertain to kings only, but also to the whole people, yea, to every member of the same according to his possibility. For that is a thing most assured that no man can mourn, lament and bewail for those things which he will not remove to the uttermost of his power. If this be required of the whole people, and of every man in his vocation, what shall be required of you, my Lords, whom God hath raised up to be princes and rulers above your brethren, whose hands He hath armed with the sword of His justice, yea, whom He hath appointed to be as bridles to repress the rage and insolence of your kings whensoever they pretend manifestly to transgress God's blessed ordinance?

NOTE.

An answer to an objection.

If any think that this my affirmation touching the punishment of idolaters be contrary to the practice of the Apostles who finding the Gentiles in idolatry did call them to repentance, requiring no such punishment, let the same man understand that the Gentiles, before the preaching of Christ, lived, as the Apostle speaketh, without God in the world, drowned in idolatry, according to the blindness and ignorance in which then they were holden as a profane nation whom God had never openly avowed to be His people, had never received in His household, neither given unto them laws to be kept in religion nor polity. And therefore did not His Holy Ghost, calling them to repentance, require of them any corporal punishment according to the rigour of the law, unto the which they were never subjects, as they that were strangers from the commonwealth of Israel. But if any think that after that the Gentiles were called from their vain conversation and, by embracing Christ Jesus, were received in the number of Abraham's children and so made one people with the Jews believing; if any think, I say, that then they were not bound to the same obedience which God required of His people Israel what time He confirmed His league and covenant with them, the same man appeareth to make Christ inferior to Moses and contrarious to the law of His heavenly Father. For if the contempt or transgression of Moses' law was worthy of death, what should we judge the contempt of Christ's ordinance to be (I mean after they be once received)? And if Christ be not come to dissolve, but to fulfil the law of His heavenly Father, shall the liberty of His Gospel be an occasion that the especial glory of His Father be trodden underfoot and regarded of no man? God forbid.

Why no law was executed against the Gentiles being idolaters.

Eph. 2.

The especial glory of God is that such as profess them to be His people should hearken to His voice. And amongst all the voices of God revealed to the world touching punishment of vices is none more evident, neither more severe, than is that which is pronounced against idolatry, the teachers and maintainers of the same. And therefore I fear not to affirm that the Gentiles (I mean every city, realm, province or nation amongst the Gentiles embracing Christ Jesus and His true religion) be bound to the same league and covenant that God made with His people Israel what time He promised to root out the nations before them in these words: 'Beware that thou make any covenant with the inhabitants of the land to the which thou comest, lest perchance that this come in ruin, that is, be destruction to thee; but thou shalt destroy their altars, break their idols and cut down their groves. Fear no strange gods, worship them not, neither yet make you sacrifice to them. But the Lord who in His great power and outstretched arm hath brought you out of the land of Egypt shall you fear, Him shall you honour, Him shall you worship, to Him shall you make sacrifice, His statutes, judgements, laws and commandments you shall keep and observe. This is the covenant which I have made with you, saith the Eternal, forget it not, neither yet fear ye other gods; but fear you the Lord your God and He shall deliver you from the hands of all your enemies.' To this same law, I say, and covenant are the Gentiles no less bound than sometime were the Jews. Whensoever God doth illuminate the eyes of any multitude, province, people or city and putteth the sword in their own hand to remove such enormities from amongst them as before God they know to be abominable, then, I say, are they no less bound to purge their dominions, cities and countries from idolatry than were the Israelites what time they received the possession of the land of Canaan. And moreover, I say, if any go about to erect and set up idolatry or to teach defection from God after that the verity hath been received and approved, that then not only the magistrates to whom the sword is committed, but also the people are bound by that oath which they have made to God to revenge to the uttermost of their power the injury done against His majesty.

The especial honour which God requireth of His people. 1 Sam. 15.

Exod. 34.12–15.

In universal defections and in a general revolt, such as was in Israel after Jeroboam, there is a diverse consideration. For then, because the whole people were together conspired against God, there could none be found that would execute the punishment which God had

[*2 Kgs.* 9.] commanded, till God raised up Jehu whom He had appointed for that purpose. And the same is to be considered in all other general defections, such as this day be in the papistry, where all are blinded and all are declined from God and that of long continuance, so that no ordinary justice can be executed, but the punishment must be reserved to God and unto such means as He shall appoint.

But I do speak of such a number as after they have received God's perfect religion do boldly profess the same, notwithstanding that some or the most part fall back (as of late days was in England). Unto such a number, I say, it is lawful to punish the idolaters with death if by any means God give them the power. For so did Joshua and [*Josh.* 32.] Israel determine to have done against the children of Reuben, Gad and Manasseh for their suspected apostasy and defection from God. And the whole tribes did in very deed execute that sharp judgement [*Judg.* 20.] against the tribe of Benjamin for a less offence than for idolatry. And the same ought to be done wheresoever Christ Jesus and His Evangel is so received in any realm, province or city that the magistrates and people have solemnly avowed and promised to defend the same, as under King Edward of late days was done in England.[7] In such places, I say, it is not only lawful to punish to the death such as labour to subvert the true religion, but the magistrates and people are bound so to do unless they will provoke the wrath of God against themselves. And therefore I fear not to affirm that it had been the duty of the nobility, judges, rulers and people of England not only to have resisted and againstanded Mary that Jezebel whom they call their queen, but also to have punished her to the death, with all the sort of her idolatrous priests, together with all such as should have assisted her what time that she and they openly began to suppress Christ's Evangel, to shed the blood of the saints of God and to erect that most devilish idolatry, the papistical abominations and his usurped tyranny, which once most justly by common oath was banished from that realm.

But because I cannot at this present discuss this argument as it appertaineth, I am compelled to omit it to better opportunity. And so returning to your Honours, I say that, if ye confess yourselves baptised in the Lord Jesus, of necessity ye must confess that the care of His religion doth appertain to your charge. And if ye know that

[7] Knox presumably has in mind here such 'public' affirmations of the reformed faith in Edward VI's reign as the two Acts of Uniformity (1549 and 1552).

in your hands God hath put the sword for the causes above expressed, then can ye not deny but that the punishment of obstinate and malapert idolaters (such as all your bishops be) doth appertain to your office, if after admonition they continue obstinate. I am not ignorant what be the vain defences of your proud prelates. They claim first a prerogative and privilege that they are exempted, and that by consent of councils and emperors, from all jurisdiction of the temporality. And secondarily, when they are convicted of manifest impieties, abuses and enormities, as well in their manners as in religion, neither fear nor shame they to affirm that things so long established cannot suddenly be reformed, although they be corrupted, but with process of time they promise to take order. But in few words I answer that no privilege granted against the ordinance and statutes of God is to be observed although all councils and men in the earth have appointed the same. But against God's ordinance it is that idolaters, murderers, false teachers and blasphemers shall be exempted from punishment, as before is declared. And therefore in vain it is that they claim for privilege when that God saith: 'The murderer shalt thou rive from my altar that he may die the death.' And as to the order and reformation which they promise, that is to be looked or hoped for when Satan, whose children and slaves they are, can change his nature.

[Exod. 21.14.]

This answer, I doubt not, shall suffice the sober and godly reader. But yet to the end that they may further see their own confusion, and that your Honours may better understand what ye ought to do in so manifest a corruption and defection from God, I ask of themselves what assurance they have for this their immunity, exemption or privilege? Who is the author of it? And what fruit it hath produced? And first, I say that of God they have no assurance neither yet can He be proved to be author of any such privilege. But the contrary is easy to be seen. For God in establishing His orders in Israel did so subject Aaron (in his priesthood being the figure of Christ) to Moses that he feared not to call him in judgement and to constrain him to give accompts of his wicked deed in consenting to idolatry, as the history doth plainly witness. For thus it is written: 'Then Moses took the calf which they had made and burned it with fire and did grind it to powder, and scattering it in the water, gave it to drink to the children of Israel' (declaring hereby the vanity of their idol and the abomination of the same). And thereafter Moses said to Aaron: 'What

God is not author of any privilege granted to papistical bishops that they be exempted from the power of the civil sword. Exod. 32. 20–1.

hath this people done to thee that thou shouldst bring upon it so great a sin?' Thus, I say, doth Moses call and accuse Aaron of the destruction of the whole people. And yet he perfectly understood that God had appointed him to be the high priest that he should bear upon his shoulders and upon his breast the names of the twelve tribes of Israel for whom he was appointed to make sacrifice, prayers and supplications. He knew his dignity was so great that only he might enter within the most holy place. But neither could his office nor dignity exempt him from judgement when he had offended. If any object Aaron at that time was not anointed and therefore was he subject to Moses, I have answered that Moses, being taught by the mouth of God, did perfectly understand to what dignity Aaron was appointed and yet he feared not to call him in judgement and to compel him to make answer for his wicked fact. But if this answer doth not suffice, yet shall the Holy Ghost witness further in the matter.

The dignity of Aaron did not exempt him from judgement.

Solomon removed from honour Abiathar, being the high priest, and commanded him to cease from all function and to live as a private man. Now if the unction did exempt the priest from jurisdiction of the civil magistrate, Solomon did offend and injured Abiathar. For he was anointed and had carried the ark before David. But God doth not reprove the fact of Solomon, neither yet doth Abiathar claim any prerogative by the reason of his office, but rather doth the Holy Ghost approve the fact of Solomon, saying: 'Solomon ejected forth Abiathar that he should not be the priest of the Lord, that the word of the Lord might be performed which he spoke upon the house of Eli.' And Abiathar did think that he obtained great favour in that he did escape the present death which by his conspiracy he had deserved. If any yet reason that Abiathar was no otherwise subject to the judgement of the king but as he was appointed to be the executor of that sentence which God before had pronounced, as I will not greatly deny that reason, so require I that every man consider that the same God who pronounced sentence against Eli and his house hath pronounced also that idolaters, whoremongers, murderers and blasphemers shall neither have portion in the kingdom of God neither ought to be permitted to bear any rule in His church and congregation. Now if the unction and office saved not Abiathar because that God's sentence must needs be performed, can any privilege granted by man be a buckler to malefactors that they shall not be subject to

1 Kgs. 2.27.

1 Sam. 3.

Note well.

Gal. 4.
1 Tim. 3.

the punishments pronounced by God? I think no man will be so foolish as so to affirm. For a thing more than evident it is that the whole priesthood in the time of the Law was bound to give obedience to the civil powers. And if any member of the same was found criminal, the same was subject to the punishment of the sword which God had put in the hand of the magistrate.

And this ordinance of His Father did not Christ disannul, but rather did confirm the same, commanding tribute to be paid for Himself and for Peter, who perfectly knowing the mind of His Master, thus writeth in his Epistle: 'Submit yourselves to all manner ordinance of man' (he excepteth such as be expressly repugning to God's commandment), 'for the Lord's sake, whether it be to king, as to the chief head, or unto rulers, as unto them that are sent by Him for punishment of evil doers and for the praise of them that do well.' The same doth the Apostle St Paul most plainly command in these words: 'Let every soul be subject to the superior powers.' Which places make evident that neither Christ neither His Apostles hath given any assurance of this immunity and privilege which men of church (as they will be termed) do this day claim. Yea, it was a thing unknown to the primitive church many years after the days of the Apostles. For Chrysostom, who served in the church at Constantinople four hundred years after Christ's ascension, and after that corruption was greatly increased, doth yet thus write upon the foresaid words of the Apostle: 'This precept (saith he) doth not appertain to such as be called seculars only, but even to those that be priests and religious men.' And after he addeth: 'Whether thou be apostle, evangelist, prophet or whosoever thou be, thou canst not be exempted from this subjection.' Hereof it is plain that Chrysostom did not understand that God had exempted any person from obedience and subjection of the civil power, neither yet that He was author of such exemption and privilege as papists do this day claim. And the same was the judgement and uniform doctrine of the primitive church many years after Christ.

Matt. 17.

1 Pet. 2.13–14.

Acts 4, 5.

Rom. 13.1.

Chrysostom, In Rom. 13 [Homilia 23].

Let papists answer Chrysostom.

Your Honours do wonder, I doubt not, from what fountain then did this their immunity, as they term it, and singular privilege spring. I shall shortly touch that which is evident in their own law and histories. When the bishops of Rome, the very Antichrists, had partly by fraud and partly by violence usurped the superiority of some places in Italy and most injustly had spoiled the emperors of their rents and

Let their own histories witness.

possessions and had also murdered some of their officers, as histories do witness, then began pope after pope to practise and devise how they should be exempted from judgement of princes and from the equity of laws. And in this point they were most vigilant, till at length iniquity did so prevail in their hands, according as Daniel had before prophesied of them, that this sentence was pronounced: 'Neither by the emperor, neither by the clergy, neither yet by the people shall the judge be judged.' 'God will (saith Symmachus) that the causes of others be determined by men, but without all question He hath reserved the bishop of this seat (understanding Rome) to His own judgement.' And hereof diverse popes and expositors of their laws would seem to give reasons. For saith Agatho: 'All the precepts of the apostolic seat are assured as by the voice of God Himself.' The author of the gloss upon their canon affirmeth that if all the world should pronounce sentence against the pope, yet should his sentence prevail. For saith he: 'The pope hath a heavenly will and therefore he may change the nature of things; he may apply the substance of one thing to another, and of nothing he may make somewhat; and that sentence which was nothing (that is, by his mind false and injust), he may make somewhat that it is true and just.' 'For (saith he) in all things that please him, his will is for reason. Neither is there any man that may ask of him why dost thou so. For he may dispense above the law, and of injustice he may make justice. For he hath the fullness of all power.'

The mouth of the beast speaking great things. Distin. 9. quest. 3.[8]

Their laws do witness. Dist. 19.[9]

De translatione titul. 7.[10]

And many other most blasphemous sentences did they pronounce every one after other, which for shortness sake I omit, till at the end they obtained this most horrible decree: 'That albeit in life and conversation they were so wicked and detestable that not only they condemned themselves, but that also they drew to hell and perdition many thousands with them, yet that none should presume to reprehend or rebuke them.' This being established for the head (albeit not without some contradiction, for some emperors did require due

Distinct. 40.[11]

Note the equity of this commandment.

[8] The first quotation is from Gratian, *Decretum (secunda pars)*, 9.3.13; the second from 9.3.14.

[9] Gratian, *Decretum (prima pars)*, 19.2.

[10] This refers to Gregory IX's *Decretals*, Lib. 1, Tit. 7 (*De translatione episcopi*), cap. 2. I have failed to locate the gloss quoted by Knox in the pre-1558 editions of the *Decretals* which I have been able to consult (Paris, 1527 and 1547), though something similar occurs in a somewhat later edition of the *Corpus iuris canonici* (Lyon, 1614), col. 217 (margin).

[11] Gratian, *Decretum (prima pars)*, 40.6.

obedience of them, as God's Word commanded and ancient bishops had given before to emperors and to their laws; but Satan so prevailed in his suit before the blind world that the former sentences were confirmed); which power being granted to the head, then began provision to be made for the rest of the members in all realms and countries where they made residence. The fruit whereof we see to be this: that none of that pestilent generation (I mean the vermin of the papistical order) will be subject to any civil magistrate, how enormous that ever his crime be, but will be reserved to their own ordinary, as they term it. And what fruits have hereof ensued, be the world never so blind, it cannot but witness. For how their head, that Roman Antichrist, hath been occupied ever since the granting of such privileges, histories do witness and of late the most part of Europe subject to the plague of God, to fire and sword, by his procurement hath felt and this day doth feel. The pride, ambition, envy, excess, fraud, spoil, oppression, murder, filthy life and incest that is used and maintained amongst that rabble of priests, friars, monks, canons, bishops and cardinals cannot be expressed.

I fear not to affirm, neither doubt I to prove, that the papistical church is further degenerate from the purity of Christ's doctrine, from the footsteps of the Apostles and from the manners of the primitive church than was the church of the Jews from God's holy statutes what time it did crucify Christ Jesus, the only Messiah, and most cruelly persecute His Apostles. And yet will our papists claim their privileges and ancient liberties. Which if you grant unto them, my Lords, ye shall assuredly drink the cup of God's vengeance with them and shall be reputed before his presence companions of thieves and maintainers of murderers, as is before declared. For their immunity and privilege whereof so greatly they boast is nothing else but as if thieves, murderers or brigands should conspire amongst themselves that they would never answer in judgement before any lawful magistrate to the end that their theft and murder should not be punished. Even such, I say, is their wicked privilege which neither they have of God the Father, neither of Christ Jesus who hath revealed His Father's will to the world, neither yet of the Apostles nor primitive church, as before is declared. But it is a thing conspired amongst themselves to the end that their iniquity, detestable life and tyranny shall neither be repressed nor reformed. And if they object that godly emperors did grant and confirm the same, I answer that

The matter is more than evident.

Whosoever maintaineth the privileges of papists shall drink the cup of God's vengeance with them.

the godliness of no man is or can be of sufficient authority to justify a foolish and ungodly fact, such I mean as God hath not allowed by His Word. For Abraham was a godly man, but the denial of his wife was such a fact as no godly man ought to imitate. The same might I show of David, Hezekiah and Josiah, unto whom I think no man of judgement will prefer any emperor since Christ in holiness and wisdom, and yet are not all their facts, not even such as they appeared to have done for good causes, to be approved nor followed. And therefore, I say, as error and ignorance remain always with the most perfect man in this life, so must their works be examined by another rule than by their own holiness if they shall be approved.

But if this answer doth not suffice, then will I answer more shortly that no godly emperor since Christ's ascension hath granted any such privilege to any such church or person as they (the whole generation of papists) be at this day. I am not ignorant that some emperors, of a certain zeal and for some considerations, granted liberties to the true church afflicted for their maintenance against tyrants. But what serveth this for the defence of their tyranny? If the law must be understood according to the mind of the lawgiver, then must they first prove themselves Christ's true and afflicted church before they can claim any privilege to appertain to them. For only to that church were the privileges granted. It will not be their glorious titles, neither yet the long possession of the name, that can prevail in this so weighty a cause. For all those had the church of Jerusalem which did crucify Christ and did condemn His doctrine. We offer to prove by their fruits and tyranny, by the Prophets and plain Scriptures of God, what trees and generation they be: to wit, unfruitful and rotten, apt for nothing but to be cut and cast in hell fire, yea, that they are the very kingdom of Antichrist of whom we are commanded to beware.

And therefore, my Lords, to return to you, seeing that God hath armed your hands with the sword of justice, seeing that His law most straitly commandeth idolaters and false prophets to be punished with death, and that you be placed above your subjects to reign as fathers over their children; and further, seeing that not only I, but with me many thousand famous, godly and learned persons, accuse your bishops and the whole rabble of the papistical clergy of idolatry, of murder and of blasphemy against God committed, it appertaineth to your Honours to be vigilant and careful in so weighty a matter. The question is not of earthly substance, but of the glory of God and of the salvation of yourselves and of your brethren subject to your charge. In which if you, after this plain admonition, be negligent, there resteth no excuse by reason of ignorance. For in the name of God I require of you that the cause of religion may be tried in your presence by the plain and simple Word of God; that your bishops be compelled to desist from their tyranny; that they be compelled to make answer for the neglecting of their office, for the substance of the poor which unjustly they usurp and prodigally they do spend; but principally for the false and deceivable doctrine which is taught and defended by their false prophets, flattering friars and other such venomous locusts. Which thing, if with single eyes ye do (preferring God's glory and the salvation of your brethren to all worldly commodity), then shall the same God, who solemnly doth pronounce to honour those that do honour Him, pour His benedictions plentifully upon you; He shall be your buckler, protection and captain, and shall repress by His strength and wisdom whatsoever Satan by his supposts shall imagine against you.

I am not ignorant that great troubles shall ensue your enterprise. For Satan will not be expelled from the possession of his usurped kingdom without resistance. But if you, as is said, preferring God's glory to your own lives, unfeignedly seek and study to obey His blessed will, then shall your deliverance be such as evidently it shall be known that the angels of the Eternal do watch, make war and fight for those that unfeignedly fear the Lord. But if you refuse this my most reasonable and just petition, what defence that ever you appear to have before men, then shall God (whom in me you contemn) refuse you. He shall pour forth contempt upon you and upon your posterity after you. The spirit of boldness and wisdom shall be taken from you, your enemies shall reign and you shall die in bondage, yea, God shall cut down the unfruitful trees when they do appear most beautifully to flourish and shall so burn the root that after of you shall neither twig nor branch again spring to glory.

Deut. 28.
Lev. 26.
Isa. 27, 30.

Hereof I need not to adduce unto you examples from the former ages and ancient histories. For your brethren the nobility of England are a mirror and glass in the which ye may behold God's just punishment. For as they have refused Him and His Evangel which once in mouth they did profess, so hath He refused them and hath taken from them the spirit of wisdom, boldness and of counsel. They see and feel their own misery and yet they have no grace to avoid it.

They hate the bondage of strangers, the pride of priests and the monstriferous empire of a wicked woman, and yet are they compelled to bow their necks to the yoke of the devil, to obey whatsoever the proud Spaniards and wicked Jezebel list to command, and finally, to stand like slaves with cap in hand till the servants of Satan, the shaven sort, call them to council. This fruit do they reap and gather of their former rebellion and unfaithfulness towards God. They are left confused in their own counsels. He whom in His members, for the pleasure of a wicked woman, they have exiled, persecuted and blasphemed, doth now laugh them to scorn, suffereth them to be pined in bondage of most wicked men, and finally, shall adjudge them to the fire everlasting, except that speedily and openly they repent their horrible treason which against God, against His Son Christ Jesus and against the liberty of their own native realm they have committed.

The same plagues shall fall upon you, be you assured, if ye refuse the defence of His servants that call for your support. My words are sharp, but consider, my Lords, that they are not mine, but that they are the threatenings of the Omnipotent who assuredly will perform the voices of His Prophets, how that ever carnal men despise His admonitions. The sword of God's wrath is already drawn which, of necessity, must needs strike when grace offered is obstinately refused. You have been long in bondage of the devil, blindness, error and idolatry prevailing against the simple truth of God in that your realm in which God hath made you princes and rulers. But now doth God of His great mercy call you to repentance before He pour forth the uttermost of His vengeance. He crieth to your ears that your religion is nothing but idolatry. He accuseth you of the blood of His saints which hath been shed by your permission, assistance and powers. For the tyranny of those raging beasts should have no force if by your strength they were not maintained. Of those horrible crimes doth now God accuse you, not of purpose to condemn you, but mercifully to absolve and pardon you, as sometime He did those whom Peter accused to have killed the Son of God, so that ye be not of mind nor purpose to justify your former iniquity.

Let England and Scotland both advert.

God calleth to repentance before He strike in His hot displeasure.

Papists had no force if princes did not maintain them.

Acts 2.

Iniquity I call not only the crimes and offences which have been and yet remain in your manners and lives. But that also which appeareth before men most holy, with hazard of my life, I offer to prove abomination before God. That is, your whole religion to be so corrupt and vain that no true servant of God can communicate with it because

No true servant of

that in so doing he should manifestly deny Christ Jesus and His eternal verity. I know that your bishops, accompanied with the swarm of the papistical vermin, shall cry: 'A damned heretic ought not to be heard.' But remember, my Lords, what in the beginning I have protested, upon which ground I continually stand: to wit, that I am no heretic nor deceivable teacher, but the servant of Christ Jesus, a preacher of His infallible verity, innocent in all that they can lay to my charge concerning my doctrine, and that therefore by them, being enemies to Christ, I am injustly damned. From which cruel sentence I have appealed and do appeal, as before mention is made. In the meantime most humbly requiring your Honours to take me in your protection, to be auditors of my just defences, granting unto me the same liberty which Ahab, a wicked king, and Israel, at that time a blinded people, granted to Elijah in the like case. That is, that your bishops and the whole rabble of your clergy may be called before you and before that people whom they have deceived, that I be not condemned by multitude, by custom, by authority or law devised by man, but that God Himself may be judge betwixt me and my adversaries. Let God, I say, speak by His law, by His Prophets, by Christ Jesus or by His Apostles, and so let Him pronounce what religion He approveth, and then, be my enemies never so many and appear they never so strong and so learned, no more do I fear victory than did Elijah being but one man against the multitude of Baal's priests.

God may communicate with the papistical religion.

An answer to the old objection, that an heretic ought not to be heard.

1 Kgs. 18.

And if they think to have advantage by their councils and doctors, this I further offer: to admit the one and the other as witnesses in all matters debatable, three things (which justly cannot be denied) being granted unto me. First, that the most ancient councils, nighest to the primitive church, in which the learned and godly fathers did examine all matters by God's Word, may be holden of most authority. Secondarily, that no determination of councils nor man be admitted against the plain verity of God's Word nor against the determination of those four chief councils whose authority hath been and is holden by them equal with the authority of the four Evangelists.[12] And last, that to no doctor be given greater authority than Augustine requireth to be given to his writings: to wit, if he plainly prove not his affirmation by God's infallible Word, that then his sentence be rejected and imputed to the error of a man. These things granted and admitted,

Touching councils and doctors.

Retractationes, prologus.

[12] That is, the councils of Nicaea (325), Constantinople (381), Ephesus (431) and Chalcedon (451).

I shall no more refuse the testimonies of councils and doctors than shall my adversaries. But and if they will justify those councils which maintain their pride and usurped authority, and will reject those which plainly have condemned all such tyranny, negligence and wicked life as bishops now do use; and if further they will snatch a doubtful sentence of a doctor and refuse his mind when he speaketh plainly, then will I say that all man is a liar, that credit ought not to be given to an unconstant witness and that no councils ought to prevail nor be admitted against the sentence which God hath pronounced.

And thus, my Lords, in few words to conclude: I have offered unto you a trial of my innocency; I have declared unto you what God requireth of you being placed above His people as rulers and princes; I have offered unto you and to the inhabitants of the realm the verity of Christ Jesus; and with the hazard of my life I presently offer to prove the religion which amongst you is maintained by fire and sword to be false, damnable and diabolical. Which things if ye refuse, defending tyrants in their tyranny, then dare I not flatter, but as it was commanded to Ezekiel boldly to proclaim, so must I cry to you that you shall perish in your iniquity, that the Lord Jesus shall refuse so many of you as maliciously withstand His eternal verity, and in the days of His apparition, when all flesh shall appear before Him, that He shall repel you from His company and shall command you to the fire which never shall be quenched, and then neither shall the multitude be able to resist, neither yet the counsels of man be able to prevail against that sentence which He shall pronounce.

Ezek. 33.

Matt. 24, 26.

Dan. 12.
Matt. 25.

God the Father of our Lord Jesus Christ, by the power of His Holy Spirit, so rule and dispose your hearts that with simplicity ye may consider the things that be offered, and that ye may take such order in the same as God in you may be glorified and Christ's flock by you may be edified and comforted to the praise and glory of our Lord Jesus Christ, whose omnipotent spirit rule your hearts in His true fear to the end.

Amen.

TO HIS BELOVED BRETHREN THE Commonalty of Scotland, John Knox wisheth grace, mercy and peace with the spirit of righteous judgement.

What I have required of the queen regent, estates and nobility, as of the chief heads (for this present)[1] of the realm, I cannot cease to require of you, dearly beloved Brethren, which be the commonalty and body of the same. To wit, that it (notwithstanding that false and cruel sentence which your disguised bishops have pronounced against me) would please you to be so favourable unto me as to be indifferent auditors of my just purgation. Which to do, if God earnestly move your hearts, as I nothing doubt but that your enterprise shall redound to the praise of His holy name, so am I assured that ye and your posterity shall by that means receive most singular comfort, edification and profit. For when ye shall hear the matter debated, ye shall easily perceive and understand upon what ground and foundation is builded that religion which amongst you is this day defended by fire and sword.

As for my own conscience, I am most assuredly persuaded that whatsoever is used in the papistical church is altogether repugning to Christ's blessed ordinance and is nothing but mortal venom, of which whosoever drinketh I am assuredly persuaded that therewith he drinketh death and damnation, except by true conversion unto God he be purged from the same. But because that long silence of

[1] That is, during Mary Stewart's minority and absence in France.

God's Word hath begotten ignorance almost in all sorts of men, and ignorance joined with long custom hath confirmed superstition in the hearts of many, I therefore in the name of the Lord Jesus desire audience as well of you the commonalty, my Brethren, as of the estates and nobility of the realm, that in public preaching I may have place amongst you at large to utter my mind in all matters of controversy this day in religion. And further I desire that ye, concurring with your nobility, would compel your bishops and clergy to cease their tyranny, and also that, for the better assurance and instruction of your conscience, ye would compel your said bishops and false teachers to answer by the Scriptures of God to such objections and crimes as shall be laid against their vain religion, false doctrine, wicked life and slanderous conversation.

Petition.

Here I know that it shall be objected that I require of you a thing most unreasonable. To wit, that ye should call your religion in doubt which hath been approved and established by so long continuance and by the consent of so many men before you. But I shortly answer that neither is the long process of time, neither yet the multitude of men, a sufficient approbation which God will allow for our religion. For as some of the most ancient writers do witness, neither can long process of time justify an error, neither can the multitude of such as follow it change the nature of the same. But if it was an error in the beginning, so is it in the end, and the longer that it be followed and the more that do receive it, it is the more pestilent and more to be avoided. For if antiquity or multitude of men could justify any religion, then was the idolatry of the Gentiles and now is the abomination of the Turks good religion. For antiquity approved the one and a multitude hath received and doth defend the other.

Answer to an objection.

Lactantius Firmianus; Tertullian; Cyprian.[2]

But otherwise to answer, godly men may wonder from what fountain such a sentence doth flow that no man ought to try his faith and religion by God's Word, but that he safely may believe and follow everything which antiquity and a multitude have approved. The spirit of God doth otherwise teach us. For the wisdom of God, Christ Jesus Himself, remitted His adversaries to Moses and the Scriptures to try by them whether His doctrine was of God or not. The Apostles Paul and Peter command men to try the religion which they profess by

John 5, 7.

Acts 17.

2 Pet. 1.

[2] It is impossible to be precise about which works of these authors Knox had in mind, but see Lactantius, *Divine Institutes*, 2.7 and 5.20; Tertullian, *Apology*, *passim*; and Cyprian's brief treatise *On the Vanity of Idols*, *passim*.

God's plain Scriptures and do praise men for so doing. St John straitly commandeth that we believe not every spirit, but willeth us to try the spirits whether they be of God or not. Now seeing that these evident testimonies of the Holy Ghost will us to try our faith and religion by the plain Word of God, wonder it is that the papists will not be content that their religion and doctrine come under the trial of the same. If this sentence of Christ be true (as it is most true, seeing it springeth from the verity itself): 'Who so evil doeth, hateth the light, neither will he come to the light lest that his evil works be manifested and rebuked', then do our papists by their own sentence condemn themselves and their religion. For in so far as they refuse examination and trial, they declare that they know some fault which the light will utter; which is a cause of their fear and why they claim to that privilege that no man dispute of their religion. The verity and truth, being of the nature of fine purified gold, doth not fear the trial of the furnace, but the stubble and chaff of man's inventions (such is their religion) may not abide the flame of the fire.

1 John 4.

John 3.20.

Why papists will not dispute of the ground of their religion.

True it is that Mahomet pronounced this sentence: that no man should in pain of death dispute or reason of the ground of his religion. Which law to this day by the art of Satan is yet observed amongst the Turks to their mortal blindness and horrible blaspheming of Christ Jesus and of His true religion. And from Mahomet (or rather from Satan, father of all lies) hath the pope and his rabble learned this former lesson. To wit, that their religion should not be disputed upon, but what the fathers have believed, that ought and must the children approve. And in so devising, Satan lacked not his foresight. For no one thing hath more established the kingdom of that Roman Antichrist than this most wicked decree: to wit, that no man was permitted to reason of his power or to call his laws in doubt. This thing is most assured, that whensoever the papistical religion shall come to examination, it shall be found to have no other ground than hath the religion of Mahomet: to wit, man's invention, device and dreams overshadowed with some colour of God's Word.

Mahomet and the pope do agree.

And therefore, Brethren, seeing that the religion is as the stomach to the body, which, if it be corrupted, doth infect the whole members, it is necessary that the same be examined, and if it be found replenished with pestilent humours (I mean with the fantasies of men), then of necessity it is that those be purged else shall your bodies and souls perish forever. For of this I would ye were most certainly persuaded,

NOTE.

Reformation of religion belongeth to all that hope for life everlasting.

that a corrupt religion defileth the whole life of man, appear it never so holy. Neither would I that ye should esteem the reformation and care of religion less to appertain to you because ye are no kings, rulers, judges, nobles, nor in authority. Beloved Brethren, ye are God's creatures, created and formed to His own image and similitude, for whose redemption was shed the most precious blood of the only beloved Son of God, to whom he hath commanded His Gospel and glad tidings to be preached, and for whom He hath prepared the heavenly inheritance, so that ye will not obstinately refuse and disdainfully contemn the means which He hath appointed to obtain the same: to wit, His blessed Evangel which now He offereth unto you to the end that ye may be saved. For the Gospel and glad tidings of the kingdom truly preached is the power of God to the salvation of every believer, which to credit and receive, you, the commonalty, are no less addebted than be your rulers and princes.

Rom. 1.

The subject is no less bound to believe in Christ than is the king. Gal. 3.

For albeit God hath put and ordained distinction and difference betwixt the king and subjects, betwixt the rulers and the common people, in the regiment and administration of civil policies, yet in the hope of the life to come He hath made all equal. For as in Christ Jesus the Jew hath no greater prerogative than hath the Gentile, the man than hath the woman, the learned than the unlearned, the lord than the servant, but all are one in Him, so is there but one way and means to attain to the participation of His benefits and spiritual graces, which is a lively faith working by charity. And therefore I say that it doth no less appertain to you, beloved Brethren, to be assured that your faith and religion be grounded and established upon the true and undoubted Word of God than to your princes or rulers. For as your bodies cannot escape corporal death if with your princes ye eat or drink deadly poison (although it be by ignorance or negligence), so shall ye not escape the death everlasting if with them ye profess a corrupt religion. Yea, except in heart ye believe and with mouth ye confess the Lord Jesus to be the only Saviour of the World (which ye cannot do except ye embrace His Evangel offered), ye cannot escape death and damnation. For as the just liveth by his own faith, so doth the unfaithful perish by his infidelity. And as true faith is engendered, nourished and maintained in the hearts of God's elect by Christ's Evangel truly preached, so is infidelity and unbelief fostered by concealing and repressing the same. And thus, if ye look for the life everlasting, ye must try if ye stand in faith, and if ye would

Hab. 2. Mark 16. John 3.

be assured of a true and lively faith, ye must needs have Christ Jesus truly preached unto you.

And this is the cause (dear Brethren) that so oft I repeat and so constantly I affirm that to you it doth no less appertain than to your king or princes to provide that Christ Jesus be truly preached amongst you, seeing that without His true knowledge can neither of you both attain to salvation. And this is the point wherein, I say, all man is equal: 'That as all be descended from Adam, by whose sin and inobedience did death enter into the world, so it behooved all that shall obtain life to be ingrafted in one, that is, in the Lord Jesus, who being the just servant doth by His knowledge justify many': to wit, all that unfeignedly believe in Him.

Wherein all man is equal. Rom. 5.12–15. Isa. 53. John 3, 5.

Of this equality, and that God requireth no less of the subject, be he never so poor, than of the prince and rich man in matters of religion, He hath given an evident declaration in the law of Moses. For when the tabernacle was builded, erected and set in order, God did provide how it and the things appertaining to the same should be sustained so that they should not fall in decay. And this provision (albeit heaven and earth obey His empire) would He not take from the secret and hid treasures which lie dispersed in the veins of the earth, neither yet would He take it from the rich and potent of His people, but He did command that every man of the sons of Israel (were he rich or were he poor) that came in compt from twenty years and upward should yearly pay half a sicle[3] for an oblation to the Lord in the remembrance of their redemption and for an expiation or cleansing to their souls, which money God commanded should be bestowed upon the ornaments and necessaries of the tabernacle of testimony. He furthermore added a precept that the rich should give no more for that use, and in that behalf, than should the poor, neither yet that the poor should give any less than should the rich in that consideration. This law to man's reason and judgement may appear very unreasonable. For some rich man might have given a thousand sicles with less hurt of his substance than some poor man might have paid the half sicle. And yet God maketh all equal, and will that the one shall pay no more than the other, neither yet the poor any less than the rich.

Exod. 30.

[Exod. 30.14–16.]

[Exod. 30.15.]

This law, I say, may appear very unequal. But if the cause which

[3] The French word for the Jewish shekel.

God addeth be observed, we shall find in the same the great mercy and inestimable wisdom of God to appear, which cause is expressed in these words: 'This money received from the children of Israel thou shalt give in the service of the tabernacle that it may be to the children of Israel for a remembrance before the Lord that He may be merciful to your souls.' This cause, I say, doth evidently declare that, as the whole multitude was delivered from the bondage of Egypt by the mighty power of God alone, so was every member of the same without respect of person sanctified by His grace, the rich in that behalf nothing preferred to the poorest. For by no merit nor worthiness of man was He moved to choose and to establish His habitation and dwelling amongst them. But their felicity, prerogative and honour, which they had above all other nations, proceeded only from the fountain of His eternal goodness, who loved them freely as that He freely had chosen them to be His priestly kingdom and holy people from all nations of the earth. Thus to honour them that He would dwell in the midst of them, He neither was moved (I say) by the wisdom of the wise, by the richest of the potent, neither yet by the virtue and holiness of any estate amongst them, but of mere goodness did He love them and with His presence did He honour that whole people. And therefore to paint out the same His common love to the whole multitude, and to cut off occasions of contention and doubts of conscience, He would receive no more from the rich than from the poor for the maintenance of that His tabernacle, by the which was represented His presence and habitation amongst them.

Exod. 30.16.

Exod. 19.

The presence of God represented in the tabernacle.

If the rich had been preferred to the poor, then as the one should have been puffed up with pride, as that he had been more acceptable to God by reason of his greater gift, so should the conscience of the other have been troubled and wounded, thinking that his poverty was an impediment, that he could not stand in so perfect favour with God as did the other because he was not able to give so much as did the rich to the maintenance of His tabernacle. But He who of mercy (as said is) did choose His habitation amongst them, and also that best knoweth what lieth within man, did provide the remedy for the one and for the other, making them equal in that behalf who in other things were most unequal. If the poor should have found himself grieved by reason of that tax, and that as much was imposed upon him as upon the rich, yet had he no small cause of joy that God Himself would please to compare him and to make him equal in the maintenance of His tabernacle to the most rich and potent in Israel.

If this equality was commanded by God for maintenance of that transitory tabernacle, which was but a shadow of a better to come, is not the same required of us who now hath the verity which is Christ Jesus, who being clad with our nature is made Immanuel, that is, God with us? 'Whose natural body, albeit it be received in the heavens, where He must abide till all be complete that is forespoken by the Prophets, yet hath He promised to be present with us to the end of the world.' And for that purpose, and for the more assurance of His promise, He hath erected amongst us here in earth the signs of His own presence with us, His spiritual tabernacle, the true preaching of His Word and right administration of His sacraments. To the maintenance whereof is no less bound the subject than the prince, the poor than the rich. For as the price which was given for man's redemption is one, so requireth God of all that shall be partakers of the benefits of the same a like duty, which is a plain confession that by Christ Jesus alone we have received whatsoever was lost in Adam. Of the prince doth God require that he refuse himself and that he follow Christ Jesus; of the subject He requireth the same. Of the kings and judges it is required that they kiss the Son, that is, give honour, subjection and obedience to Him; and from such reverence doth not God exempt the subject that shall be saved. And this is that equality which is betwixt the kings and subjects, the most rich or noble and betwixt the poorest and men of lowest estate: to wit, that as the one is obliged to believe in heart and with mouth to confess the Lord Jesus to be the only Saviour of the World, so also is the other.

Heb. 9.

Isa. 8.

Acts 3.21.

Matt. 28.20.

The spiritual tabernacle and signs of Christ's presence with us.

[*Ps.* 2.10–12.]

Neither is there any of God's children (who hath attained to the years of discretion) so poor but that he hath thus much to bestow upon the ornaments and maintenance of their spiritual tabernacle when necessity requireth; neither yet is there any so rich of whose hand God requireth any more. For albeit that David gathered great substance for the building of the temple, that Solomon with earnest diligence and incredible expenses erected and finished the same, that Hezekiah and Josiah purged the religion which before was corrupted, yet to them was God no further debtor in that respect than He was to the most simple of the faithful posterity of faithful Abraham. For their diligence, zeal and works gave rather testimony and confession before men what honour they did bear to God, what love to His

NOTE.

1 Chr. 29.

2 Chr. 3, 4, 5.

2 Chr. 29, 30, 35.

Word and reverence to His religion than that any work proceeding from them did either establish or yet increase God's favour towards them, who freely did love them in Christ His Son before the foundation of the world was laid. So that these forenamed by their notable works gave testimony of their unfeigned faith, and the same doth the poorest that unfeignedly and openly professeth Christ Jesus, that doth embrace His glad tidings offered, that doth abhor superstition and flee from idolatry. The poorest, I say, and most simple that this day in earth, in the days of this cruel persecution, firmly believeth in Christ and boldly doth confess Him before this wicked generation, is no less acceptable before God, neither is judged in His presence to have done any less in promoting Christ His cause, than is the king that by the sword and power which he hath received of God rooteth out idolatry and so advanceth Christ's glory.

But to return to our former purpose, it is no less required, I say, of the subject to believe in Christ and to profess His true religion than of the prince and king. And therefore I affirm that in God's presence it shall not excuse you to allege that ye were no chief rulers, and therefore that the care and reformation of religion did not appertain unto you. Ye dear Brethren (as before is said) are the creatures of God, created to His own image and similitude, to whom it is commanded to hear the voice of your heavenly Father, to embrace His Son Christ Jesus, to flee from all doctrine and religion which He hath not approved by His own will revealed to us in His most blessed Word. To which precepts and charges, if ye be found inobedient, ye shall perish in your iniquity as rebels and stubborn servants that have no pleasure to obey the good will of their sovereign Lord who most lovingly doth call for your obedience. And therefore, Brethren, in this behalf it is your part to be careful and diligent. For the question is not of things temporal which, although they be endangered, yet by diligence and process of time may after be redressed, but it is of the damnation of your bodies and souls and of the loss of the life everlasting, which once lost can never be recovered. And therefore I say that it behooveth you to be careful and diligent in this so weighty a matter, lest that ye, contemning this occasion which God now offereth, find not the like, although that after with groaning and sobs ye languish for the same. And that ye be not ignorant of what occasion I mean, in few words I shall express it.

Matt. 17.

Note.

Not only I, but with me also diverse other godly and learned men, do offer unto you our labours faithfully to instruct you in the ways of the Eternal our God and in the sincerity of Christ's Evangel, which this day by the pestilent generation of Antichrist (I mean by the pope and by his most ungodly clergy) are almost hid from the eyes of men. We offer to jeopard our lives for the salvation of your souls and by manifest Scriptures to prove that religion which amongst you is maintained by fire and sword to be vain, false and diabolical. We require nothing of you but that patiently ye will hear our doctrine, which is not ours, but is the doctrine of salvation revealed to the world by the only Son of God; and that ye will examine our reasons by the which we offer to prove the papistical religion to be abominable before God. And last we require that by your power the tyranny of those cruel beasts (I mean of priests and friars) may be bridled till we have uttered our minds in all matters this day debatable in religion. If these things in the fear of God ye grant to me, and unto others that unfeignedly for your salvation and for God's glory require the same, I am assured that of God ye shall be blessed whatsoever Satan shall devise against you. But and if ye contemn or refuse God, who thus lovingly offereth unto you salvation and life, ye shall neither escape plagues temporal, which shortly shall apprehend you, neither yet the torment prepared for the devil and for his angels, except by speedy repentance ye return to the Lord whom now ye refuse if that ye refuse the messengers of His Word.

The offer of John Knox to his native realm.

What he requireth.

But yet I think ye doubt what ye ought and may do in this so weighty a matter. In few words I will declare my conscience in the one and in the other. Ye ought to prefer the glory of God, the promoting of Christ His Evangel and the salvation of your souls to all things that be in earth; and ye, although ye be but subjects, may lawfully require of your superiors, be it of your king, be it of your lords, rulers and powers, that they provide for you true preachers and that they expel such as under the names of pastors devour and destroy the flock, not feeding the same as Christ Jesus hath commanded. And if in this point your superiors be negligent, or yet pretend to maintain tyrants in their tyranny, most justly ye may provide true teachers for yourselves, be it in your cities, towns or villages; them ye may maintain and defend against all that shall persecute them and by that means shall labour to defraud you of that most comfortable food of your souls, Christ's Evangel truly preached. Ye may moreover withhold the fruits and profits which your false bishops and clergy most

An answer to two questions.

Subjects may lawfully require true preachers of their rulers.

injustly receive of you unto such time as they be compelled faithfully to do their charge and duties, which is to preach unto you Christ Jesus truly, rightly to minister His sacraments according to His own institution, and so to watch for the salvation of your souls, as is commanded by Christ Jesus Himself and by His Apostles Paul and Peter.

John 21. Acts 20.

If God shall move your hearts in His true fear to begin to practise these things and to demand and crave the same of your superiors, which most lawfully ye may do, then I doubt not but of His great mercy and free grace He shall illuminate the eyes of your minds that His undoubted verity shall be a lantern to your feet to guide and lead you in all the ways which His godly wisdom doth approve. He shall make your enemies tremble before your faces, He shall establish His blessed Evangel amongst you to the salvation and perpetual comfort of yourselves and of your posterity after you. But and if (as God forbid) the love of friends, the fear of your princes and the wisdom of the world draw you back from God, and from His Son Christ Jesus, be ye certainly persuaded that ye shall drink the cup of His vengeance, so many I mean as shall contemn and despise this loving calling of your heavenly Father. It will not excuse you (dear Brethren) in the presence of God, neither yet will it avail you in the day of His visitation, to say: 'We were but simple subjects; we could not redress the faults and crimes of our rulers, bishops and clergy. We called for reformation, and wished for the same, but lords' brethren were bishops, their sons were abbots, and the friends of great men had the possession of the church, and so were we compelled to give obedience to all that they demanded.' These vain excuses, I say, will nothing avail you in the presence of God who requireth no less of the subjects than of the rulers, that they decline from evil and that they do good, that they abstain from idolatry, superstition, blasphemy, murder and other such horrible crimes which His law forbiddeth and yet nonetheless are openly committed and maliciously defended in that miserable realm.

Things that may draw men back from the sincerity of Christ's Evangel.

And if ye think that ye are innocent because ye are not the chief authors of such iniquity, ye are utterly deceived. For God doth not only punish the chief offenders, but with them doth He damn the consenters to iniquity; and all are judged to consent that knowing impiety committed give no testimony that the same displeaseth them. To speak this matter more plain, as your princes and rulers are

Rom. 1.

Note.

criminal with your bishops of all idolatry committed, and of all the innocent blood that is shed for the testimony of Christ's truth, and that because they maintain them in their tyranny, so are you (I mean so many of you as give no plain confession to the contrary) criminal and guilty with your princes and rulers of the same crimes, because ye assist and maintain your princes in their blind rage and give no declaration that their tyranny displeaseth you.

Princes and bishops are alike criminal.

This doctrine I know is strange to the blind world, but the verity of it hath been declared in all notable punishments from the beginning. When the original world perished by water, when Sodom and Gomorrah were consumed by fire, and finally when Jerusalem was horribly destroyed, doth any man think that all were alike wicked before the world? Evident it is that they were not if they shall be judged according to their external facts. For some were young and could not be oppressors, neither yet could defile themselves with unnatural and beastly lusts; some were pitiful and gentle of nature and did not thirst for the blood of Christ nor of His Apostles. But did any escape the plagues and vengeance which did apprehend the multitude? Let the Scriptures witness and the histories be considered, which plainly do testify that by the waters all flesh in earth at that time did perish (Noah and his family reserved), that none escaped in Sodom and in the other cities adjacent except Lot and his two daughters. And evident it is that in that famous city Jerusalem, in that last and horrible destruction of the same, none escaped God's vengeance except so many as before were dispersed. And what is the cause of this severity, seeing that all were not alike offenders? Let flesh cease to dispute with God and let all man by these examples learn betimes to flee and avoid the society and company of the proud contemners of God if that they list not to be partakers of their plagues.

How subjects offend with their princes.

Gen. 7, 19. Josephus. Aegesippus.[4]

The cause is evident if we can be subject without grudging to God's judgements which in themselves are most holy and just. For in the original world none was found that either did resist tyranny and oppression that universally was used either yet that earnestly reprehended the same. In Sodom was none found that did againstand that furious and beastly multitude that did compass about and besiege the house of Lot. None would believe Lot that the city should be

Why all perished in the flood, in Sodom and Gomorrah.

[4] As subsequently becomes clear, Knox is referring here to the destruction of Jerusalem in AD 70 described in Josephus, *Jewish War*, 7.1, and Hegesippus, *Historia de bello Judaico*.

destroyed. And finally in Jerusalem was none found that studied to repress the tyranny of the priests who were conjured against Christ and His Evangel, but all fainted (I except ever such as gave witness with their blood or their flying that such impiety displeased them), all kept silence, by the which all approved iniquity and joined hands with the tyrants, and so were all arrayed and set as it had been in one battle against the Omnipotent and against His Son Christ Jesus. For whosoever gathereth not with Christ in the day of His harvest is judged to scatter. And therefore of one vengeance temporal were they all partakers.

Which thing, as before I have touched, ought to move you to the deep consideration of your duties in these last and most perilous times. The iniquity of your bishops is more than manifest; their filthy lives infect the air; the innocent blood which they shed crieth vengeance in the ears of our God; the idolatry and abomination which openly they commit and without punishment maintain doth corrupt and defile the whole land; and none amongst you doth unfeignedly study for any redress of such enormities. Will God in this behalf hold you as innocents? Be not deceived, dear Brethren. God hath punished not only the proud tyrants, filthy persons and cruel murderers, but also such as with them did draw the yoke of iniquity, was it by flattering their offences, obeying their injust commandments or in winking at their manifest iniquity. All such, I say, hath God once punished with the chief offenders. Be ye assured, Brethren, that as He is immutable of nature, so will He not pardon in you that which so severely He hath punished in others; and now the less, because He hath plainly admonished you of the dangers to come and hath offered you His mercy before He pour forth His wrath and displeasure upon the inobedient.

What subjects shall God punish with their princes.

God the Father of our Lord Jesus Christ, who is Father of glory and God of all consolation, give you the spirit of wisdom and open unto you the knowledge of Himself by the means of His dear Son, by the which ye may attain to the esperance and hope that, after the troubles of this transitorious life, ye may be partakers of the riches of that glorious inheritance which is prepared for such as refuse themselves and fight under the banner of Christ Jesus in the day of this His battle; that in deep consideration of the same ye may learn to prefer the invisible and eternal joys to the vain pleasures that are present. God further grant you His Holy Spirit, righteously to consider what I in His name have required of your nobility, and of you the subjects, and move you all together so to answer that my petition be not a testimony of your just condemnation when the Lord Jesus shall appear to revenge the blood of His saints and the contempt of His most holy Word. Amen.

Sleep not in sin, for vengeance is prepared against all inobedient. Flee from Babylon if ye will not be partakers of her plagues.

Be witness to my Appellation.
Grace be with you.
From Geneva.
The 14 of
July,
1558.

Your brother to command in godliness
JOHN KNOX

JOHN KNOX TO THE READER.

Because many are offended at the *First Blast of the Trumpet*, in which I affirm that to promote a woman to bear rule or empire above any realm, nation or city is repugnant to nature, contumely to God, and a thing most contrarious to His revealed and approved ordinance; and because also that some hath promised (as I understand) a confutation of the same,[1] I have delayed the *Second Blast* till such time as their reasons appear, by the which I either may be reformed in opinion or else shall have further occasion more simply and plainly to utter my judgement. Yet in the meantime, for the discharge of my conscience, and for avoiding suspicion which might be engendered by reason of my silence, I could not cease to notify these subsequent propositions, which by God's grace I purpose to entreat in the *Second Blast* promised.

1. It is not birth only nor propinquity of blood that maketh a king lawfully to reign above a people professing Christ Jesus and His eternal verity, but in his election must the ordinance which God hath established in the election of inferior judges be observed.

2. No manifest idolater nor notorious transgressor of God's holy precepts ought to be promoted to any public regiment, honour or dignity in any realm, province or city that hath subjected the self to Christ Jesus and to His blessed Evangel.

3. Neither can oath nor promise bind any such people to obey and maintain tyrants against God and against His truth known.

4. But if either rashly they have promoted any manifest wicked person, or yet ignorantly have chosen such a one as after declareth himself unworthy of regiment above the people of God (and such be

[1] Presumably Knox is referring here to John Aylmer's *An Harborowe*, which was to be published in Strasburg in 1559.

all idolaters and cruel persecutors), most justly may the same men depose and punish him that unadvisedly before they did nominate, appoint and elect.

MATT. 6.22.

'If the eye be single, the
whole body shall be clear.'

PART II
KNOX AND SCOTLAND 1557–1564

Knox and the Protestant nobility, March–December 1557

[After his successful mission to Scotland in the winter of 1555–6, Knox returned to Geneva from where he continued to correspond with the Protestant nobility with whom he had made contact in his homeland. The following extract from his *History of the Reformation* (Laing MS, fos. 90v–94r; Laing, vol. I, pp. 267–74; Dickinson, vol. I, pp. 131–7) begins with a letter from the Protestant nobility of 10 March 1557 inviting Knox to return to Scotland, continues with Knox's response to discovering that by October they had changed their minds and culminates with the signing of the First Band or Covenant on 3 December 1557.]

At this same time,[1] some of the nobility directed their letters to call JOHN KNOX from Geneva, for their comfort, and for the comfort of their brethren the preachers, and others that then courageously fought against the enemies of God's truth. The tenor of their letter is this:

Grace, Mercy and Peace, for Salutation, etc.

The second vocation of John Knox by letters of the lords.

Dearly beloved in the Lord, the faithful that are of your acquaintance in these parts (thanks be unto God) are steadfast in the belief whereunto ye left them and has a godly thirst and desire, day by day, of your presence again; which, if the spirit of God will so move and permit time unto you, we will heartily desire you, in the name of the Lord, that ye will return again in these parts, where ye shall find all faithful that ye left behind you, not only glad to hear your doctrine, but will be ready to jeopard lives and goods in the forward setting of

[1] That is, March 1557. In reading what follows it should be borne in mind that throughout the *History* Knox normally refers to himself in the third person.

the glory of God, as He will permit time. And albeit the magistrates in this country be as yet but in the state ye left them, yet at the making hereof, we have no experience of any more cruelty to be used nor was before; but rather we have belief that God will augment His flock, because we see daily the friars, enemies to Christ's Evangel, in less estimation both with the queen's grace and the rest of the nobility of our realm. This in few words is the mind of the faithful being present, and others absent. The rest of our minds this faithful bearer will show you at length. Thus, fare ye well in the Lord.

Of Stirling, the tenth of March, Anno 1557.[2] (This is the true copy of the bill, being subscribed by the names underwritten:)

Sic subscribitur, GLENCAIRN
LORNE
ERSKINE
JAMES STEWART[3]

These letters were delivered to the said John in Geneva by the hands of James Sim, who now resteth with Christ, and of James Baron, that yet liveth, in the month of May immediately thereafter. Which received, and advised upon, he took consultation as well with his own church as with that notable servant of God, John Calvin, and with other godly ministers, who all with one consent said that he could not refuse that vocation unless he would declare himself rebellious unto his God and unmerciful to his country. And so he returned answer with promises to visit them with reasonable expedition and so soon as he might put order to that dear flock that was committed to his charge. And so, in the end of the next September after, he departed from Geneva and came to Dieppe, where there met him contrary letters; as by this his answer thereto we may understand.

The spirit of wisdom, constancy and strength be multiplied with you, by the favour of God our Father, and by the grace of our Lord Jesus Christ.

According to my promise, Right Honourable, I came to Dieppe, the 24 of October, of full mind, by the good will of God, with the first

[2] 1556 in the original old-style reckoning.

[3] That is, Alexander Cunningham, fifth earl of Glencairn; Archibald Campbell, Lord Lorne (later fifth earl of Argyll); John Erskine of Dun; and James Stewart, prior of St Andrews (later earl of Moray).

ships to have visited you. But because two letters, not very pleasing to the flesh, were there presented unto me, I was compelled to stay for a time.[4] The one was directed to myself from a faithful brother, which made mention that new consultation was appointed for final conclusion of the matter before purposed, and willed me therefore to abide in these parts till the determination of the same. The other letter was directed from a gentleman to a friend, with charge to advertise me that he had communed with all those that seemed most frack and fervent in the matter and that into none did he find such boldness and constancy as was requisite for such an enterprise; but that some did (as he writeth) repent that ever any such thing was moved, some were partly ashamed, and others were able to deny that ever they did consent to any such purpose, if any trial or question should be taken thereof, etc.

Which letters, when I had considered, I partly was confounded and partly was pierced with anguish and sorrow. Confounded I was that I had so far travailed in the matter, moving the same to the most godly and most learned that this day we know to live in Europe, to the effect that I might have their judgements and grave counsels, for assurance as well of your consciences as of mine, in all enterprises. And then that nothing should succeed of so long consultation cannot but redound either to your shame or mine; for either it shall appear that I was marvellous vain, being so solist where no necessity required, or else that such as were my movers thereto lacked the ripeness of judgement in their first vocation. To some it may appear a small and light matter that I have cast off, and as it were abandoned, as well my particular care as my public office and charge, leaving my house and poor family destitute of all head, save God only, and committing that small (but to Christ dearly beloved) flock, over the which I was appointed one of the ministers, to the charge of another. This, I say, to worldly men may appear a small matter, but to me it was, and yet is, such that more worldly substance than I will express could not have caused me willingly behold the eyes of so many grave men weep at once for my cause as that I did in taking of my last good night from them. To whom, if it please God that I return, and question be demanded, 'What was the impediment of my purposed journey?', judge you what I shall answer.

[4] These letters have not survived.

The cause of my dolour and sorrow (God is witness) is for nothing pertaining either to my corporal contentment or worldly displeasure; but it is for the grievous plagues and punishments of God which assuredly shall apprehend, not only you, but every inhabitant of that miserable realm and isle, except that the power of God, by the liberty of His Evangel, deliver you from bondage. I mean not only that perpetual fire and torment prepared for the devil, and for such as denying Christ Jesus and His known verity do follow the sons of wickedness to perdition (which most is to be feared); but also that thraldom and misery that shall apprehend your own bodies, your children, subjects and posterity, whom ye have betrayed (in conscience, I can except none that bear the name of nobility), and presently do fight to betray them and your realm to the slavery of strangers.[5] The war begun (although I acknowledge it to be the work of God) shall be your destruction, unless that, betime, remedy be provided.[6] God open your eyes that ye may espy and consider your own miserable estate.

My words shall appear to some sharp and undiscreetly spoken; but as charity ought to interpret all things to the best, so ought wise men to understand that a true friend cannot be a flatterer, especially when the questions of salvation, both of body and soul, are moved; and that not of one nor of two, but as it were of a whole realm and nation. What are the sobs, and what is the affection of my troubled heart, God shall one day declare. But this will I add to my former rigour and severity: to wit, if any persuade you, for fear of dangers that may follow, to faint in your former purpose, be he never esteemed so wise and friendly, let him be judged of you both foolish and your mortal enemy. Foolish, for because he understandeth nothing of God's approved wisdom; and enemy unto you, because he laboureth to separate you from God's favour, provoking His vengeance and grievous plagues against you, because he would that ye should prefer your worldly rest to God's praise and glory, and the friendship of the wicked to the salvation of your brethren.

[5] That is, to the French.

[6] Knox is referring here to the war between the Catholic powers of Spain and France in which England had become embroiled through the marriage of Mary Tudor to Philip II of Spain. In the autumn of 1557, Mary of Guise assembled an army intent on invading England on France's behalf. In the event, the Scottish nobility refused to cross the border.

I am not ignorant that fearful troubles shall ensue your enterprise (as in my former letters I did signify unto you); but O joyful and comfortable are those troubles and adversities which man sustaineth for accomplishment of God's will revealed by His Word! For how terrible that ever they appear to the judgement of the natural man, yet are they never able to devour nor utterly to consume the sufferers. For the invisible and invincible power of God sustaineth and preserveth, according to His promise, all such as with simplicity do obey Him. The subtle craft of Pharaoh, many years joined with his bloody cruelty, was not able to destroy the male children of Israel; neither were the waters of the Red Sea, much less the rage of Pharaoh, able to confound Moses and the company which he conducted; and that because the one had God's promise that they should multiply and the other had His commandment to enter into such dangers. I would your wisdoms should consider that our God remaineth one and is immutable; and that the church of Christ Jesus hath the same promise of protection and defence that Israel had of multiplication; and farther, that no less cause have ye to enter in your former enterprise than Moses had to go to the presence of Pharaoh. For your subjects, yea, your brethren, are oppressed, their bodies and souls holden in bondage, and God speaketh to your consciences (unless ye be dead with the blind world) that you ought to hazard your own lives (be it against kings or emperors) for their deliverance.

[*Exod. 1.*]

[*Exod. 14.*]

The duty of the nobility.

For only for that cause are ye called princes of the people and ye receive of your brethren honour, tribute and homage at God's commandment; not by reason of your birth and progeny (as the most part of men falsely do suppose), but by reason of your office and duty, which is to vindicate and deliver your subjects and brethren from all violence and oppression to the uttermost of your power. Advise diligently, I beseech you, with the points of that letter which I directed to the whole nobility and let every man apply the matter and case to himself.[7] For your conscience shall one day be compelled to acknowledge that the reformation of religion, and of public enormities, doth appertain to more than to the clergy, or chief rulers called kings.

That letter lost by negligence and troubles.

The mighty spirit of the Lord Jesus rule and guide your counsels

[7] Although, as the sidenote indicates, this letter to the nobility has been lost, the argument Knox is pursuing here is elaborated on at length in the *Appellation*.

to His glory, your eternal comfort, and to the consolation of your brethren. Amen.

From Dieppe, the 27 of October 1557.

These letters received and read, together with others directed to the whole nobility and some particular gentlemen, as to the lairds of Dun and Pittarrow,[8] new consultation was had what was best to be done. And in the end it was concluded that they would follow forward their purpose once intended and would commit themselves, and whatsoever God had given unto them, in His hands, rather than they would suffer idolatry so manifestly to reign and the subjects of that realm so to be defrauded, as long they had been, of the only food of their souls, the true preaching of Christ's Evangel. And that every one should be the more assured of other, a common band was made, and by some subscribed, the tenor whereof follows:

WE, perceiving how Satan in his members, the Antichrists of our time, cruelly doth rage, seeking to downthring and to destroy the Evangel of Christ and His Congregation, ought, according to our bounden duty, to strive in our Master's cause, even unto the death, being certain of the victory in Him. The which our duty being well considered, we do promise before the majesty of God, and His Congregation, that we (by His grace) shall with all diligence continually apply our whole power, substance and our very lives, to maintain, set forward and establish the most blessed Word of God and His Congregation; and shall labour at our possibility to have faithful ministers purely and truly to minister Christ's Evangel and sacraments to His people. We shall maintain them, nourish them and defend them, the whole Congregation of Christ, and every member thereof, at our whole powers and waring of our lives, against Satan, and all wicked power that does intend tyranny or trouble against the foresaid Congregation. Unto the which Holy Word and Congregation we do join us, and also do forsake and renounce the congregation of Satan, with all the superstitious abomination and idolatry thereof; and moreover, shall declare ourselves manifestly enemies thereto, by this our faithful promise before God, testified to His Congregation, by our subscriptions at these presents:

[8] Erskine of Dun and Wishart of Pittarrow.

At Edinburgh, the third day of December, the year of God 1557 years. God called to witness:

Sic subscribitur ARGYLL
GLENCAIRN
MORTON
LORNE
ERSKINE OF DUN
Et cetera.[9]

[9] In fact, there were no other signatories of the First Band. Those who did sign were Archibald Campbell, fourth earl of Argyll; Alexander Cunningham, fifth earl of Glencairn; James Douglas, fourth earl of Morton; Archibald Campbell, Lord Lorne (later fifth earl of Argyll); and John Erskine of Dun.

Knox to the Protestant nobility, 17 December 1557

[Knox remained in Dieppe for some months before returning to Geneva in the spring of 1558. He presumably did not know of the drawing up of the First Band when he penned the following letter (Laing, vol. IV, pp. 276–86) two weeks later on 17 December 1557.]

To the Lords and Others Professing the Truth in Scotland.
The secrets of the Lord are revealed to those that fear Him.

The Holy Ghost, by the mouth of David and Solomon (Right Honourable Lords), for two reasons calleth 'the fear of the Lord the beginning of all wisdom'. First, because without the same, all that appeareth to be wisdom perisheth, and most commonly turneth to the perdition of those that are esteemed and do esteem themselves most wise. For wisdom natural, not ruled nor bridled by the fear of God, as it is but extreme foolishness, so is it a poison and venom most deadly, which in the end commonly bringeth the worldly wise to worldly confusion, as the experience of all ages has taught us; where, by the contrary, the fear of the Lord preserveth His servants in their greatest extremities even before the world. But this is not the chief cause why the fear of the Lord hath the forenamed title. For evident it is that not only the worldly wise once suffer death and come to confusion, but also, as David does witness, even those that altogether be fools and enraged with madness; yea, it is statute to all men once to die. But because that where the fear of the Lord is once deeply grafted in the heart, that there also is the graces of the Holy Spirit from time to time added to the further instruction, comfort and confirmation of God's chosen children in all godliness; therefore, it is justly and chiefly called 'the beginning of wisdom', by which man attaineth to eternal felicity, and so doth escape death and confusion. For this is the conclusion of the Holy Ghost, most certain and infal-

[*Ps. 111.10.*]

[*Ps. 49.10.*]

lible: that where God of His great mercy and infinite goodness once begins to touch the heart with His true fear, and as it were to change it from the natural rebellion to give unfeigned reverence to His holy majesty, that there He will (yea, even against the puissance and rage of the ports of hell) perform the work of our redemption, to the manifestation of His own glory, and to the everlasting joy of those to whom he appointeth His Holy Spirit schoolmaster and instructor.

And albeit that this His favour and fatherly care be common to all His children in things appertaining to life everlasting (every one receiving such portion and measure of His grace as His wisdom knoweth to be expedient for finishing and confirmation of that good work begun), yet in distributing temporal benedictions, His majesty takes most especial care upon those whom He hath determined and appointed to be rulers, comforters and maintainers of others. To Joseph He gave not only favour in the eyes of strangers in time of his bondage, but also in his young age He did show unto him most notable visions, to the perfect understanding and knowledge whereof did neither his father, neither yet himself, fully attain many days after. To Solomon, likewise, were superabundantly given riches, honour and worldly rest, besides the wisdom which he required. And to Daniel, above all mortal men of that age, was given the knowledge and revelation of secret and hid things to come. Which singular privileges (in which they did far excel their brethren) did not so mekill serve for themselves as for the commodity and profit of others, to whom God made them instructors, rulers, defenders and stewards. For the interpretation of dreams and visions given unto Joseph did more profit the commonwealth of Egypt than it did serve for his eternal salvation; and the same may be said of those notable prerogatives given to Solomon and Daniel. For by the felicity of the one was the people of Israel living in his age repute blessed, and by the revelation granted to the other is the whole kirk of God this day assured of things bypast and that are to come. And therefore, I say, that such singular and rare privileges and graces are given to a few for the comfort, instruction and defence of many.

But one thing is to be here marked and diligently to be observed, which is this: that before all these superexcellent graces, we plainly may perceive that the fear of God was planted in their hearts. For in Joseph we may espy a hatred of sin and iniquity which his brethren committed, in so far as he reveals the same to his and their father, whose authority he judged sufficient to have repressed the same. In [*Gen.* 37.]

[*1 Kgs.* 4.] Solomon we see a desire of wisdom, whereby he might rule and govern with equity and justice the people committed to his charge. [*Dan.* 1.]. And in Daniel doth evidently appear the horror and fear that he had to pollute and defile himself with meats forbidden by the law of the Lord his God. And thus, I say, that the fear of the Lord is the beginning and continuance of wisdom. Of wisdom, I say, which is worthy the name of wisdom, and is the most singular gift of God given to those by whom He purposeth to work any notable work to His glory. But further must I admonish that I mean not that those only who have these singular privileges or revelations of secret things given unto them, immediately given of God, have in their hearts His true fear, and that no other besides hath any motion thereof. But I mean also that they whose hearts God does so mollify and move, that with reverence they receive the counsel and admonitions given unto them by God's messengers, and do determine with themselves to obey His holy will revealed unto them, albeit the same appear far to pass their power and engine; these men, I say, how ignorant that ever they appear to be of God, cannot be judged altogether empty and void of His true fear, neither shall they be destitute of wisdom and power to perform those things which God requireth of them.

For in so far as Pharaoh did fear the things that were not seen, [*Gen.* 41.] and at the counsel and commandment of Joseph did make provision for the danger which the natural man could neither have believed nor feared; in so doing, I say, he did declare himself mekill to esteem the messenger of God, by whose spirit, power and providence were such things not only revealed, but also should be performed and brought to pass. Which things I mean (to reverence God's messengers, heartily to embrace and study to obey the precepts and charges which they give, to study also to magnify God and to make His providence and wondrous works known unto men) can no man do from an unfeigned heart, except that some spark of God's true fear rest in the same. The like is to be noted in Nebuchadnezzar who, being the golden head and only monarch in the earth in his days, [*Dan.* 2.] ashamed not to stoop and to fall down (hearing the interpretation of his own dreams) before the feet of Daniel, and openly to confess that there was no God who ruleth the heaven and the earth except the God of Israel. And, moreover, he did not only promote Daniel, being a stranger, captive and prisoner, above all the princes of his realm, but also, at his request, the king promoted to honours and offices his fellows, and was beneficial to the rest of the Jews then afflicted in his dominions. Which confession, obedience, love and liberality did, no doubt, spring from the secret and hid fear of God which was planted in his heart and, no doubt, had some root in the same when he appeared ignorant of God, and greatest enemy to His people.

What further graces and commodities (not only to themselves, but also to many other) did ensue this their obedience, the Holy Ghost doth not conceal. For by the one, to wit, by Pharaoh, was not only his own people fed and preserved in the days of famine, but also by that godly provision made in his realm was the lives of many others preserved; yea, the lives of the whole kirk of God which that day was known to be upon the earth – I mean of Jacob and his household. And albeit that Nebuchadnezzar did fall, and in many things offend most horribly, yet still we find that the mercy of God did so overcome his malice that after long punishment and dejection from all honours he was restored again, not only to the form, reason and understanding of man (of the which he was deprived for a time), but also to his former dignity, honours and empire, to the great manifestation of God's glory, and to the most singular erudition, admonition and comfort to others. For what erudition and doctrine was preached to the world by the publication of his confession, and of the most wondrous work of God declared upon him, which he did notify to many realms and nations [which heretofore] were drowned in idolatry, and did live without any perfect knowledge of the living God; what admonition might, and this day may and should, earthly rulers and princes receive by his punishment; and what singular comfort is left to penitent sinners in his most notable restitution to honours again; the matter, I say, cannot be expressed by the wit or engine of man.

[*Gen. 42, 43.*]

[*Dan. 4.*]

And therefore, yet again I say that wheresoever the true fear of God is planted in the heart, that there shall also after be added wisdom and other graces necessary and profitable not only to the receiver but also to others. But this root of virtue and wisdom (the true fear of God, I mean) being absent from the heart, as there can be no obedience which is acceptable unto God, neither yet any love to His messengers of any long continuance, so can there be no wisdom to search and seek for things profitable, neither yet grace to follow God's will how manifestly that ever it be revealed. But rather are the wholesome counsels and admonitions given for reformation of manifest iniquity, and also for temporal commodities and conservation of realms and commonwealths, not marked nor perfectly understood, or else when God's messengers do plainly speak to princes and rulers, their counsels and admonitions are disdainfully contemned. The counsel, no doubt, of Moses to proud Pharaoh had been to the salvation of himself and to the safeguard of his people, if after many plagues he could have given obedience. But as the sun did long shine before the blind, so in the end, without all light and wisdom, was he and his army in their cruel rage drowned by the waters of the Red Sea. [*Exod.* 14.]

The admonition and counsel of Jeremiah to King Zedekiah (although it appeared sharp, for he commanded him to render and subject himself in the power of the king who besieged him), yet had it not been a little profitable to him and to that commonwealth if he had obeyed and followed the commandment of the Prophet. But because the king and his council in the end agreed to follow their own imaginations, and so to rebel against God and His messenger Jeremiah, the one and the other, I mean the king and his councillors, did taste the bitter cup of God's vengeance, which so oft was pronounced by the mouth of the same Prophet. For the eyes of Zedekiah was compelled to behold his councillors, yea, and his own sons, slain in his presence, and immediately was his own eyes put out, so that ever [after] that he never saw light nor comfort on earth. Jerusalem was burned with fire and the whole land was laid waste, and all this calamity came upon them because the counsel of God, proclaimed by His Prophets, was mocked and contemned. And yet in this most miserable and universal visitation mercy was shown to such as feared God and had been obedient and shown mercy to His Prophet. For besides the multitude, which at the commandment of Jeremiah did subject themselves to the king of Babylon, and so was saved from that present vengeance, Ebedmelech, the Blackamoor or Ethiopian, by whose intercession and bald request unto the king, the Prophet was delivered from death and prison; and Baruch, the scribe, by whom was written and presented to the prince and councillors the sermons and preachings of Jeremiah; these two, I say, in the midst of that same fire of God's vengeance which consumed many thousands, found favour and grace, and did obtain their lives for a prey. [*Jer.* 52.] [*Jer.* 39.] [*Jer.* 43.]

These things I briefly touch, Right Honourables, not so mekill to instruct you, as to animate and to encourage you in that most godly work which once ye have purposed. Ye were of mind (and my good hope is that so ye yet remain) to jeopard and hazard in the cause of Christ Jesus, and for the deliverance of your brethren from this Babylonical and Antichristian bondage, your lives, your honours, and whatsoever ye have received in temporal things of God's hands. This matter ye have communicated with me, and I, as I must answer in the presence of the Lord Jesus, hath given unto you such counsel as His Holy Spirit assured me is for the manifestation of God's glory, and also to your eternal comfort, whatsoever flesh and blood do judge in the matter; as in my former letters more fully is expressed.[1] But this your former purpose, and my counsel also, notwithstanding, if the true fear of God have not some root in your hearts, all is vain and labour lost. For of this one thing I will that assuredly ye persuade yourselves: that the floods shall come, the winds shall blow, the storms and tempests shall arise, and with violent rage they altogether shall assault your fortress; and then, except ye be builded upon the sure rock, Christ Jesus, who hath commanded you to forsake yourselves and to follow Him, impossible it is that ye can remain constant in your godly purpose, but in a moment shall your whole building and house be overthrown. For flesh and blood cannot deny the self, neither yet can it be made able to endure and abide the fire of afflictions, except that it be convicted of its own affirmity, and therefore be strengthened and confirmed by the power of another.

For this order does God most commonly keep in appointing and sending to battle His best and most approved soldiers: first, to deject them from all confidence which they may have, either in themselves, either yet in the arm of any man, and thereafter to erect and raise them up in boldness of His strength, and by the free promises of His mercy, somewhat does He remeid the trouble of their conscience. And this dejection, humiliation and refusal of themselves, He worketh both in conscience and in confidence of worldly power; He embases and beateth down the conscience, opening the eyes of their minds that they may behold the miseries of their own nature, and their just condemnation which their sins deserveth. In deep contemplation whereof, God bringeth them, as it were, to the ports of hell, to an unfeigned hatred of themselves and of sin (and this is the first entrance to the true fear of God); but in this estate He leaveth them not, but manifesting to them His undeserved love and favour in

[1] Presumably the same (lost) letters to which Knox refers in his letter of 27 October 1557 above, pp. 137–8.

Christ Jesus, His only Son, He relieveth and somewhat raiseth up their conscience, so that in all assaults they rest upon His free mercy. Thus did He beat down the pride of Peter and the confidence which he had in his own strength; and the glory also which Paul had in the justice of the law; and yet was the one appointed preacher to the Jews and the other chief Apostle to the Gentiles. And such as it [pleased] God to appoint to deliver His people oppressed by worldly calamities, He commonly doth so entreat for a long season, to the end that they have no cause to glory in any thing appertaining to the flesh. For albeit Moses in his youthhood was nourished in Pharaoh's house, yet before he was known to be the appointed messenger of God for the deliverance of Israel afflicted, he was forty years banished, yea, and ashamed not to keep the sheep of his father-in-law. The low and simple estate of Gideon, the contemned youth and infancy of David, are not concealed by the Holy Ghost, to instruct us: first, that the eye of God in appointing of His messengers looketh not to such things as the world most esteemeth; and secondly, to beat down the arrogance and pride of all flesh that no man glory of such works as God does work by him whom He hath chosen from the dunghill (as David speaketh) and placed him with the princes of His people, without all merit or deserving of themselves, either yet of any of their progenitors.

[*Exod.* 2.]

[*Judg.* 8.]

[*1 Sam.* 17.]

[*Ps.* 113.7–8.]

The same I might prove by more examples; but these histories I may not apply lest that I be compelled to exceed the measure of a missive. Those that thus be taught of God, and by plain and clear sight of their infirmity and wretched nature, are unfeignedly moved to rest upon the power of God, and upon His free and undeserved mercy, have from time to time augmentation and increase of His Holy Spirit, and wisdom in abundance, joined with constancy, ministered unto them in the midst of all afflictions, to perform the good work which in God's name they begin. And so potently does He sometimes work, even by such as have sometimes appeared abject, and of no estimation, that by one He comforteth, maintaineth and delivereth many thousands. If ye have tasted of this spirit (Right Honourable), and by the motion of the same put your hands to the Lord's work, then whatsoever any creature imagine in your contrary, yet shall ye so prosper that in the end ye shall be called the blessed of the Lord. For as such as labour to suppress God's glory shall leave their names in execration to the posterity following, so shall those that unfeignedly seek to promote the same have their names written, not only in the book of life, but also shall have them here kept and registered in special recommendation. But in all things I wish your eyes to be single, beholding only in your enterprise the glory of God, your duty, and the salvation of your brethren.

But now, no further to trouble you at this present, I will only advertise you of such bruit as I hear in these parts uncertainly noised; which is this, that contradiction and rebellion is made to the authority by some in that realm. In which point my conscience will not suffer me to keep back from you my counsel, yea, my judgement and commandment, which I communicate with you in God's fear, and by the assurance of His truth. Which is that none of you that seek to promote the glory of Christ do suddenly disobey or displease the established authority in things lawful; neither yet that ye assist or fortify such as for their own particular cause and worldly promotion would trouble the same. But in the bowels of Christ Jesus I exhort you that with all simplicity and lawful obedience, joined with boldness in God, and with open confession of your faith, ye seek the favours of the authority, that by it (if possible be) the cause in which ye labour may be promoted, or at the least not persecuted; which thing, after all humble request if ye cannot attain, then, with open and solemn protestation of your obedience to be given to the authority in all things not plainly repugning to God, ye lawfully may attempt the extremity, which is to provide, whether the authority will consent or no, that Christ's Evangel may be truly preached and His holy sacraments rightly ministered unto you, and to your brethren, the subjects of that realm.

And further, ye lawfully may, yea, and thereto is bound to defend your brethren from persecution and tyranny, be it against princes or emperors, to the uttermost of your power, providing always, as I have said, that neither yourself deny lawful obedience, neither yet that ye assist nor promote those that seek authority and pre-eminence of worldly glory, yea, of the oppression and destruction of others: I mean of him[2] who in the beginning of his authority and government began to profess Christ's truth, but suddenly sliding back, became a cruel persecutor of Christ's members, a manifest and open oppressor of all true subjects, and a maintainer of all mischievous men; in which horrible vices he and his faction and assisters, I mean his nearest

[2] Knox is clearly referring here to James Hamilton, duke of Châtelherault.

kinsmen,[3] chiefest counsel to this day, do continue, and malign according to their power, which God of His just judgement shall shortly suppress. For not only the blood of those constant martyrs of Christ Jesus, Mr George Wishart, simple Adam Wallace, and of others which did suffer for Christ's cause only, but also the blood of those which, under the title of civil crimes, was most injustly shed, shall cry in the ears of the Lord of Hosts till a just and open vengeance be poured forth upon all those that sought the same; but chiefly upon him that then was in authority, except that unfeigned and speedy repentance prevent God's judgements. I shall be judged sharp; but be ye admonished to flee all confederacy with that generation; for I speak and write in the presence of Him before whose eyes the blood of His saints is so precious that no worldly power was ever found able to maintain long, or defend such as delighted in the shedding of the same. And therefore, unto such time as ye see some signs of repentance in them, I say yet again, avoid over great familiarity with them.

That now I persuade you to give lawful obedience to the authority is nothing repugnant to that which I wrote before touching the war begun; for a great difference there is betwixt lawful obedience and a fearful flattering of princes, or an injust accomplishment of their desires in things which be required or devised for the destruction of a commonwealth. But this article I omit for this present.

The mighty spirit of the Lord Jesus rule your hearts in the true fear of God, open your eyes to consider your duties, and give you strength to execute the same. Amen.

From Dieppe, the 17th of December 1557.

Yours to command in godliness,

JOHN KNOX

[3] Primarily John Hamilton, archbishop of St Andrews, half-brother of Châtelherault, and Gavin Hamilton, commendator of Kilwinning.

Letters to the regent and nobility, 22 May 1559

[Shortly after his final return to Scotland on 2 May 1559, there was an outbreak of iconoclastic rioting in the town of Perth (St Johnston) inspired by Knox's preaching against idolatry. As a result Mary of Guise began to concentrate troops around the town to suppress the Protestant rebels. The following extract from Knox's *History* (Laing MS, fos. 113v–118r; Laing, vol. 1, pp. 325–36; Dickinson, vol. 1, pp. 164–72) shows the Congregation preparing their ideological defences in the form of letters to the regent and the nobility. It is not certain that Knox wrote them, but the style and content make it extremely likely.]

The certainty hereof[1] coming to our knowledge, some of us repaired to the town again, about the 22 day of May, and there did abide for the comfort of our brethren. Where, after invocation of the name of God, we began to put the town and ourselves in such strength as we thought might best [serve] for our just defence. And because we were not utterly despaired of the queen's favours, we caused to form a letter to her grace, as followeth:

To the Queen's Grace Regent, all humble obedience and duty premised.

As heretofore, with jeopard of our lives, and yet with willing hearts, we have served the authority of Scotland, and your Grace, now regent in this realm, in service to our bodies dangerous and painful; so now, with most dolorous minds, we are constrained by injust tyranny purposed against us to declare unto your Grace that, except this cruelty be stayed by your wisdom, we will be compelled to take the sword of just defence against all that shall pursue us for the matter

[1] That is, of military action being taken against the Protestant Congregation in Perth.

of religion, and for our conscience sake, which ought not nor may not be subject to mortal creatures further than by God's Word man be able to prove that he hath power to command us. We signify moreover unto your Grace that, if by rigour we be compelled to seek the extreme defence, that we will not only notify our innocency and petitions to the king of France, to our mistress and to her husband,[2] but also to the princes and council of every Christian realm, declaring unto them that this cruel, injust and most tyrannical murder, intended against towns and multitudes, was and is the only cause of our revolt from our accustomed obedience, which, in God's presence, we faithfully promise to our sovereign mistress, to her husband, and unto your Grace Regent; provided that our consciences may live in that peace and liberty which Christ Jesus hath purchased till us by His blood, and that we may have His Word truly preached and holy sacraments rightly ministered unto us, without which we firmly purpose never to be subject to mortal man.

For better, we think, to expone our bodies to a thousand deaths than to hazard our souls to perpetual condemnation by denying Christ Jesus and His manifest verity; which thing not only do they that commit open idolatry, but also all such as seeing their brethren injustly pursued for the cause of religion, and having sufficient means to comfort and assist them, do nonetheless withdraw from them their debtful support. We would not your Grace should be deceived by the false persuasions of those cruel beasts, the churchmen, who affirm that your Grace needeth not greatly to regard the loss of us that profess Christ Jesus in this realm. If (as God forbid) ye give ear to their pestilent counsel, and so use against us this extremity pretended, it is to be feared that neither ye, neither yet your posterity, shall at any time after this find that obedience and faithful service within this realm which at all times you have found in us. We declare our judgements freely, as true and faithful subjects. God move your Grace's heart favourably to interpret our faithful meaning.

Further advertising your Grace that the self same thing, together with all things that we have done, or yet intend to do, we will notify by our letters to the king of France; asking of you, in the name of the eternal God, and as your Grace tenders the peace and quietness of this realm, that ye invade us not with violence till we receive answer

[2] That is, to Mary Queen of Scots, her husband, Francis, and the latter's father, Henry II, king of France.

from our mistress, her husband, and from their advised council there. And thus we commit your Grace to the protection of the Omnipotent.

From St Johnston, the 22 of May 1559.

(*Sic subscribitur*)

Your Grace's obedient subjects in all things not repugnant to God,

The Faithful Congregation of Christ Jesus in Scotland.

In the same tenor we wrote to Monsieur d'Oysel in French, requiring of him that by his wisdom he would mitigate the queen's rage, and the rage of the priests; otherwise that flame, which then began to burn, would so kindle that, when some men would, it could not be slakened. Adding further that he declared himself no faithful servant to his master the king of France if for the pleasure of the priests he would persecute us, and so compel us to take the sword of just defence. In like manner we wrote to Captain Serra la Burse,[3] and to all other captains and French soldiers in general, admonishing them that their vocation was not to fight against us natural Scottishmen; neither yet that they had any such commandment of their master. We besought them therefore not to provoke us to enmity against them, considering that they had found us favourable in their most extreme necessities. We declared further unto them that, if they entered in hostility and bloody war against us, that the same should remain longer than their and our lives, to wit, even in all posterity to come, so long as natural Scottishmen should have power to revenge such cruelty and most horrible ingratitude.

These letters were caused [to] be spread abroad in great abundance to the end that some might come to the knowledge of men. The queen regent her letter was laid upon her cushion in the chapel royal at Stirling where she [was] accustomed to sit at mass. She looked upon it and put it in the pocket of her gown. Monsieur d'Oysel and the captains received theirs delivered even by their own soldiers (for some among them were favourers of the truth), who after the reading of them began to rive their own beards; for that was the modest behaviour of Monsieur d'Oysel when truth was told unto him, so that it repugn to his fantasy. These our letters were suppressed to the uttermost of their power, and yet they came to the knowledge of

[3] Corbeyran de Cardaillac-Sarlabous, commander of the French garrison at Dunbar.

many. But the rage of the queen and priests could not be stayed; but forward they move[d] against us, who then were but a very few and mean number of gentlemen in St Johnston. We perceiving the extremity to approach did write to all brethren to repair towards us for our relief; to the which we found all men so ready bent that the work of God was evidently to be espied. And because that we would omit no diligence to declare our innocency to all men, we formed a letter to those of the nobility who then persecuted us, as after followeth:

To the nobility of Scotland, the Congregations of Christ Jesus within the same desire the spirit of righteous judgement.

Because we are not ignorant that the nobility of this realm who now persecute us, employing their whole study and force to maintain the kingdom of Satan, of superstition and idolatry, are yet nonetheless divided in opinion; WE, the Congregation of Christ Jesus, by you injustly persecuted, have thought good, in one letter, to write unto you severally.

Ye are divided, we say, in opinion; for some of you think that we who have taken upon us this enterprise to remove idolatry, and the monuments of the same, to erect the true preaching of Christ Jesus in the bounds committed to our charges, are heretics, seditious men, and troublers of this commonwealth, and therefore that no punishment is sufficient for us. And so, blinded with this rage, and under pretence to serve the authority, ye proclaim war and threaten destruction without all order of law against us. To you, we say, that neither your blind zeal, neither yet the colour of authority, shall excuse you in God's presence, who commandeth none to suffer death till that he be openly convicted in judgement to have offended against God and against His law written, which no mortal creature is able to prove against us. For whatsoever we have done, the same we have done at God's commandment, who plainly commands idolatry and all monuments of the same to be destroyed and abolished. Our earnest and long request hath been, and is, that in open assembly it may be disputed in presence of indifferent auditors whether that these abominations, named by the pestilent papists religion, which they by fire and sword defend, be the true religion of Christ Jesus or not? Now, this our humble request denied unto us, our lives are sought in most cruel manner.

[*Deut.* 17.6.]

The perpetual request of the Protestants of Scotland.

And ye, the nobility (whose duty is to defend innocents, and to bridle the fury and rage of wicked men, were it of princes or emperors) do notwithstanding follow their appetites, and arm yourselves against us, your brethren and natural countrymen; yea, against us that be innocent and just, as concerning all such crimes as be laid to our charges. If ye think that we be criminal because that we dissent from your opinion, consider, we beseech you, that the Prophets under the Law, the Apostles of Christ Jesus after His ascension, His primitive church and holy martyrs did disassent from the whole world in their days; and will ye deny but that their action was just, and that all those that persecuted them were murderers before God? May not the like be true this day? What assurance have ye this day of your religion which the world that day had not of theirs? Ye have a multitude that agree with you, and so had they. Ye have antiquity of time, and that they lacked not. Ye have councils, laws and men of reputation that have established all things, as ye suppose. But none of all these can make any religion acceptable unto God, which only dependeth upon His own will, revealed to man in His most sacred Word.

Is it not then a wonder that ye sleep in so deadly a security in the matter of your own salvation, considering that God giveth unto you so manifest tokens that ye and your leaders are both declined from God? For if 'the tree shall be judged by the fruit' (as Christ Jesus affirmeth that it must be), then of necessity it is that your prelates, and the whole rabble of their clergy, be evil trees. For if adultery, pride, ambition, drunkenness, covetousness, incest, unthankfulness, oppression, murder, idolatry, and blasphemy be evil fruits, there can none of that generation, which claim to themselves the title of churchmen, be judged good trees; for all these pestilent and wicked fruits do they bring forth in greatest abundance. And if they be evil trees (as ye yourselves must be compelled to confess they are), advise prudently with what consciences ye can maintain them to occupy the room and place in the Lord's vineyard. Do ye not consider that in so doing ye labour to maintain the servants of sin in their filthy corruption; and so consequently ye labour that the devil may reign and still abuse this realm by all iniquity and tyranny, and that Christ Jesus and His blessed Evangel be suppressed and extinguished?

[Matt. 12.38.]

Probation against the papists.

The name and the cloak of the authority, which ye pretend, will nothing excuse you in God's presence; but rather shall ye bear double condemnation, for that ye burden God, as that His good ordinance

Against such as under colour of

authority persecute their brethren.

were the cause of your iniquity. All authority which God hath established is good and perfect, and is to be obeyed of all men, yea, under the pain of damnation. But do ye not understand that there is a great difference betwixt the authority which is God's ordinance and the persons of those which are placed in authority? The authority and God's ordinance can never do wrong; for it commandeth that vice and wicked men be punished, and virtue, with virtuous men and just, be maintained. But the corrupt person placed in this authority may offend, and most commonly doth the contrary hereof; and is then the corruption of the person to be followed by reason that he is clad with the name of the authority? Or shall those that obey the wicked commandment of those that are placed in authority be excusable before God? Not so; not so. But the plagues and vengeances of God taken upon kings, their servants and subjects, do witness to us the plain contrary.

Difference betwixt the person and the authority. [*Rom.* 13.]

[*Exod.* 1, 5.]

Pharaoh was a king, and had his authority of God, who commanded his subjects to murder and torment the Israelites, and at last most cruelly to persecute their lives. But was their obedience (blind rage it should be called) excusable before God? The universal plague doth plainly declare that the wicked commander, and those that obeyed, were alike guilty before God. And if the example of Pharaoh shall be rejected because he was an Ethnic, then let us consider the facts of Saul. He was a king anointed of God, appointed to reign over His people; he commanded to persecute David because (as he alleged) David was a traitor and usurper of the crown; and likewise commanded Ahimelech the high priest and his fellows to be slain. But did God approve any part of this obedience? Evident it is that He did not. And think ye that God will approve in you that which He did damn in others? Be not deceived: with God there is no such partiality. If ye obey the injust commandments of wicked rulers, ye shall suffer God's vengeance and just punishment with them. And therefore, as ye tender your own salvation, we most earnestly require of you moderation, and that ye stay yourselves, and the fury of others, from persecuting of us, till our cause be tried in lawful and open judgement.

The fact of King Saul. [1 *Sam.* 18, 19.] [1 *Sam.* 22.]

And now, to you that are persuaded of the justice of our cause, that sometime have professed Christ Jesus with us, and that also have exhorted us to this enterprise, and yet have left us in our extreme necessity, or at the least look through your fingers in this our trouble, as that the matter appertained not unto you; we say, that unless (all fear and worldly respects set aside) ye join yourselves with us, that as of God ye are reputed traitors, so shall ye be excommunicated from our society, and from all participation with us in the administration of sacraments. The glory of this victory, which God shall give to His church, yea, even in the eyes of men, shall not appertain to you; but the fearful judgement which apprehended Ananias and his wife Sapphira shall apprehend you and your posterity. Ye may perchance contemn and despise the excommunication of the church, now by God's mighty power erected amongst us, as a thing of no force; but yet doubt we nothing but that our church, and the true ministers of the same, have the same power which our Master, Christ Jesus, granted to His Apostles in these words: 'Whose sins ye shall forgive, shall be forgiven; and whose sins ye shall retain, shall be retained'; and that because they preach and we believe the same doctrine which is contained in His most blessed Word. And therefore except that ye will contemn Christ Jesus, ye neither can despise our threatening, neither yet refuse us calling for your just defence.

[*Acts* 5.]

[*John* 20.23.]

By your fainting, and by extracting of your support, the enemies are encouraged, thinking that they shall find no resistance. In which point, God willing, they shall be deceived. For if they were ten thousand, and we but one thousand, they shall not murder the least of our brethren, but we (God assisting us) shall first commit our lives in the hands of God for their defence. But this shall aggravate your damnation; for ye declare yourselves both traitors to the truth once professed and murderers of us, and of your brethren, from whom ye draw your debtful and promised support, whom your only presence (to man's judgement) might preserve from this danger. For our enemies look not to the power of God, but to the force and strength of man. When the number is mean to resist them, then rage they as bloody wolves; but a party equal or able to resist them in appearance doth bridle their fury. Examine your own consciences and weigh that sentence of our Master, Christ Jesus, saying: 'Whosoever denyeth me, or is ashamed of me before men, I shall deny him before my Father.' Now is the day of His battle in this realm. If ye deny us, your brethren, suffering for His name's sake, ye do also deny Him, as Himself doth witness in these words: 'Whatsoever ye did to any

[*Matt.* 10.33.]

of these little ones, that ye did to me; and what ye did not to one of those little ones, that ye did not to me.'[4] If these sentences be true, as concerning meat, drink, clothing and such things as appertain to the body, shall they not be likewise true in these things that appertain to the preservation of the lives of thousands, whose blood is now sought, for profession of Christ Jesus?

And thus shortly leave we you, who sometimes have professed Christ Jesus with us, to the examination of your own consciences. And yet once again, of you who, blinded by superstition, persecute us, we require moderation, till our cause may be tried, which if ye will not grant unto us for God's cause, yet we desire you to have respect to the preservation of our common country, which we cannot sooner betray in the hands of strangers than that one of us destroy and murder another. Consider our petitions, and call for the spirit of righteous judgement.

[4] I can find no exact equivalent of this, but it is possibly a paraphrase of Matthew 18.1–6.

The regent and the Congregation, August 1559

[Although the rebellion – and civil war – may be said to have begun in May 1559, neither side was in a position to force a decisive engagement that might resolve the issue. Instead, having fortified the port of Leith, the regent sought further military support from France, while the Congregation appealed for the intervention of England. The result was a temporary truce – the Appointment of Leith of 24 July 1559 – the terms of which became an immediate focus of dispute. The following extract from Knox's *History* (Laing MS, fos. 143r–149v; Laing, vol. I, pp. 397–412; Dickinson, vol. I, pp. 217–28) begins with a proclamation of the regent defending the arrival of French reinforcements and continues with the Congregation's response to the regent's arguments. Again, it is not clear that Knox himself was the author of the latter document, but the 'supplement' to the public letter, essentially a defence of the Protestant preachers' attitude to the 'authority', bears distinctive Knoxian hallmarks.]

A proclamation set out by the queen regent to blind the vulgar people.

FORSAMEKLE as we understand that certain seditious persons has invented and blown abroad diverse rumours and evil bruits, tending thereby to stir up the hearts of the people, and so to stop all reconciliations betwixt us and our subjects, being of the number of the Congregation, and consequently to kindle and nourish continual strife and division in this realm, to the manifest subversion of the whole estates thereof; and amongst other purposes, has maliciously devised for that effect, and has persuaded to many, that we have violated the Appointment lately tane, in so far as any more Frenchmen sensyne are come in; and that we are minded to draw in great forces of men of war forth of France to suppress the liberty of this realm, oppress the inhabitants thereof, and make up strangers with their lands and goods; which reports are all (God knows) most vain, feigned and untrue. For it is of truth, that nothing has been done on our part since the said Appointment, whereby it may be alleged that any point thereof has been contravened; nor yet was at that time anything communed or concluded to stop the sending in of Frenchmen, as may clearly appear by inspection of the said Appointment, which the bearer hereof has presently to show.[1] What[ever] number of men of war be arrived, we [have] such regard to our honour, and quietness of this realm, that in case in the room of every one Frenchman that is in Scotland there were a hundred at our command, yet should not for that any jot that is promised be broken, or any alteration be made by our provocation; but the said proclamation[2] truly and surely observed in every point, if the said Congregation will in like manner faithfully keep their part thereof.

Nor yet mean we to trouble any man in the peaceable possession of their goods and rooms, nor yet to enrich the crown, and far less any stranger, with your substance; for our dearest son and daughter, the king and queen, are by God's provision placed in the room, where all men of judgement may well consider they have no need of any man's goods. And for our self, we seek nothing but debtful obedience unto them, such as good subjects ought to give to their sovereigns, without diminution of your liberties and privileges, or alteration of your laws. Therefore, we thought good to notify unto you our good mind foresaid, and desires you not to give ear nor credit to such vain imaginations, whereof, before God, no part ever entered in our conceit; nor suffer yourselves be thereby led from your due obedience; assuring you, ye shall ever find with us truth in promises, and a motherly love towards all, you behaving yourselves our obedient subjects.

But of one thing we give you warning, that whereas some preachers of the Congregation, in their public sermons, speaks irreverently and slanderously, as well of princes in general as of our self in particular, and of the obedience to the higher powers; inducing the people, by that part of their doctrine, to defection from their duty, which pertains nothing to religion, but rather to sedition and tumult, things direct

[1] The fifth clause of the Appointment as drawn up by the Congregation had stipulated that no more Frenchmen should be brought into the country without the consent of the nobility and parliament. This clause, however, appears to have been dropped from the final document drawn up at Leith.

[2] That is, the Appointment.

contrary to religion; therefore, we desire you to take order in your town and bounds, that when the preachers repair there, they use themselves more modestly in these behalfs, and in their preaching not to mell so mekle with civil policy and public governance, nor yet name us, or other princes, but with honour and reverence, otherwise it will not be suffered. Attour, since ye have presently the declaration of our intention, we desire to know likewise what shall be your part to us, that we may understand what to lippin for at your hands; whereof we desire a plain declaration in writ, with this bearer, without excuse or delay.

At Edinburgh, the 28 of August 1559.

*****

The answer to this former proclamation was made in form as follows:

To the nobility, burghs and community of this realm of Scotland, the lords, barons and others, brethren of the Christian Congregation, wishes increase of wisdom, with the advancement of the glory of God, and of the commonwealth, etc., etc.

The love of our native country craves, the defence of our honours requires, and the sincerity of our consciences compels us (dearest Brethren) to answer some part to the last writings and proclamations set forth by the Queen's Grace Regent, no less to make us and our cause odious, than to abuse your simplicity to your final destruction, conspired of old, and now already put to work.

And first, where she alleges certain seditious persons have of malice invented and blown abroad diverse rumours, [tending] thereby (as she alleges) to stir up the hearts of the people to sedition, by reason that the Frenchmen are croppin in of late in our country; true it is (dear Brethren) that all such as bear natural love to their country, to you, their brethren, inhabitants thereof, to our houses, wives, bairns, the esperance of your posterity, and shortly to your commonwealth, and the ancient laws and liberties thereof, cannot but in heart lament, with mouth and tears complain, the most crafty assaults devised and practised, to the utter ruin of all these things forenamed; and that so manifestly is gone to work, that even in our eyes our dearest brethren, true members of our commonwealth, are most cruelly oppressed by strangers, in so far that some are banished their own houses, some robbed and spulzied of their substance, conqueist by their just labours in the sweat of their brows; some cruelly murdered at the pleasure of these inhuman soldiers; and altogether have their lives in such fear and dreddour, as if the enemy were in the midst of them; so that nothing can seem pleasing unto them which they possess in the bowels of their native country; so near judges every man (and not but just cause) the practice used upon their brethren to approach next unto them their selves, wives, bairns, houses and substances, which altogether are cassin at the feet of strangers, men of war, to be by them thus abused at their unbridled lust's desire.

Now, if it be sedition (dear Brethren) to complain, lament and pour forth before God the sorrows [and] sobs of our dolorous hearts, crying to Him for redress of these enormities (which elsewhere is not to be found); and these altogether do [proceed] of the unlawful holding of strange soldiers over the heads of our brethren; if this to complain be sedition, then indeed (dear Brethren) can none of us be purged of that crime; for as in very heart we damn such inhuman cruelty, with the wicked and crafty pretence thereof, so can we, nor dare we not, neither by mouths speaking nor yet by keeping of silence, justify the same. Neither do we here aggrege the breaking of the Appointment made at Leith (which always has manifestly been done); but when we remember what oath we have made to our commonwealth, and how the duty we owe to the same compels us to cry out that her Grace, by wicked and ungodly counsel, goes most craftily about utterly to oppress the same, and the ancient laws and liberties thereof, as well against the king of France's promise, her own duty, in respect of the high promotions that she received thereby, which justly should have caused her to have been indeed that which she would be called (and is nothing less in verity), to wit, a careful mother over this commonwealth; but what motherly care she has used towards you, ye cannot be ignorant. Have ye not been, even from the first entres of her reign, ever smited and oppressed with unaccustomed and exorbitant taxations, [more] than ever were used within this realm? Yea, and how far was it sought here to have been brought in upon you and your posterity, under colour to have been laid up in store for the wars? The inquisition tane of all your goods, movable and immovable, by way of testament; the seeking of the whole coal and salt of this realm, to have been laid up in store and girnall, and she alone to have been merchant thereof, does teach you by experience some of her motherly care.

Again, what care over your commonwealth does her Grace instantly bear, when even now presently, and of a long time bygone, by the ministry of some (who better deserve the gallows than ever did Cochrane), she does so corrupt the layit money,[3] and has brought it in such baseness, and such quantity of scruiff,[4] that all men that has their eyes open may perceive an extreme beggary to be brought therethrough upon the whole realm, so that the whole exchange and traffic to be had with foreign nations (a thing most necessary in all commonwealths) shall thereby be utterly extinguished; and all the gains received thereby is that she therewith entertains strangers upon our heads. For, Brethren, ye know that her money has served for no other purpose in our commonwealth this long time bygone; and the impunity of these wicked ministers (whom lately we spake of) has brought the matter to such a licentious enormity, and plain contempt of the commonwealth, that now they spare not plainly to break down and convert the good and stark money, cunzied in our sovereign's less age, into this their corrupted scruiff and baggage of hard-heads and non-sunts,[5] most like that she and they had conspired to destroy all the whole good cunzie of this realm, and consequently that part of the commonwealth. Besides all this, their clipped and rounged sous,[6] which had no passage these three years past in the realm of France, are commanded to have course in this realm to gratify thereby her new come soldiers. And all these things together are done without the advice or consent of the nobility and council of this realm, and manifestly therethrough against our ancient laws and liberties.

Thirdly, her last and most weighty proceeding more fully declares her motherly care her Grace bears to our commonwealth and us, when in time of peace, but any occasion of foreign wars, thousands of strangers are laid here and there upon the necks of our poor members of this commonwealth; their idle bellies fed upon the poor substance of the community, conqueist by their just labours in the painful sweat of their brows. Which to be true, Dunbar, North Berwick, Tranent, Prestonpans, Musselburgh, Leith, Canongate,

[3] 'Layit money' was base money made from alloy.

[4] 'Scruiff' or 'scruff' literally means encrusted skin or a scab, hence its meaning here of base coinage with a thin covering of precious metal.

[5] 'Hard-heads' or 'lions' were small coins of base metal with the royal cipher, crowned, on one side and a lion rampant on the other. 'Non-sunts' were similarly of base metal, bearing the arms of Francis and Mary and deriving their name from the legend on the obverse: *iam non sunt duo sed una caro*.

[6] That is, French coinage that had been clipped or worn away by a file.

Kinghorn, Kirkcaldy, Dysart, with the depauperate souls that this day dwell therein, can testify; whose oppression, as doubtless it is entered in before the justice seat of God, so ought it justly to move our hearts to have ruth and compassion upon these our poor brethren, and at our powers to provide remedy for the same. And albeit her strangers had been garnissed with money (as ye know well they were not), yet can their here lying be no ways but most hurtful to our commonwealth, seeing that the fertility of this realm has never been so plenteous that it was able of any continuance to sustain the self, and inhabitants thereof, without support of foreign countries; far less able, besides the same, to sustain thousands of strangers wherewith it is burdened to the dearthing of all vivers, as the murmur and complaint of Edinburgh this day does testify. But to what effect the commonwealth is this way burdened, the end does declare; for shortly were there brought to the fields against our sovereign's true lieges, even us your brethren, who (God knows) sought not else but peace of conscience, under protection of our sovereign, and reformation of these enormities, for no other cause but that we would not renounce the Evangel of Jesus Christ and subdue our necks under the tyranny of that man of sin, the Roman Antichrist, and his forsworn shavelings, who at all times most tyrannically oppressed our souls with hunger of God's true Word, and reft our goods and substances, to waste the same upon their foul lust and stinking harlots.

But (O dear Brethren) this was not the chief pretence and final scope of her proceedings (as these days do well declare); for had not God given in our hearts to withstand that oppression with weapons of most just defence, thou, O St Johnston and Dundee, had been in no better estate nor your sister of Leith is this day. For though we in very deed (God is witness) meant then nothing but, in the simplicity of our hearts, the maintenance of true religion, and safety of our brethren professors of the same, yet lay there another serpent lurking in the breast of our adversaries, as this day (praise to God) is plainly opened to all that list behold, to wit, to bring you and us both under the perpetual servitude of strangers. For we being appointed, as ye know, touching religion to be reasoned in the council at the day affixed,[7] and no occasion made to break the same on our side (as is

[7] The first clause of the Leith Appointment as drawn up by the Congregation specified that a parliament was to be held on 10 January 1560 to decide the religious controversy.

well known), yet come there forth writings and complaints that this day and that day we were prepared to invade her Grace's person (when in very truth there was never such thing thought, as the very deed has declared); but because she was before deliberate to bring in Frenchmen to both our destructions, that ye should not stir therewith, she made you to understand that those bands came only for the safety of her own person.

O craft, Brethren! O subtlety! But behold the end. They are come (yet [not] so many, no, not the sixth part that she desired and looked for), and how? Not only with weapons to defend her Grace's person, but with wives and bairns, to plant in your native rooms, as they have already begun in the town of Leith, the principal port and staple of all this realm, the girnall and furnitour of the council and seat of justice; and here will they dwell while they may reinforce them with greater number of their fellow soldiers, to subdue then the rest, if God withstand not. And yet her Grace feared nor ashamed not to write: 'If they were a hundred Frenchmen for every one of them that is in Scotland, yet they should harm no man.' Tell thou now, Leith! if that be true; if this be not a crafty entry to a manifest conquest, forethought of old, judge you, dear Brethren! Thus to fort our towns, and even the principal port of our realm, and to lay so strong garrisons of strangers therein, without any consent of the nobility and council of this realm, but express against their mind (as our writings sent to her Grace bears record), if this be not to oppress the ancient laws and liberties of our realm, let all wise men say to it. And further, to take the barnyards new gathered, the girnalls replenished, the houses garnissed, and to sit down therein, and by force to put the just possessors and ancient inhabitants therefrom, with their wives, bairns and servants, to shift [for] themselves in begging, if there be no other means, they being true Scotsmen, members of our commonwealth, and our dear brethren and sisters, born, fostered and brought up in the bowels of our common and native country; if this be not the manifest declaration of their old pretence and mind to the whole Scots nation, let your own conscience (Brethren) be judge herein. Was all Leith of the Congregation? No, I think not; yet were all alike served.

The cause of the Frenchmen's coming with wife and bairns.

Let this motherly care then be tried by the fruits thereof. First, by the great and exorbitant taxations used upon you, and yet ten times greater pressed at, as ye know. Secondly, the utter depravation of our cunzie, to conqueiss thereby money to entertain strangers, French soldiers, upon you, to make them strongholds, lest ye should sometime expel them out of your native rooms. Thirdly, by the daily reinforcing of the said French soldiers, in strength and number, with wives and bairns, planting in your brethren's houses and possessions. Indeed, her Grace is, and has been at all times, careful to procure by her craft of fair words, fair promises, and sometimes buds, to allure your simplicity to that point, to join yourself to her soldiers, to danton and oppress us, that ye the remanent (we being cut off) may be an easy prey to her sleights, which God, of His infinite goodness, has now discovered to the eyes of all that list to behold. But credit the works (dear Brethren) if ye will not credit us; and lay the example of foreign nations, yea, of your own brethren, before your eyes, and procure not your own ruin willingly. If ye tender true religion, ye see how her Grace bears her[self] plain enemy thereto, and maintains the tyranny of their idle bellies, the bishops, against God's kirk. If religion be not persuaded unto you, yet cast ye not away the care ye ought to have over your commonwealth, which ye see manifestly and violently ruined before your eyes. If this will not move you, remember your dear wives, children and posterity, your ancient heritages and houses; and think well these strangers will regard no more your right thereunto than they have done your brethren's of Leith, whenever occasion shall serve.

But if ye purpose, as we doubt not but that all they that either have wit or manhood will declare and prove indeed, to brook your ancient rooms and heritages, conquered most valiantly, and defended by your most noble progenitors against all strangers, invaders of the same, as the French pretends plainly this day; if ye will not be slaves unto them, and to have your lives, your wives, your bairns, your substance, and whatsoever is dear unto you, cassin at their feet, to be used and abused at the pleasure of strange soldiers, as ye see your brethren's at this day before your eyes; if ye will not have experience some day hereof in your own persons (as we suppone the least of you would not gladly have, but rather would choose with honour to die in defence of his own native room than live and serve so shameful a servitude); then, Brethren, let us join our forces, and both with wit and manhood resist these beginnings or else our liberties hereafter shall be dearer bought. Let us surely be persuaded, 'when our neighbour's house be on fire, that we dwell not without danger'. Let no man withdraw himself herefrom; and if any will be so unhappy and mischievous (as

A proverb.

we suppone none to be), let us altogether repute, hold and use him (as he is indeed) for an enemy to us, and to himself and to his commonweal.

The eternal and omnipotent God, the true and only revenger of the oppressed, be our comfort and our protector against the fury and rage of the tyrants of this world; and especially from the insatiable covetousness of the Guisian's generation. AMEN.

Besides this, our public letter, some men answered certain heads of her said proclamation on this manner:

If it be seditious to speak the truth in all sobriety, and to complain when they are wounded, or to call for help against unjust tyranny before that their throats be cut, then can we not deny but we are criminal and guilty of tumult and sedition. For we have said that our commonwealth is oppressed, that we and our brethren are hurt by the tyranny of strangers, and that we fear bondage and slavery, seeing that multitudes of cruel murderers are daily brought in our country without our counsel or knowledge and consent. We dispute not so mekill whether the bringing in of more Frenchmen be violating of the Appointment (which the Queen nor her faction cannot deny to be manifestly broken by them, in more cases than one), as that we would know if that the heaping of strangers upon strangers above us, without our counsel or consent, be a thing that may stand with the liberty of our realm, and with the profit of our commonwealth. It is not unknown to all men of judgement that the fruits of our country, in the most common years, be no more than sufficient reasonable to nourish the born inhabitants of the same. But now, seeing that we have been vexed with wars, taken upon us at the pleasure of France, by the which the most fruitful portion of our country in corns has been wasted; what man is so blind but that he may see that such bands of ungodly and idle soldiers can be nothing else but an occasion to famish our poor brethren? And in this point we refuse not (which is the chief) the judgement of all natural Scotsmen.

The Queen Regent alleged that, although there were a hundred Frenchmen for one in Scotland, yet she is not minded to trouble any in his just possession. Whereto we answer that we dispute not what she intends (which nonetheless, by probable conjectures, is to be suspected); but always we affirm that such a multitude of Frenchmen is a burden, not only unprofitable, but also intolerable to this poor realm, especially being entreated as they are by her and Monsieur d'Oysel; for if their wages be paid out of France, then are they both (the Queen, we say, and Monsieur d'Oysel) traitors to the king and council; for the poor commons of this realm have sustained them with the sweat of their brows, since the contracting of peace, and somewhat before.

What motherly affection she has declared to this realm, and to the inhabitants of the same, her works have evidently declared, even since the first hour that she has borne authority; and albeit men will not this day see what danger hangs over their heads, yet fear we that, or it be long, experience shall teach some that we fear not without cause. The cruel murder and oppression used by them whom now she fosters is to us a sufficient argument what is to be looked for when her number is so multiplied that our force shall not be able to gainstand their tyranny.

The doctrine of our preachers concerning obedience to be given to magistrates.

Where she complains of our preachers, affirming that irreverently they speak of princes in general and of her in particular, inducing the people thereby to defection from their duty etc., and therefore that such thing cannot be suffered; because this accusation is laid[8] against God's true ministers, we cannot but witness what tred and order of doctrine they have kept and yet keep in that point. In public prayers they commend to God all princes in general, and the magistrates of this our native realm in particular. In open audience they declare the authority of princes and magistrates to be of God; and therefore they affirm that they ought to be honoured, feared, obeyed, even for conscience sake, provided that they command nor require nothing expressly repugning to God's commandment and plain will, revealed in His Holy Word. Moreover, they affirm that if wicked persons, abusing the authority established by God, command things manifestly wicked, that such as may and do bridle their inordinate appetites of princes, cannot be accused as resisters of the authority, which is God's good ordinance. To bridle the fury and rage of princes in free kingdoms and realms, they affirm it appertains to the nobility, sworn and born counsellors of the same, and also to the barons and people, whose votes and consent are to be required in all great and weighty matters of the commonwealth. Which if they do not, they

[8] Laing MS: occasion is had.

declare themselves criminal with their princes, and so subject to the same vengeance of God, which they deserve for that, that they pollute the seat of justice, and do, as it were, make God author of iniquity. They proclaim and they cry that the same God who plagued Pharaoh, repulsed Sennacherib, struck Herod with worms, and made the bellies of dogs the grave and sepulchre of despiteful Jezebel, will not spare the cruel princes, murderers of Christ's members in this our time.

On this manner they speak of princes in general and of your Grace in particular. This only we have heard one of our preachers say, rebuking the vain excuse of such as flatter themselves, by reason of the authority: 'Many now a days (said he) will have no other religion nor faith than the Queen and the authority has. But is it [not] possible that the Queen be so far blinded that she will have no religion nor no other faith than may content to the cardinal of Lorraine?[9] And may it not likewise be able that the cardinal be so corrupt that he will admit no religion which does not establish the pope in his kingdom? But plain it is that the pope is lieutenant to Satan, and enemy to Christ Jesus, and to His perfect religion. Let men therefore consider what danger they stand in if their salvation shall depend upon the Queen's faith and religion.' Further we have never heard any of our preachers speak of the Queen Regent, neither publicly nor privately. Where her Grace declares: 'It will not be suffered that our preachers mell with policy, nor speak of her nor of other princes but with reverence', we answer that as we will justify and defend nothing in our preachers which we find not God to have justified and allowed in His messengers before them, so dare we not forbid them openly to reprehend that which the Spirit of God, speaking in the Prophets and Apostles, has reprehended before them. Elijah did personally reprove Ahab and Jezebel of idolatry, of avarice, of murder; and such like Isaiah the Prophet called the magistrates of Jerusalem in his times companions to thieves, princes of Sodom, bribe-takers and murderers. He complained that their silver was turned into dross, that their wine was mingled with water, and that justice was bought and sold. Jeremiah said that the bones of King Jehoiakim should wither with the sun. Christ Jesus called Herod a fox; and Paul called the high priest a painted wall, and prayed unto God that He should

The Prophets have meddled with policy, and has reproved the corruption thereof. [*1 Kgs 18; Isa. 1.*] [*Jer. 8.1–2.; 22.18–19.*] [*Luke 13.32.*]

[9] That is, the regent's brother, Charles of Guise, cardinal of Lorraine.

[*Acts* 23.3.] strike him, because that against justice he commanded him to be smitten. Now if the like or greater corruptions be in to the world this day, who dare enterprise to put silence to the Spirit of God, which [will] not be subject to the appetites of wicked princes?

The suspension of the regent, October 1559

[By October 1559, while the regent continued to fortify Leith, the Congregation – reinforced by the accession of the duke of Châtelherault to their ranks – were in possession of Edinburgh and contemplating military action against the regent's French troops. The following extract from Knox's *History* (Laing MS, fos. 163r–167r; Laing, vol. I, pp. 441–9; Dickinson, vol. I, pp. 249–55) gives details of the debate among the Congregation preceding their decision formally to 'suspend' the regent's authority. In fact, the subsequent siege of Leith proved wholly abortive and the Congregation were never in a position to enforce their deposition.]

The order of the suspension of the Queen Regent from the authority within Scotland.

The whole nobility, barons and burghs then present were commanded to convene in the Tolbooth of Edinburgh the same 21 day of October for deliberation of these matters. Where the whole cause being exponed by the Lord Ruthven, the question was proponed: 'Whether she that so contemptuously refused the most humble request of the born counsellors of the realm, being also but a regent, whose pretences threatened the bondage of the whole commonwealth, ought to be suffered so tyrannously to empire above them?' And because that this question had not been before disputed in open assembly, it was thought expedient that the judgement of the preachers should be required; who being called and instructed in the case, John Willock, who before had sustained the burden of the church in Edinburgh, commanded to speak, made discourse as followeth, affirming:

The discourse of John Willock.

1. 'First, that albeit magistrates be God's ordinance, having of Him power and authority, yet is not their power so largely extended but that [it] is bounded and limited by God in His Word.

2. 'And secondarily, that as subjects are commanded to obey their magistrates, so are magistrates commanded to give some duty to the subjects; so that God by His Word has prescribed the office of the one and of the other.

3. 'Thirdly, that albeit God hath appointed magistrates His lieutenants on earth, and has honoured them with His own title, calling them gods, that yet He did never so establish any but that for just causes they might have been deprived.

4. 'Fourthly, that in deposing of princes, and those that had been in authority, God did not always use His immediate power; but sometimes He used other means which His wisdom thought good and justice approved, as by Asa He removed Maachah his own mother from honour and authority which before she had brooked; by Jehu He destroyed Jehoram and the whole posterity of Ahab; and by diverse others He had deposed from authority those whom before He had established by His own Word.'

[2 Chr. 15.16.]

[2 Kgs. 9.]

And hereupon concluded he: 'That since the Queen Regent denied her chief duty to the subjects of this realm, which was to minister justice unto them indifferently, to preserve their liberties from invasion of strangers, and to suffer them have God's Word freely and openly preached amongst them; seeing, moreover, that the Queen Regent was an open and obstinate idolatress, a vehement maintainer of all superstition and idolatry; and, finally, that she utterly despised the counsel and requests of the nobility, he could see no reason why they, the born counsellors, nobility and barons of the realm, might not justly deprive her from all regiment and authority amongst them.'

The causes.

The judgement of John Knox in the deposition of the Queen Regent.

Hereafter was the judgement of John Knox required, who, approving the sentence of his brother, added:

1. 'First, that the iniquity of the Queen Regent and [her] misorder ought in no wise to withdraw neither our hearts, neither yet the hearts of other subjects, from the obedience due unto our sovereigns.

2. 'Secondarily, that and if we deposed the said Queen Regent rather of malice and private envy than for the preservation of the commonwealth, and for that her sins appeared incurable, that we should not escape God's just punishment, howsoever that she had deserved rejection from honours.

3. 'And thirdly, he required that no such sentence should be pronounced against her, but that upon her known and open repentance,

and upon her conversion to the commonwealth and submission to the nobility, place should be granted unto her of regress to the same honours from the which, for just causes, she justly might be deprived.'

The votes of every man particularly by himself required, and every man commanded to speak, as he would answer to God, what his conscience judged in that matter, there was none found amongst the whole number who did not by his own tongue consent to her deprivation. Thereafter was her process committed to writ and registered as followeth:

At Edinburgh, the 21 day of October 1559. The nobility, barons and burghs convened to advise upon the affairs of the commonweal, and to aid, support and succour the same, perceiving and lamenting the enterprised destruction of their said commonweal, and overthrow of the liberty of their native country, by the means of the Queen Regent and certain strangers her privy councillors, plain contrary our sovereign lord and lady's mind, and direct against the counsel of the nobility, to proceed by little and little even unto the uttermost, so that the urgent necessity of the commonweal may suffer no longer delay, and earnestly craves our support. Seeing [t]herefore that the said Queen Regent (abusing and overpassing our sovereign lord and lady's commission, given and granted to her) has in all her proceedings pursued the barons and burghs within this realm, with weapons and armour of strangers, but any process or order of law, they being our sovereign lord and lady's true lieges and never called nor convicted in any crime by any judgement lawful; as first at St Johnston, in the month of May, she assembled her army against the town and inhabitants thereof, never called nor convicted in any crime, for that they professed true worship of God, conform to His most sacred Word; and likewise in the month of June last, without any lawful order or calling going before, invaded the persons of sundry noblemen and barons with force of arms convened at St Andrews, only for cause of religion, as is notoriously known, they never being called nor convicted in any crime. Attour laid garrisons the same month upon the inhabitants of the said town of St Johnston, oppressing the liberties of the queen's true lieges; for fear of which her garrisons, a great part of the inhabitants thereof fled of the town and durst not resort

The enormities committed by the Queen Regent.

again unto their houses and heritages, while they were restored by arms, they notwithstanding never being called nor convicted in any crime. And further, that same time did thrust in upon the heads of the inhabitants of the said town provost and bailies, against all order of election; as lately, in this last month of September, she had done in the towns of Edinburgh and Jedburgh, and diverse other places, in manifest oppression of our liberties. Last of all, declaring her evil mind toward the nobility, commonty and whole nation, has brought in strangers, and daily pretends to bring in greater force of the same; pretending a manifest conquest of our native rooms and country, as the deed itself declares.

In so far as she, having brought in the said strangers, but any advice of the council and nobility, and contrary [to] their express mind sent to her Grace in writ, has placed and planted her said strangers in one of the principal towns and ports of the realm, sending continually for greater forces, willing thereby to suppress the commonweal and liberty of our native country, to make us and our posterity slaves to strangers forever; which, as it is intolerable in commonwealths and free countries, so is it very prejudicial to our sovereign lady, and her heirs whatsomever, in case our sovereign lord decease but heirs of her Grace's person; and to perfurnish these her wicked enterprises, conceived (as appears) of inveterate malice against our whole country and nation, causes (but any consent or advice of the council and nobility) cunzie layit money, so base, and of such quantity, that the whole realm shall be depauperate, and all traffic with foreign nations everted thereby. And attour, her Grace places and maintains, contrary [to] the pleasure of the council of this realm, a stranger in one of the greatest offices of credit within this realm, that is, in keeping of the great seal thereof,[1] whereunto great perils may be ingenerate to the commonweal and liberty thereof; and further, lately sent the said great seal furth of this realm by the said stranger, contrary [to] the advice of the said council, to what effect God knows; and has else by his means altered the old law and consuetude of our realm, ever observed in the graces and pardons granted by our sovereigns to all their lieges being repentant of their offences committed against their highness or the lieges of the realm; and has introduced a new captious style and form of the said pardons and remis-

[1] Yves de Rubay.

sions, attending to the practice of France, tending thereby to draw the said lieges of this realm, by process of time, in a deceivable snare; and further, shall creep in the whole subversion and alteration of the remanent laws of this realm, in contrary the contents of the Appointment of Marriage;[2] and also peace being accorded amongst the princes, retains the great army of strangers, after command sent by the king of France to retire the same, making excuse that they were retained for suppressing of the attempts of the lieges of this realm, albeit the whole subjects thereof, of all estates, is and ever has been ready to give all debtful obedience to their sovereigns, and their lawful ministers, proceeding by God's ordinance. And the said army of strangers not being paid of wages, was laid by her Grace upon the necks of the poor community of our native country, who was compelled by force to defraud themselves, their wives and bairns, of that poor substance which they might conquiess with the sweat of their brows, to satisfy their hunger and necessities, and quit the same to sustain the idle bellies of these strangers. Through the which in all parts rose such heavy lamentation and complaint of the community, accusing the nobility and council of their sleuth, that as the same oppression we doubt not has entered in before the justice seat of God, so has it moved our hearts to ruth and compassion.

And for redressing of the same, with other great offences committed against the public weal of this realm, we have convened here, as said is; and, as oft times of before, has most humbly, and with all reverence, desired and required the said Queen Regent to redress the said enormities, and especially to remove her strangers from the necks of the poor community, and to desist from enterprising or fortification of strengths within this realm, against the express will of the nobility and council of the same. Yet we being convened the more stark for fear of her strangers, whom we saw presume no other thing but with arms to pursue our lives and possessions, besought her Grace to remove the fear of the same, and make the town patent to all our sovereign lord and lady's lieges; the same on nowise would her Grace grant unto; but when some of our company in peaceable manner went to view the said town, there was both great and small munition shot forth at them. And seeing therefore that neither access

[2] The Articles and Instructions drawn up on 15 April 1558 at the time of the marriage of Mary and Francis guaranteed the ancient laws and liberties of Scotland and similar promises were made in letters patent signed by Henry II and Francis on 19 April.

was granted to be used, nor yet her Grace would join herself to us, to consult upon the affairs of our commonweal, as we that be born counsellors to the same, by the ancient laws of the realm; but fearing the judgement of the council would reform, as necessity required, the foresaid enormities, she refuses all manner of assistance with us, and by force and violence intends to suppress the liberties of our commonweal, and of us the favourers of the same.

We, therefore, so many of the nobility, barons and provost of burghs as are touched with the care of the commonweal (unto the which we acknowledge ourselves not only born, but also sworn protectors and defenders, against all and whatsomever invaders of the same), and moved by the foresaid proceedings notorious, and with the lamentable complaint of oppression of our community, our fellow members of the same; perceiving further that the present necessity of our commonweal may suffer no delay, being convened (as said is) presently in Edinburgh, for support of our commonweal, and ripely consulted and advised, taking the fear of God before our eyes, for the causes foresaid, which are notorious, with one consent and common vote, each man in order his judgement being required, in name and authority of our sovereign lord and lady, suspends the said commission granted by our said sovereigns to the said Queen Dowager; discharging her of all administration or authority she has or may have thereby, unto the next parliament to be set by our advice and consent; and that because the said Queen, by the foresaid faults notorious, declares herself enemy to our commonweal, abusing the power of the said authority, to the destruction of the same. And likewise, we discharge all members of her said authority from henceforth; and that no cunzie be cunzied from henceforth without express consent of the said council and nobility, conform to the laws of this realm, which we maintain. And ordains this to be notified and proclaimed by officers of arms in all head burghs within the realm of Scotland. In witness of the which, our common consent and free vote, we have subscribed this present Act of Suspension with our hands, day, year and place foresaid.[3]

[3] The Laing MS has a blank half page at this point where the names of the subscribers were to be added. Other MSS and later published versions add: '(*Sic subscribitur*) By us, the Nobility and Commons of the Protestants of the Church of Scotland'.

Knox and Mary Queen of Scots, September 1561

[Mary Stewart's arrival in Scotland on 19 August 1561 prompted Knox to preach a series of sermons inveighing against the queen's idolatry and the reintroduction of the mass to the very heart of the realm. As a result, on Thursday 4 September, he was summoned to the queen's presence for the first of several personal 'reasonings' or interviews. The following extract from the *History* (Laing MS, fos. 305r–308r; Laing, vol. II, pp. 277–86; Dickinson, vol. II, pp. 13–20) is Knox's own summary of a long interview 'whereof we only touch a part'.]

Whether it was by counsel of others, or of the Queen's own desire, we know not; but the Queen spake with John Knox, and had long reasoning with him, none being present except the Lord James[1] (two gentlewomen stood in the other end of the house). The sum of their reasoning was this. The Queen accused him that he had raised a part of her subjects against her mother, and against herself; that he had written a book against her just authority (she meant the treatise against the Regiment of Women),[2] which she had, and should cause the most learned in Europe to write against it; that he was the cause of great sedition and great slaughter in England; and that it was said to her that all which he did was by necromancy, etc.

The first reasoning betwixt the Queen and John Knox.

To the which the said John answered: 'Madam, it may please your majesty patiently to hear my simple answers. And first (said he), if to teach the truth of God in sincerity, if to rebuke idolatry, and to will a people to worship God according to His Word, be to raise subjects against their princes, then cannot I be excused; for it has pleased God of His mercy to make me one (amongst many) to disclose unto

[1] Lord James Stewart.
[2] That is, *The First Blast of the Trumpet*.

this realm the vanity of the papistical religion, and the deceit, pride and tyranny of that Roman Antichrist. But, Madam, if the true knowledge of God and His right worshipping be the chief causes that must move men from their heart to obey their just princes (as it is most certain that they are) wherein can I be reprehended? I think, and am surely persuaded, that your Grace have had, and presently have, as unfeigned obedience of such as profess Jesus Christ within this realm as ever your father or other progenitors had of those that were called bishops. And touching that book which seemeth so highly to offend your majesty, it is most certain that I wrote it, and am content that all the learned of the world judge of it. I hear that an Englishman hath written against it, but I have not read him.[3] If he have sufficiently improved my reasons, and established his contrary proposition with as evident testimonies as I have done mine, I shall not be obstinate, but shall confess my error and ignorance. But to this hour I have thought, and yet thinks, myself alone to be more able to sustain the things affirmed in that my work than any ten in Europe shall be able to confute it.'

'Ye think then (quod she) that I have no just authority?'

'Please your majesty (said he) that learned men in all ages have had their judgements free, and most commonly disagreeing from the common judgement of the world; such also have they published, both with pen and tongue, and yet, notwithstanding, they themselves have lived in the common society with others, and have borne patiently with the errors and imperfections which they could not amend. Plato, the philosopher, wrote his books of the commonwealth,[4] in the which he damneth many things that then were maintained in the world and required many things to have been reformed; and yet, notwithstanding, he lived even under such policies as then were universally received without further troubling of any estate. Even so, Madam, am I content to do, in uprightness of heart and with a testimony of a good conscience. I have communicated my judgement to the world. If the realm finds no inconvenience from the regiment of a woman, that which they approve shall I not further disallow than within my own breast, but shall be as well content to live under your Grace as Paul was to live under Nero; and my hope is that, so long as that ye

[3] A reference to John Aylmer's *An Harborowe* (1559).

[4] *The Republic.*

defile not your hands with the blood of the saints of God, that neither I nor that book shall either hurt you or your authority; for in very deed, Madam, that book was written most especially against that wicked Jezebel of England.'[5]

'But (said she) ye speak of women in general.'

'Most true it is, Madam (said the other), and yet it appeareth to me that wisdom should persuade your Grace never to raise trouble for that which to this day hath not troubled your majesty, neither in person nor yet in authority. For of late years many things which before were holden stable have been called in doubt; yea, they have been plainly impugned. But yet, Madam (said he), I am assured that neither Protestant nor papist shall be able to prove that any such question was at any time moved in public or in secret. Now, Madam (said he), if I had intended to have troubled your estate because ye are a woman, I might have chosen a time more convenient for that purpose than I can do now, when your own presence is within the realm.

'But now, Madam, shortly to answer to the other two accusations. I heartily praise my God, through Jesus Christ, that Satan, the enemy of mankind, and the wicked of the world, have no other crimes to lay to my charge than such as the very world itself knoweth to be most false and vain. For in England I was resident only the space of five years. The places were Berwick, where I abode two years; so long in the New Castle; and a year in London. Now, Madam, if in any of these places, during the time that I was there, any man shall be able to prove that there was either battle, sedition or mutiny I shall confess that I myself was the malefactor and the shedder of the blood. I ashame not, Madam, further to affirm that God so blessed my weak labours that in Berwick (where commonly before there used to be slaughter by reason of quarrels that used to arise amongst soldiers) there was a[s] great quietness all the time that I remained there as there is this day in Edinburgh. And where they slander me of magic, necromancy, or of any other art forbidden of God, I have witnesses (besides my own conscience), all congregations that ever heard me, what I speak both against such arts and against those that use such impiety. But seeing the wicked of the world said that my Master, the Lord Jesus, was possessed with Beelzebub, I must

[5] Mary Tudor.

patiently bear, albeit that I, wretched sinner, be injustly accused of those that never delighted in the verity.'

The Queen's second objection.

'But yet (said she) ye have taught the people to receive another religion than their princes can allow. And how can that doctrine be of God seeing that God commands subjects to obey their princes?'

Answer.

'Madam (said he), as right religion took neither original, strength nor authority from worldly princes but from the Eternal God alone, so are not subjects bound to frame their religion according to the appetites of their princes. For oft it is that princes are the most ignorant of all others in God's true religion, as we may read in the histories as well before the death of Christ Jesus as after. If all the seed of Abraham should have been of the religion of Pharaoh, whom to they were long subjects, I pray you, Madam, what religion should there have been in the world? Or, if all men in the days of the Apostles should have been of the religion of the Roman emperors, what religion should there have been upon the face of the earth? Daniel and his fellows were subjects to Nebuchadnezzar and unto Darius, and yet, Madam, they would not be of their religion, neither of the one nor of the other. For the three children said: "We make it known unto thee, O king, that we will not worship thy gods"; and Daniel did pray publicly unto his God against the expressed commandment of the king. And so, Madam, ye may perceive that subjects are not bound to the religion of their princes, albeit they are commanded to give them obedience.'

[*Dan. 3.*]

The third objection.

'Yea (quod she), but none of those men raised the sword against their princes.'

Answer.

'Yet Madam (quod he), ye cannot deny but that they resisted; for those that obey not the commandments that are given, in some sort resist.'

Question.

'But yet (said she), they resisted not by the sword?'

Answer.

'God (said he), Madam, had not given unto them the power and the means.'

'Think ye (quod she) that subjects having power may resist their princes?'

'If their princes exceed their bounds (quod he), Madam, and do against that wherefore they should be obeyed, it is no doubt but they may be resisted, even by power. For there is neither greater honour nor greater obedience to be given to kings or princes than God has commanded to be given unto father and mother. But so it is, Madam, that the father may be stricken with a frenzy in the which he would slay his own children. Now, Madam, if the children arise, join themselves together, apprehend the father, take the sword or other weapons from him, and finally bind his hands, and keep him in prison till that his frenzy be overpast, think ye, Madam, that the children do any wrong? Or think ye, Madam, that God will be offended with them that have stayed their father to commit wickedness? It is even so (said he), Madam, with princes that would murder the children of God that are subject unto them. Their blind zeal is nothing but a very mad frenzy; and therefore, to take the sword from them, to bind their hands, and to cast themselves in prison till that they be brought to a more sober mind, is no [dis]obedience against princes, but just obedience, because that it agreeth with the will of God.'

Question to answer the former.

At these words, the Queen stood, as it were, amazed more than the quarter of an hour. Her countenance altered, so that Lord James began to entreat her and to demand: 'What has offended you, Madam?'

The Queen's conclusion.

At length, she said: 'Well, then, I perceive that my subjects shall obey you and not me, and shall do what they list and not what I command; and so must I be subject to them, and not they to me.'

'God forbid (answered he) that ever I take upon me to command any to obey me, or yet to set subjects at liberty to do what pleaseth them. But my travail is that both princes and subjects obey God. And think not (said he), Madam, that wrong is done unto you when ye are willed to be subject unto God, for it is He that subjects people under princes and causes obedience to be given unto them; yea, God craves of kings that they be, as it were, foster-fathers to His church, and commands queens to be nurses unto His people. And this subjection, Madam, unto God, and unto His troubled church, is the greatest dignity that flesh can get upon the face of the earth, for it shall carry them to everlasting glory.'

The Queen's kirk.

'Yea (quod she), but ye are not the kirk that I will nourish. I will defend the kirk of Rome for I think it is the true kirk of God.'

'Your will (quod he), Madam, is no reason; neither doth your thought make that Roman harlot to be the true and immaculate spouse of Jesus Christ. And wonder not, Madam, that I call Rome a harlot; for that church is altogether polluted with all kind of spiritual fornication, as well in doctrine as in manners. Yea, Madam, I offer myself further to prove that the church of the Jews that crucified

Christ Jesus was not so far degenerated from the ordinances and statutes which God gave by Moses and Aaron unto His people when that they manifestly denied the Son of God as that the church of Rome is declined, and more than five hundred years hath declined, from the purity of that religion which the Apostles taught and planted.'

'My conscience (said she) is not so.'

'Conscience, Madam (said he), requires knowledge, and I fear that right knowledge ye have none.'

'But (said she) I have both heard and read.'

'So (said he), Madam, did the Jews that crucified Christ Jesus read both the law and the prophets and heard the same interpreted after their manner. Have ye heard (said he) any teach but such as the pope and his cardinals have allowed? And ye may be assured that such will speak nothing to offend their own estate.'

Question. 'Ye interpret the Scriptures (said she) in one manner and they interpret in another. Whom shall I believe? And who shall be judge?'

Answer. 'Ye shall believe (said he) God that plainly speaketh in His Word; and further than the Word teaches you, ye neither shall believe the one nor the other. The Word of God is plain in the self; and if there appear any obscurity in one place, the Holy Ghost, which is never contrarious to Himself, explains the same more clearly in other places, so that there can remain no doubt but unto such as obstinately will remain ignorant. And now (said he), Madam, to take one of the chief points which this day is in controversy betwixt the papists and us for example. The papists allege, and boldly have affirmed, that *Mass.* the mass is the ordinance of God and the institution of Jesus Christ, and a sacrifice for the sins of the quick and the dead. We deny both the one and the other and affirm that the mass as it is now used is nothing but the invention of man, and therefore is an abomination before God and no sacrifice that ever God commanded. Now, Madam, who shall judge betwixt us two thus contending? It is no reason that either of the parties be further believed than they are able to prove by insuspect witnessing. Let them lay down the book of God, and by the plain words thereof prove their affirmatives, and we shall give unto them the plea granted. But so long as they are bold to affirm, and yet do prove nothing, we must say that, albeit all the world believed them, yet believe they not God, but receives the lies of men for the truth of God. What our Master Jesus Christ did, we know by His Evangelists; what the priest doth at his mass, the world seeth. Now, doth not the Word of God plainly assure us that Christ Jesus neither said nor yet commanded mass to be said at His Last Supper, seeing that no such thing as their mass is made mention of within the whole Scriptures?'

'Ye are over sore for me (said the Queen), but and if they were here that I have heard, they would answer you.'

'Madam (quod the other), would to God that the learnedest papist in Europe, and he that ye would best believe, were present with your Grace to sustain the argument, and that ye would patiently abide to hear the matter reasoned to the end. For then I doubt not, Madam, but that ye should hear the vanity of the papistical religion and how small ground it hath within the Word of God.'

'Well (said she), ye may perchance get that sooner than ye believe.'

'Assuredly (said the other), if ever I get that in my life, I get it sooner than I believe. For the ignorant papists cannot patiently reason; and the learned and crafty papist will never come in your audience, Madam, to have the ground of their religion searched out, for they know that they are never able to sustain an argument, except fire and sword and their own laws be judges.'

'So say ye (quod the Queen), but I can [not] believe that.'

'It has been so to this day (quod he). For how oft have the papists in this and other realms been required to come to conference, and yet could it never be obtained unless that themselves were admitted for judges? And therefore, Madam, I must yet say again that they dare never dispute but where themselves are both judge and party. And whensoever that ye shall let me see the contrary, I shall grant myself to have been deceived in that point.'

And with this the Queen was called upon to dinner, for it was after noon. At departing, John Knox said unto her: 'I pray God, Madam, that ye may be as blessed within the commonwealth of Scotland, if it be the pleasure of God, as ever Deborah was in the commonwealth of Israel.'

The debate at the General Assembly, June 1564

[The meeting of the General Assembly in June 1564 brought the dispute over the legitimacy of the queen's mass to a head. While the majority of the Protestant nobility were unwilling to alienate the queen by forbidding her to worship as a Catholic, the more radical ministers were adamant in their opposition to what they construed as idolatry. On the first day of the Assembly, the 'courtiers' (as Knox calls the politique noblemen) invited a small group of ministers to confer with them in order to avoid a full public debate of the matter. Reluctantly, the ministers agreed, though only on condition that nothing should be voted upon or concluded without the knowledge and advice of the Assembly as a whole. The following extract from Knox's *History* (Laing MS, fos. 370r–387r; Laing, vol. II, pp. 425–61; Dickinson, vol. II, pp. 108–34) gives a detailed account of the ensuing debate – primarily between Knox and the queen's secretary, William Maitland of Lethington – over Knox's uncompromising attitude to the mass, and, more broadly, over the general principle of resistance to ungodly rulers.]

Lethington's harangue at the assembly in June 1564 years.

Secretary Lethington began the harangue which contained these heads: first, how much we were addebted unto God by whose providence we had liberty of religion under the Queen's Majesty, albeit that she was not persuaded in the same; secondly, how necessary a thing it was that the Queen's Majesty, by all good offices (so spake he) of the part of the kirk, and of the ministers principally, should be retained in that constant opinion, that they unfeignedly favoured her advancement, and procured her subjects to have a good opinion of her; and last, how dangerous a thing it was that ministers should be noted and to disagree one from another in form of prayer for her Majesty or in doctrine concerning obedience to her authority. 'And in these two last heads (said he) we desire you all to be circumspect; but especially we must crave of you, our brother, John Knox, to moderate yourself, as well in form of praying for the Queen's Majesty as in doctrine that ye propone touching her estate and obedience. Neither shall ye take this (said he) as spoken to your reproach, *quia nevus interdum in corpore pulchro*,[1] but because that others, by your example, may imitate the like liberty, albeit not with the same modesty and foresight; and what opinion that may ingather in the people's heads, wise men do foresee.'

The said John prepared him for answer as follows: 'If such as fear God have occasion to praise Him, that because that idolatry is maintained, the servants of God despised, wicked men placed again in honour and authority (Mr Henry Sinclair was of short time before made president,[2] who before durst not have sitten in judgement); and, finally (said he), if we ought to praise God because that vice and impiety overfloweth this whole realm without punishment, then have we occasion to rejoice and to praise God. But if those and the like use to provoke God's vengeance against realms and nations, then in my judgement the godly within Scotland ought to lament and mourn, and so to prevent God's judgements, lest that He, finding all in a like secret, strike in His hot indignation, beginning perchance at such as think they offend not.'

'That is a head', said Lethington, 'whereinto ye and I never agreed; for how are ye able to prove that ever God struck or plagued a nation or people for the iniquity of their prince, if that themselves lived godly?'

'I looked', said he, 'my Lord, to have audience till that I had absolved the other two parts; but seeing it pleases your Lordship to cut me off before the midst, I will answer to your question. The Scripture of God teaches me that Jerusalem and Judah was punished for the sin of Manasseh; and if ye will allege that they were punished because that they were wicked and offended with their king, and not because their king was wicked, I answer that albeit the Spirit of God makes for me, saying in expressed words, "for the sin of Manasseh", yet will I not be so obstinate as to lay the whole sin and plagues that

[*2 Kgs. 21; 2 Chr. 33.*]

[1] Meaning literally 'because moles sometimes occur on a beautiful body'.

[2] That is, president of the court of session. According to Knox, Sinclair was 'a perfect hypocrite and a conjured enemy to Christ Jesus' (Laing, vol. II, p. 398).

thereof followed upon the king, and utterly absolve the people; but I will grant with you that the whole people offended with the king, but how, and [in] what fashion, I fear that I and ye shall not agree. I doubt not but the great multitude accompanied him in all abominations which he did, for idolatry and a false religion hath ever been, is, and will be pleasing to the most part of men. But to affirm that all Judah committed really the acts of his impiety is but to affirm that which neither has certainty nor yet appearance of a truth; for who can think it to be possible that all those of Jerusalem should so shortly turn to external idolatry, considering the notable reformation lately before had in the days of Hezekiah? But yet, says the text: "Manasseh made Judah and the inhabitants of Jerusalem to err." True it is; for the one part, as I have said, willingly followed him in his idolatry, and the other, by reason of his authority, suffered him to file Jerusalem, and the temple of God, with all abominations, and so were they all criminal of his sin; the one by act and deed, the other by suffering and permission: even as whole Scotland is guilty this day of the Queen's idolatry, and ye, my Lords, specially above all others.'

2 Chr. 33.9.

'Well', said Lethington, 'that is the chief head wherein we never agreed; but of that we shall speak hereafter. What will ye say as touching the moving of the people to have a good opinion of the Queen's Majesty, and as concerning obedience to be given to her authority, as also of the form of the prayer which commonly ye use', etc.

'My Lord', said he, 'more earnestly to move the people, or yet otherwise to pray than heretofore I have done, a good conscience will not suffer me; for He who knows the secrets of hearts, knows that privily and publicly I have called to God for her conversion, and have willed the people to do the same, showing them the dangerous estate wherein not only she herself stands, but also the whole realm, by the reason of her indurate blindness', etc.

'That is [it]', said Lethington, 'wherein we find greatest fault. Your extremity against her mass in particular passes measure. Ye call her a slave to Satan; ye affirm that God's vengeance hangs over the realm by reason of her impiety; and what is this else but to raise up the heart of the people against her Majesty, and against them that serve her.'

The Master of Maxwell's

There was heard an acclamation of the rest of the flatterers, that such extremity could not profit. The Master of Maxwell said in plain words: 'If I were in the Queen's Majesty's place, I would not suffer such things as I hear.'

words in the Assembly.

'If the words of preachers', said John Knox, 'shall always be wrest to the worst part, then will it be hard to speak anything [so] circumspectly, provided that the truth be spoken, which shall not escape the censure of the calumniator. The most vehement and, as ye speak, excessive manner of prayer that I use in public is this: "O Lord, if thy pleasure be, purge the heart of the Queen's Majesty from the venom of idolatry, and deliver her from the bondage and thraldom of Satan, in the which she has been brought up, and yet remains, for the lack of true doctrine; and let her see, by the illumination of thy Holy Spirit, that there is no mean to please thee but by Jesus Christ thy only Son, and that Jesus Christ cannot be found but in thy Holy Word, nor yet received but as it prescribes; which is to renounce our own wits and preconceived opinion, and worship thee as thou commands; that in so doing she may avoid that eternal damnation which abides all obstinate and impenitent unto the end; and that this poor realm may also escape that plague and vengeance which inevitably follows idolatry, maintained against thy manifest Word, and the open light thereof." This (said he) is the form of my common prayer, as yourselves can witness. Now, what is worthy [of] reprehension in it I would hear?'

John Knox his prayer for the Queen.

'There are three things', said Lethington, 'that never liked unto me. And the first is, ye pray for the Queen's Majesty with a condition, saying: "Illuminate her heart, if thy good pleasure be", whereby it may appear that ye doubt of her conversion. Where have ye the example of such prayer?'

'Wheresoever the examples are', said the other, 'I am assured of the rule, which is this; "If we shall ask anything according to His will, He shall hear us"; and our Master, Christ Jesus, commanded us to pray unto our Father: "Thy will be done."'

[Matt. 6.10.]

'But', said Lethington, 'where ever find ye any of the Prophets so to have prayed?'

'It sufficeth me', said the other, 'my Lord, that the Master and Teacher of both Prophets and Apostles has taught me so to pray.'

'But in so doing', said he, 'ye put a doubt in the people's head of her conversion.'[3]

[3] Laing MS: conversation.

'Not I, my Lord', said the other, 'but her own obstinate rebellion causes more than me to doubt of her conversion.'

'Whereinto', said he, 'rebels she against God?'

'In all the actions of her life', said he, 'but in these two heads especially: former, that she will not hear the preaching of the blessed Evangel of Jesus Christ; and secondly, that she maintains that idol the mass.'

'She thinks not that rebellion', said Lethington, ['but good religion.']

'So thought they', said the other, 'that sometimes offered their children unto Molech, and yet the Spirit of God affirms that they offered them unto devils and not unto God. And this day the Turks think to have a better religion than the papists have; and yet, I think, ye will excuse neither of them both from committing rebellion against God; neither yet justly can ye do the Queen, unless that ye will make God to be partial.'

[*Lev.* 20.]

'But yet', said Lethington, 'why pray ye not for her without moving any doubt?'

'Because', said the other, 'I have learned to pray in faith. Now faith, ye know, depends upon the Word[4] of God, and so it is that the Word teaches me that prayers profit the sons and daughters of God's election, of which number, whether she be one or not, I have just cause to doubt; and, therefore, I pray God "illuminate her heart, if his good pleasure be."'

'But yet', said Lethington, 'ye can produce the example of [none] that so has prayed before you.'

'Thereto I have already answered', said John Knox, 'but yet for further declaration, I will demand a question, which is this: whether if ye think that the Apostles prayed themselves as they commanded others to pray?'

'Who doubts of that?' said the whole company that were present.

'Well then', said John Knox, 'I am assured that Peter said these words to Simon Magus: "Repent therefore of this thy wickedness, and pray to God that, if it be possible, the thought of your heart may be forgiven thee." Here we may clearly see that Peter joins a condition with his commandment: that Simon should repent and pray, to wit, if it were possible that his sin might be forgiven; for he was not

[*Acts* 8.22.]

[4] Laing MS: words.

ignorant that some sins were unto the death, and so without all hope of repentance or remission. And think ye not, my Lord Secretary (said he), but the same doubt may touch my heart, as touching the Queen's conversion, that then touched the heart of the Apostle?'

'I would never', said Lethington, 'hear you or any other call that in doubt.'

'But your will', said the other, 'is no assurance to my conscience. And to speak freely, my Lord, I wonder if ye yourself doubt not of the Queen's conversion; for more evident signs of induration have appeared, and still do appear in her, than Peter outwardly could have espied in Simon Magus. For albeit sometimes he was a sorcerer, yet joined he with the Apostles, believed, and was baptised; and albeit that the venom of avarice remained in his heart, and that he would have bought the Holy Ghost, yet when he heard the fearful threatenings of God pronounced against him, he trembled, desired the assistance of the prayers of the Apostles, and so humbled himself, so far as the judgement of man could pierce, like a true penitent; and yet we see that Peter doubts of his conversion. [Why then may not all the godly justly doubt of the conversion] of the Queen, who has used idolatry, which is no less odious in the sight of God than is the other, and still continues in the same, yea, that despises all threatenings, and refuses all godly admonitions?'

'Why say ye that she refuses admonition?' said Lethington. 'She will gladly hear any man.'

'But what obedience', said the other, 'to God or to His Word ensues of all that is spoken unto her? When shall she be seen to give her presence to the public preaching?'

'I think never', said Lethington, 'so long as she is thus entreated.'

'And so long', said the other, 'ye and all others must be content that I pray so as I may be assured to be heard of my God, that His good will may be done, either in making her comfortable to His kirk, or if that He has appointed her to be a scourge to the same, that we may have patience, and she may be bridled.'

'Well', said Lethington, 'let us come to the second head. Where find ye that the Scripture calls any the bound slaves to Satan or that the Prophets of God speak so irreverently of kings and princes?'

'The Scripture', said John Knox, 'says, that "by nature we are all the sons of wrath". Our Master, Christ Jesus, affirms "that such as do sin are servants to sin" and that it is the only Son of God that [*Eph.* 2.3.] [*John* 8.4.]

sets men at freedom. Now what difference there is betwixt the sons of wrath and the servants of sin and the slaves to the devil, I understand not, except I be taught; and if the sharpness of the term offended you, I have not invented that phrase of speech, but have learned it out of God's Scripture; for those words I find spoken unto Paul: "Behold, I send thee to the Gentiles to open their eyes that they may turn from darkness to light, and from the power of Satan unto God." Mark these words, my Lord, and sture not at the speaking of the Holy Ghost. And the same Apostle writing to his scholar Timothy, says: "Instruct with meekness those that are contrary minded, if that God at any time will give them repentance, that they may know the truth, and that they may come to amendment out of the snare of the devil, which are taken of him at his will." If your Lordship rightly consider these sentences, ye shall not only find my words to be the words of the Holy Ghost, but also the condition which I use to add to have the assurance of God's Scriptures.'

Acts 26.17–18.

2 Tim. 2.24–6.

'But they spake nothing against kings in especial', said Lethington, 'and yet your continual crying is: "The Queen's idolatry, the Queen's mass, will provoke God's vengeance."'

'In the former sentences', said the other, 'I hear not kings and queens excepted, but all unfaithful are pronounced to stand in one rank and to be in bondage to one tyrant, the devil. But belike, my Lord, ye little regard the estate wherein they stand when ye would have them so flattered that the danger thereof[5] should neither be known, neither yet declared to the poor people.'

'Where will ye find', said Lethington, 'that any of the Prophets did so entreat kings and queens, rulers or magistrates?'

'In more places than one', said the other. 'Ahab was a king, and Jezebel was a queen, and yet what the Prophet Elijah said to the one and to the other, I suppose ye be not ignorant?'

'That was not cried out before the people', said Lethington, 'to make them odious unto their subjects.'

'That Elijah said, "Dogs shall lick the blood of Ahab"', said John Knox, '"and [eat] the flesh of Jezebel", the Scriptures assure me; but that it was whispered in their own ear, or in a corner, I read not. But the plain contrary appears to me, which is that both the people and the court understood well enough what the Prophet had prom-

[1 Kgs. 21.19, 23.]

[5] Laing MS: therefor.

ised; for so witnessed Jehu, after that God's vengeance had stricken Jezebel.'

'They were singular motions of the Spirit of God', said Lethington, 'and appertain nothing to this our age.'

'Then has the Scripture far deceived me', said the other, 'for St Paul teaches me that: "Whatsoever is written within the Holy Scriptures, the same is written for our instruction." And my Master said that: "Every learned and wise scribe brings forth his treasure, both things old and things new." And the Prophet Jeremiah affirms that: "Every realm and every city that likewise offends, as then did Jerusalem, should likewise be punished."[6] Why then that the facts of the ancient Prophets, and the fearful judgements of God executed before us upon the disobedient, appertain not unto this our age, I neither see nor yet can understand. But now, to put end to this head, my Lord (said he), the Prophets of God has not spared to rebuke wicked kings, as well in their face as before the people and subjects. Elisha feared not to say to King Jehoram: "What have I to do with thee? Get thee [to the Prophets of thy father, and] to the Prophets of thy mother; for as the Lord of Hosts lives, in whose sight I stand, if it were not that I regard the presence of Jehoshaphat, the king of Judah, I would not have looked toward thee, nor seen thee." Plain it is that the Prophet was a subject in the kingdom of Israel, and yet how little reverence he gives to the king, we hear. Jeremiah the Prophet was commanded to cry to the king and to the queen and to say: "Behave yourselves lowly; execute justice and judgement; or else your carcagies shall be cassin to the heat of the day, and unto the frost of the night." Unto Coniah, Shallum and Zedekiah, he speaks in special, and shows unto them in his public sermons their miserable ends; and therefore ye ought not to think[7] it strange, my Lord (said he), albeit that the servants of God mark the vice of kings and queens, even as well as of other offenders, and that because their sins be more noisome to the commonwealth than are the sins of inferior persons.'

[*Rom.* 15.4.]

[*Matt.* 13.52.]

[2 *Kgs.* 3.13–14.]

[*Jer.* 36.30.]

[*Jer.* 21, 22.]

The most part of this reasoning, Secretary Lethington leaned upon the Master of Maxwell's breast, who said: 'I am almost weary; I would that some other would reason in the chief head, which is not touched.'

Then the Earl of Morton, Chancellor, commanded Mr George

[6] Possibly Jeremiah 25.18, but the quote is far from exact.
[7] Laing MS: make.

Hay to reason against John Knox in the head of obedience due unto magistrates, who began so to do. Unto whom John Knox said: 'Brother, that ye shall reason in my contrary I am well content, because I know you both a man of learning and of modesty; but that ye shall oppone yourself in the truth whereof,[8] I suppose, your own conscience is no less persuaded[9] than is mine, I cannot well approve; for I would be sorry that I and ye should be reputed to reason as two scholars of Pythagoras, to show the quickness of our engine, as it were to reason on both the parts. I protest here before God that, whatsoever I sustain, the same [I do] of conscience; yea, I dare no more sustain a proposition known unto myself untrue than that I dare teach false doctrine in the public place. And therefore, Brother, if conscience move you to oppone yourself to that doctrine which ye have heard of my mouth in that matter, do it boldly; it shall never offend me. But that ye shall be found to oppone yourself unto me, ye being persuaded in the same truth, I say yet again, it pleases me not; for therein may be greater inconvenient than either ye or I do consider for the present.'

The said Mr George answered, 'That I would oppone myself unto you as willing to impugn or confute that head of doctrine which not only ye, but many others, yea, and I myself have affirmed, far be it from me; for so should I be found contrarious [to] myself. For my Lord Secretary knows my judgement in that head.'

'Marry!' said the Secretary, 'Ye are the well worst of the two, for I remember well your reasoning when the Queen was in Carrick.'[10]

'Well', said John Knox, 'seeing, Brother, that God has made you to occupy the chair of verity, wherein, I assure, we will agree in all principal heads of doctrine, let it never be said that we disagree in disputation.' John Knox was moved thus to speak because he[11] understood more of the craft than the other did.

[8] Laing MS: wherefor.

[9] Laing MS: dead.

[10] Mary visited the south-west of Scotland on progress in the summer of 1563, but there is no evidence that she then witnessed in 'reasoning' involving George Hay who had been appointed commissioner of Carrick by the General Assembly in 1562, but had been posted the following year to Aberdeen and Banff. It is possible that Lethington is conflating the queen's visit to the area with the disputation which took place at Maybole in Ayrshire in 1562 during which both Hay and Knox crossed swords with Quintin Kennedy, abbot of Crossraguel (Laing, vol. II, pp. 351–2).

[11] Laing MS: they.

'Well', said Lethington, 'I am somewhat better provided in this last head than I was in the other two. Mr Knox (said he), yesterday we heard your judgement upon the 13th [chapter] to the Romans; *[Rom. 13.]* we heard the mind of the Apostle well opened; we heard the causes why God has established powers upon the earth; we heard the necessity that mankind has of the same; and we heard the duty of magistrates sufficiently declared. But in two things I was offended, and I think some more of my Lords that then were present. The one was, ye made difference betwixt the ordinance of God and the persons that were placed in authority, and ye affirmed that men might refuse the persons and yet not to offend against God's ordinance. This is the one; the other ye had no time to explain, but this methought ye meant: that subjects were not bound to obey their princes if they commanded unlawful things, but that they might refuse their princes and were not ever bound to suffer.'

'In very deed', said the other, 'ye have rightly both marked my words and understood my mind; for [of] that same judgement I have long been, and so yet I remain.'

'How will ye prove your division and difference', said Lethington, 'and that the person placed in authority may be resisted and God's ordinance not transgressed, seeing that the Apostle says: "He that *[Rom. 13.2.]* resists, resisteth the ordinance of God."'

'My Lord', said he, 'the plain words of the Apostle make the difference, and the facts of many approved by God, prove my affirmative. First, the Apostle affirms that the powers are ordained of God [for the preservation of quiet and peaceable men, and for the punishment of malefactors; whereof it is plain that the ordinance of God] and the power given unto man is one thing, and the person clad with the power or with the authority is another; for God's ordinance is the conservation of mankind, the punishment of vice, the maintaining of virtue, which is in itself holy, just, constant, stable and perpetual. But men clad with the authority are commonly profane and unjust; yea, they are mutable and transitory, and subject to corruption, as God threateneth them by His Prophet David, saying: "I have said ye are *[Ps. 82.6–7.]* gods, and every one of you [the sons of] the Most Highest; but ye shall die as men, and the princes shall fall like others." Here I am assured that persons, the soul and body [of] wicked princes, are threatened with death. I think that so ye will not affirm is the authority, the ordinance and the power, wherewith God endued such persons; for as I have said, as it is holy, so it is the permanent will of God. And now, my Lord, that the prince may be resisted and yet the ordinance of God not violated, it is evident; for the people resisted Saul when he had sworn by the living God that Jonathan should die. The people (I say) swore in the contrary and delivered Jonathan, so that a hair of [his] head fell not. Now, Saul was the anointed king and they were his subjects, and yet they so resisted him that they made him no better than mansworn.'

[*1 Sam.* 14.44–5.]

'I doubt', said Lethington, '[if] in so doing the people did well.'

'The Spirit of God', said the other, 'accuses them not of any crime, but rather praises them, and damns the king, as well for his foolish vow and law made without God, as for his cruel mind, that so severely would have punished an innocent man. But herein I shall not stand; this that follows shall confirm the former. This same Saul commanded Ahimelech and the priests of the Lord to be slain because they had committed treason, as he alleged, for intercommuning with David. His guard and principal servants would not obey his unjust commandment, but Doeg the flatterer put the king's cruelty to execution. I will not ask your judgement whether that the servants of the king, in not obeying his commandment, resisted God or not. Or whether Doeg, in murdering the priests, gave obedience to a just authority. For I have the Spirit of God, speaking by the mouth of David, to assure me of the one as well as of the other. For he, in his 52nd Psalm, damns that fact as a most cruel murder, and affirms that God would punish, not only the commander, but also the merciless executor. And therefore I conclude that they who gainstood his commandment resisted not the ordinance of God.

[*1 Sam.* 22.]

[*Ps.* 52.]

'And now, my Lord, to answer to the place of the Apostle who affirms "that such as resists the power, resists the ordinance of God", I say that the power in that place is not to be understood of the unjust commandment of men, but of the just power wherewith God has armed His magistrates and lieutenants to punish sin and maintain virtue. As if any man should enterprise to take from the hands of a lawful judge a murderer, an adulterer or any malefactor that by God's law deserved death, this same man resisted God's ordinance, and procured to himself vengeance and damnation because that he stayed God's sword to strike. But so it is not if that men in the fear of God oppone themselves to the fury and blind rage of princes; for so they resist not God, but the devil, who abuses the sword and authority of God.'

[*Rom.* 13.2.]

'I understand sufficiently', said Lethington, 'what ye mean; and to the one part I will not oppone myself. But I doubt of the other. For if the Queen would command me to slay John Knox because she is offended at him, I would not obey her. But, and she would command others to do it, or yet by a colour of justice take his life from him, I cannot tell if I be found to defend him against the Queen and against her officers.'

'Under protestation', said the other, 'that the auditor think not that I seek favours to myself, I say, my Lord, that if ye be persuaded of my innocency, and if God has given unto you such a power and credit as might deliver me, and yet suffered me to perish, that in so doing ye should be criminal and guilty of my blood.'

'Prove that and win the play', said Lethington.

'Well, my Lord', said the other, 'remember your promise and I shall be short of my probation. The Prophet Jeremiah was apprehended by the priests and prophets (who were a part of the authority within Jerusalem) and by the multitude of the people, and this sentence was pronounced against him: "Thou shall die the death, for thou has said, This house shall be like Shiloh, and this city shall be desolate without an habitant." The princes hearing the uproar came from the king's house and sat down in judgement in the entry of the new gate of the Lord's house, and there the priests and the prophets, before the princes and before all the people, attended their accusation in these words: "This man is worthy to die, for he has prophesied against this city, as your ears have heard." Jeremiah answered: "That whatsoever he had spoken proceeded from God; and therefore (said he) as for me, behold, I am in your hands, do with me as ye think good and right. But know ye for certain that [if] ye put me to death, ye shall surely bring innocent blood upon your souls, and upon this city, and upon the habitations thereof; for of truth, the Lord has sent me unto you to speak all these words." Now, my Lord, if the princes and the whole people should have been guilty of the Prophet's blood, how shall ye or others be judged innocent before God if ye shall suffer the blood of such as have not deserved death to be shed when that ye may save it?'

Jer. 26.8–9.

[Jer. 26.11.]

[Jer. 26.12–15.]

'The cases are nothing like', said Lethington.

'And I would learn', said the other, 'wherein the dissimilitude stands.'

'First', said Lethington, 'the king had not condemned him to the death. And next, the false prophets and the priests and the people accused him without a cause, and therefore they could not [but] be guilty of his blood.'

'Neither of these', said John Knox, 'fights against my argument; for albeit the king was neither present nor yet had condemned him, yet were the princes and chief counsellors there sitting in judgement, who presented the king's person and authority, hearing the accusation laid unto the charge of the Prophet; and therefore he forewarns them of the danger, as before I said, to wit, that in case he should be condemned, and so put to death, that the king, the council, and the whole city of Jerusalem, should be guilty of his blood, because he had committed no crime worthy of death. And if ye think that they should have been all criminal only because that they all accused him, the plain text witnesses the contrary; for the princes defended him, and so no doubt did a great part of the people; and yet he boldly affirms that they should be all guilty of his blood if that he should be put to death. And the Prophet Ezekiel gives the reason why all are guilty of a common corruption: "Because", says he, "I sought a man amongst them that should make the hedge, and stand in the gap before me for the land that I should not destroy it, but I found none; therefore, have I poured my indignation upon them." Hereof, my Lord (said he), it is plain that God craves not only that man do no iniquity in his own person, but also that he oppone[12] himself to all iniquity, so far forth as into him lies.'

[*Ezek.* 22.30–1.]

'Then will ye', said Lethington, 'make subjects to control their princes and rulers?'

'And what harm', said the other, 'should the commonwealth receive if that the corrupt affections of ignorant rulers were moderated and so bridled by the wisdom and discretion of godly subjects that they should do wrong nor violence to no man?'

'All this reasoning', said Lethington, 'is not of the purpose, for we reason as if the Queen should become such an enemy to our religion that she should persecute it and put innocent men to death; which I am assured she never thought nor never will do. For if I should see her begin at that end, yea, if I should suspect any such thing in her, I should be as far forward in that argument as ye or any other within this realm. But there is not such a thing. Our question is whether that we may and ought to suppress the Queen's mass? Or whether that her idolatry shall be laid to our charge?'

[12] Laing MS: that to heap upon.

'What ye may', said the other, 'by force, I dispute not; but what ye may and ought to do by God's express commandment, that I can tell. Idolatry ought not [only] to be suppressed, but the idolater ought to die the death, unless that we will accuse God.'

'I know', said Lethington, 'the idolater is commanded to die the death; but by whom?'

'By the people of God,' said the other, 'for the commandment was given to Israel, as ye may read: "Hear, Israel", says the Lord, "the statutes and the ordinances of the Lord thy God", etc. Yea, a commandment was given that if it be heard that idolatry is committed in any one city, inquisition shall be taken; and if it be found true that then the whole body of the people shall arise and destroy that city, sparing in it neither man, woman nor child.' [*Deut.* 5.1.]

'But there is no commandment given to the people', said the Secretary, 'to punish their king if he be an idolater.'

'I find no more privilege granted unto kings', said the other, 'by God, more than unto the people, to offend God's majesty.'

'I grant', said Lethington, 'but yet the people may not be judges unto their king to punish him, albeit he be an idolater.'

'God', said the other, 'is Universal Judge, as well unto the king as to the people; so that what His Word commands to be punished in the one is not to be absolved in the other.'

'We agree in that', said Lethington, 'but the people may not execute God's judgement, but must leave it unto Himself, who will either punish it by death, by war, by imprisonment, or by some other plagues.'

'I know the last part of your reason', said John Knox, 'to be true; but for the first, to wit, that the people, yea, or a part of the people, may not execute God's judgements against their king, being an offender, I am assured ye have no other warrant except your own imagination and the opinion of such as more fear to offend princes than God.'

'Why say ye so?' said Lethington. 'I have the judgements of the most famous men within Europe, and of such as ye yourself will confess both godly and learned.'

And with that he called for his papers, which produced by Mr Robert Maitland, he began to read with great gravity the judgements of Luther, Melanchthon, the minds of Bucer, Musculus and Calvin, how Christians should behave themselves in time of persecution; yea, the Book of Baruch was not omitted[13] with his conclusion. 'The gathering of these things', said he, 'has cost me more travail than I took this seven years in reading of any commentaries.'

'The more pity', said the other, 'and yet what ye have profited your own cause, let others judge. But as for my argument, I am assured ye have infirmed [it] nothing; for your first two witnesses speak against the Anabaptists, who deny that Christians should be subject to magistrates, or yet that [it] is lawful for a Christian to be a magistrate; which opinion I no less abhor than ye do, or any other that lives do.[14] The others speak of Christians subject unto tyrants and infidels, so dispersed that they have no other force but only to sob to God for deliverance. That such indeed should hazard any further than these godly men wills them, I cannot hastily be of counsel. But my argument has another ground; for I speak of the people assembled together in one body of a commonwealth unto whom God has given sufficient force, not only to resist, but also to suppress all kind of open idolatry; and such a people, yet again I affirm, are bound to keep their land clean and unpolluted. And that this my division shall not appear strange unto you, ye shall understand that God required one thing of Abraham and of his seed when he and they were strangers and pilgrims in Egypt and Canaan; and another thing required he of them when they were delivered from the bondage of Egypt and the possession of the land of Canaan [was] granted unto them. At the first, and during all the time of their bondage, God craved no more but that Abraham should not defile himself with idolatry. Neither was he nor yet his posterity commanded to destroy the idols that were in Canaan or in Egypt. But when God gave unto them the possession of the land, He gave unto them this strait commandment: "Beware that you make league or confederacy with the inhabitants of this land; give not thy sons unto their daughters, nor yet give thy daughters unto their sons. But this shall ye do unto them: cut down their groves, destroy their images, break down their altars, and leave thou no kind of remembrance of those abominations which the inhabitants of the land used before; for thou art a holy people unto the Lord thy God. Defile not thyself therewith with their gods."

[*Exod.* *24.12–16.*]

[13] Laing MS: admitted. Jeremiah's scribe, Baruch, was credited with the authorship of a number of apocryphal books.

[14] In 1560, Knox had himself published a lengthy polemic against the Anabaptists entitled *An Answer to the Cavillations of an Adversary respecting the Doctrine of Predestination* (Laing, vol. v, pp. 9–468).

'To this same commandment, I say, [are] ye, my Lords, and all such as have professed the Lord Jesus within this realm bound. For God has wrought no less miracle upon you, both spiritual and corporal, than He did unto the carnal seed of Abraham. For in what estate your bodies, and this poor realm was, within this seven year, yourselves cannot be ignorant. You and it were both in bondage of a strange nation; and what tyrants rang over your conscience, God perchance may let you feel, because that ye do not rightly acknowledge the benefit received. When our poor brethren before us gave their bodies to the flames of fire for the testimony of the truth, and when scarcely could ten be found into a country that rightly knew God, it had been foolishness to have craved either of the nobility or of the mean subjects the suppressing of idolatry; for that had been nothing but to have exponed the simple sheep in a prey to the wolves. But since that God has multiplied knowledge, yea, and has given the victory to His truth, even in the hands of His servants, if ye suffer the land again to be defiled, ye and your Princess shall both drink the cup of God's indignation, she for her obstinate abiding in manifest idolatry in this great light of the Evangel of Jesus Christ, and ye for your permission and maintaining her in the same.'

Lethington said: 'In that point we will never agree; and where find ye, I pray you, that ever any of the Prophets or of the Apostles taught such a doctrine that the people should be plagued for the idolatry of the prince; or yet that the subjects might suppress the idolatry of their rulers or punish them for the same?'

'What was the commission given to the Apostles', said he, 'my Lord, we know: it was to preach and plant the Evangel of Jesus Christ where darkness afore had dominion; and therefore it behoved them first to let them see the light before that they should will them to put to their hands to suppress idolatry. What precepts the Apostles gave unto the faithful in particular, other than that they commanded all to flee from idolatry, I will not affirm. But I find two things which the faithful did: the one was, they assisted their preachers, even against the rulers and magistrates; the other was, they suppressed idolatry wheresoever God gave unto them force, asking no leave at the emperor nor of his deputies. Read the ecclesiastical history and ye shall find example sufficient. And as to the doctrine of the Prophets, we know they were interpreters of the law of God, and we know they spake as well to the kings as to the people. I read that neither of both would hear them; and therefore come the plague of

God upon both. But [that] they more flattered kings than that they did the people, I cannot be persuaded. Now, God's law pronounces death, as before I have said, to idolaters without exception of any person. Now, how the Prophets could rightly interpret the law and show the causes of God's judgements, which ever they threatened should follow[15] idolatry, and for the rest of [the] abominations that accompany it (for it is never alone, but still corrupt religion brings with it a filthy and corrupt life); how, I say, the Prophets could reprove the vices, and not show the people their duty, I understand not; and therefore I constantly believe that the doctrine of the Prophets was so sensible that the kings understood their own abominations, and the people understood what they have ought to have done in punishing and repressing them. But because that the most part of the people were no less rebellious unto God than were their princes, therefore the one and the other convened against God and against His servants. And yet, my Lord, the facts of some Prophets are so evident that thereof we may collect what doctrine they taught; for it were no small absurdity to affirm that their facts should repugn to their doctrine.'

'I think', said Lethington, 'ye mean of the history of Jehu. What will ye prove thereby?'

'The chief head', said John Knox, 'that ye deny, to wit, that the Prophets never taught that it appertained to the people to punish the idolatry of their kings; the contrary whereof I affirm. And for the probation, I am ready to produce the fact of a Prophet; for ye know, my Lord, said he, that Elisha sent one of the children of the Prophets to anoint Jehu, who gave him in commandment to destroy the house of his master Ahab for the idolatry committed by him and for the innocent blood that Jezebel his wicked wife had shed; which he obeyed, and put in full execution, for the which God promised unto him the stability of the kingdom to the fourth generation. Now, said he, here is the fact of a Prophet that proves that subjects were commanded to execute judgements upon their king and prince.'

[*2 Kgs. 9, 10.*]

'There is enough', said Lethington, 'to be answered thereto; for Jehu was a king before he put anything in execution; and besides this, the fact is extraordinary and ought not to be imitated.'

'My Lord', said the other, 'he was a mere subject and no king

[15] Laing MS: fall for.

when the Prophet's servant came unto him; yea, and albeit that his fellow captains, hearing of the message, blew the trumpet, and said, "Jehu is king", yet I doubt not but Jezebel both thought and said, "He was a traitor", and so did many others that were in Israel and in Samaria. And as touching that ye allege that the fact was extraordinary and is not to be imitated, I say that it had ground of God's ordinary judgement, which commands the idolater to die the death; and, therefore, I yet again affirm that it is to be imitated of all those that prefer the true honour, the true worship and glory of God, to the affections of flesh, and of wicked princes.'[16]

[2 *Kgs.* 9.13.]

'We are not bound to imitate extraordinary examples', said Lethington, 'unless we have the like commandment and assurance.'

'I grant', said the other, 'if the example repugn to the law; and if an avaricious and deceitful man would borrow [gold,] silver, raiment, or [any] other necessaries from his neighbour, and withhold the same, alleging that so he might do and not offend God, because that the Israelites did so [to] the Egyptians at their departure forth of Egypt. The example served to no purpose unless that they could produce the like cause, and the like commandment that the Israelites had, and that because their fact repugned to this commandment of God: "Thou shall not steal". But where the example agrees with the law, and is, as it were, the execution of God's judgements expressed in the same, I say that the example approved of God stands to us in place of [a] commandment; for, as God of His nature is constant [and] immutable, so can He not damn in the ages subsequent that which He has approved in His servants before us. But in His servants before us, He by His own commandment has approved that subjects has not only destroyed their kings for idolatry, but also has rooted out their whole posterity, so that none of that race was left after to empire above the people of God.'

[*Exod.* 20.15.]

'Whatsoever they did', said Lethington, 'was done at God's commandment.'

'That fortifies my argument', said the other, 'for by God's commandment He approved that subjects punish their princes for idolatry and wickedness by them committed.'

'We have not the like commandment', said Lethington.

[16] In the Laing MS the words of this sentence are so awkwardly transposed as to render it unintelligible. I have followed Laing, vol. II, p. 446.

'That I deny', said the other, 'for the commandment, "The idolater shall die the death",[17] is perpetual, as [ye] yourself has granted. You[18] doubted only who should be executors against the king; and I said the people of God, and has sufficiently proven, as I think, that God has raised up the people, and by His Prophet has anointed a king to take vengeance upon the king and upon his posterity. Which fact, God since that time has never retreated; and, therefore, to me it remains for a constant and clear commandment to all the people professing God, and having the power to punish vice, what they ought to do in the like case. If the people had enterprised anything without God's commandment, we might have doubted whether they had done well or evil; but seeing that God did bring the execution of His law again in practice, after that it was come in oblivion and contempt, what reasonable man can doubt now of God's will, unless we will doubt of all things which God renews not unto us by miracles, as it were, from age to age. But I am assured that the answer of Abraham unto the rich man, who being into[19] hell desired that Lazarus, or some of the dead, should be sent unto his brethren and friends to forewarn them of his incredible [pain and] torments, and that they should behave themselves, so that they should not come in that place of torment; the answer, I say, given him shall confound such as crave further approbation of God's will than is already expressed within His Holy Scriptures; for Abraham said: "They have Moses and the Prophets, whom if they will not believe, neither will they believe albeit that one of the dead should rise." Even so, I say, my Lord, that such as will not be taught what they ought to do, by commandment of God once given, and once put in practice, will not believe nor obey, albeit that God should send angels from heaven to instruct that doctrine.'

[*Luke 16.19–31.*]

[*Luke 16.31.*]

'Ye have but produced one example', said Lethington.

'One sufficeth', said the other, 'but yet, God be praised, we lack not others; for the whole people conspired against Amaziah, king of Judah, after that he had turned away from the Lord, followed him to Lachish and slew him, and took Uzziah and anointed him king

2 Chr. 25, 26.[20]

[17] For injunctions against idolatry, see Exodus 20.4 and 22.20, but Knox probably has in mind here Ezekiel 33.8.

[18] Laing MS: The.

[19] Laing MS: unto.

[20] The reference in the original to 2 Chr. 2 is clearly an error.

instead of his father. The people had not altogether [for]gotten the league and covenant which was made betwixt their king and them at the inauguration of Joash, his father, to wit: "that the king and the people should be the people of the Lord", and then should they be His faithful subjects. From the which covenant, when that first the father, and after the son declined, they were both punished to the death, Joash by his own servants, and Amaziah by the whole people.' *[2 Chr. 23.16.]* *[2 Chr. 24.25.]* *[2 Chr. 25.27.]*

'I doubt', said Lethington, 'whether they did well or not.'

'It shall be free for you', said the other, 'to doubt as ye please; but where I find execution according to God's laws, and God Himself not to accuse the doers, I dare not doubt of the equity of their cause. And further, it appears unto me that God gave[21] sufficient approbation and allowance to their fact, for He blessed them with victory, peace and prosperity the space of fifty-two years thereafter.'

'But prosperity', said Lethington, 'does not always prove that God approves the facts of men.'

'Yes', said the other, 'when the facts[22] of men agree with the law of God and are rewarded [according] to God's own promise expressed in His law, I say that the prosperity succeeding the fact is most infallible assurance that God has approved that fact. Now so it is that God has promised in His law that when His people shall exterminate and destroy such as decline from Him, that He will bless them, and multiply them, as He has promised unto their fathers. But so it is that Amaziah turned from God, for so the text do witness; and plain it is the people slew their king; and like plain it is that God blessed them. Therefore yet again conclude I that God approved their fact, in so far as it was done according to His commandment, was blessed according to His promise.'

'Well', said Lethington, 'I think not the ground so sure as I durst build my conscience thereupon.'

'I pray God', said the other, 'that your conscience have no worse ground than is this whensoever ye shall begin that like work which God in your own eyes has already blessed. And now, my Lord (said he), I have but one example to produce, and then I will put end to my reasoning, because I weary longer to stand.' (Commandment was given that he should sit down, but he refused it, and said, 'Melan-

[21] Laing MS: have.
[22] Laing MS: faults.

choly[23] reasons would have some mirth intermixed.') 'My last example (said he), my Lord, is this: Uzziah the king, not content of his royal estate, malapertly took upon him to enter within the temple of the Lord to burn incense upon the altar of incense: "And Azariah the priest went in after him, and with him eighty priests of the Lord, valiant men, and they withstood Uzziah the king, and said unto him, It pertaineth thee not, Uzziah, to burn incense unto the Lord, but to the priests, the sons of Aaron, that are consecrated to offer incense. Go forth of the sanctuary, for thou has transgressed, and you shall have no honour of the Lord God." Hereof, my Lord, I conclude that subjects not only may, but also ought to withstand and resist their princes, whensoever they do anything that expressly repugns to God, His law or holy ordinance.'

[*2 Chr. 26, 16–18.*]

'They that withstood the king', said Lethington, 'were not simple subjects, but were the priests of the Lord, and figures of Christ, and such priests have we none this day to withstand kings if they do wrong.'

'That the high priest was the figure of Christ', said the other, 'I grant; but that he was not a subject, that I deny. For I am assured that he in his priesthood had no prerogative above those that had passed before him. Now, so it is that Aaron was subject unto Moses and called him his lord. Samuel, being both prophet and priest, subject himself to Saul after he was inaugurated of the people. Zadok bowed before David; and Abiathar was deposed from the priesthood by Solomon; which all confessed themselves subjects to the kings, albeit that therewith they ceased not to be the figures of Christ. And whereas ye say [that] we have no such priests this day, I might answer that neither have we such kings this day as then were anointed at God's commandment, and sat upon the seat of David, and were no less the figure of Christ Jesus in their just administration than were the priests in their appointed office; and such kings,[24] I am assured, we have not now more than that we have such priests; for Christ Jesus being anointed in our nature, of God His Father, both king, priest and prophet, has put [an] end to all external unction. And yet, I think, ye will not say that God has now diminished His graces for those whom He appoints ambassadors betwixt Him and His people, [more] than that He does from kings and princes; and therefore, why

[*1 Sam. 10.*]

[*1 Kgs. 1, 2.*]

[23] Laing MS: melankourelie.

[24] Laing MS: things.

that the servants of Jesus Christ may not also justly withstand kings and princes that this day no less offended God's majesty than Uzziah did, I see not, unless that ye will say that we, in the brightness of the Evangel, are not so straitly bound to regard God's glory, nor yet His commandments, as were the fathers that lived under the dark shadows of the Law.'

'Well', said Lethington, 'I will dip no further in that head. But how resisted the priests the king? They only spake unto him without further violence intended.'

'That they[25] withstood him', said the other, 'the text assures me; but that they did nothing but speak, I cannot understand; for the plain text affirms the contrary, to wit, that they caused him hastily to depart from the sanctuary, yea, and that he was compelled to depart; which manner of speaking, I am assured, in the Hebrew tongue imports other thing than exhorting or commanding by word.' [2 *Chr.* 26.18.]

'They did that', said Lethington, 'after that he was espied leprous.'

'They withstood him before', said the other, 'but yet their last fact confirms my proposition so evidently that such as will oppone[26] them unto it must needs oppone them unto God; for my assertion is that kings have no privilege more than has the people to offend God's majesty; and if that so they do, they are no more exempted from the punishment of the law than is any other subject; yea, and that subjects may not only lawfully oppone themselves to their kings, whensoever they do anything that expressedly repugns to God's commandment, but also that they may execute judgement upon them according to God's law; so that [if] the king be a murderer, adulterer or idolater, he should suffer according to God's law, not as a king, but as an offender. And that the people may put God's laws in execution this history clearly proves: for how soon that the leprosy appeared in his forehead, he was not only compelled to depart out of the sanctuary, but also he was removed from all public society and administration of the kingdom and was compelled to dwell in a house apart, even as the law commanded, and got no greater privilege in that case than any other of the people should have done; and this was executed by the people; for it is no doubt more were witnesses of his leprosy than the priests alone. But we find none oppone themselves to the sentence of God pronounced in His law against the leprous; and therefore, [2 *Chr.* 26.19–21.]

[25] Laing MS: They that.
[26] Laing MS: opprove.

yet again say I that the people ought to execute God's law even against their princes, when that their open crimes by God's law deserve death, but especially when they are such as may infect the rest of the multitude. And now, my Lords, (said he) I will reason no longer, for I have spoken more than I intended.'

'And yet', said Lethington, 'I cannot tell what can be concluded.'

'Albeit ye cannot', said the other, 'yet I am assured what I have proven, to wit: that subjects have delivered an innocent from the hands of their king, and thereintil offended not God; that subjects have refused to strike innocents when a king commanded, and in so doing denied no just obedience; that such as struck at the commandment of the king before God were reputed murderers; that God has not only of a subject made a king, but also has armed subjects against their natural kings, and commanded them to take vengeance upon them according to His law; and last, that God's people has executed God's law against their king, having no further regard to him in that behalf than if he had been the most simple subject within this realm. And therefore, albeit ye will not understand what should be concluded, yet I am assured that not only may God's people, but also that they are bound to do the same where the like crimes are committed, and when He gives unto them the like power.'

1.
2.
3.
4.
5.

'Well', said Lethington, 'I think ye shall not have many learned men of your opinion.'

'My Lord', said the other, 'the truth ceases not to be the truth, howsoever it be that men misknow it or yet gainstand it. And yet (said he) I praise my God, I lack not the consent of God's servants in that head.' And with that he presented unto the Secretary the Apology of Magdeburg, and willed him to read the names of the ministers who had subscribed the defence of the town to be a most just defence; and therewith added: 'that to resist a tyrant is not to resist God nor yet His ordinance'.

Which when he had read, he scripped and said, '*Homines obscuri*'. The other answered, '*Dei tamen servi*'.[27]

And [so] Lethington arose and said: 'My Lords, ye have heard the reasons upon both parties; it becomes you now to decide, and [to]

[27] That is, according to Lethington, they were 'men of little consequence', though for Knox they were 'nevertheless, servants of God'. On the Apology of Magdeburg, see the Introduction, p. xix.

put an order unto preachers, that they be uniform in doctrine. May we, think ye, take the Queen's mass from her?'

While that some began to give their votes, for some were appointed, as it were, leaders to the rest, John Knox said: 'My Lords, I suppose that ye will not [do] contrary to your promise made to the whole Assembly, which was that nothing should be voted in secret till that the first all matters should be debated in public, and that then the votes of the whole Assembly should put [an] end to the controversy. Now have I only sustained the argument, and have rather shown my conscience in most simple manner than that I have insisted upon the force and vehemence of any one argument. And therefore I, for my part, utterly disassent from all voting till that the whole Assembly have heard the propositions and the reasons of both parties. For I unfeignedly acknowledge that many in this company are more able to sustain the argument than I am.'

'Think ye it reasonable', said Lethington, 'that such a multitude [as] are now convened should reason and vote in these heads and matters that concern the Queen's Majesty's own person and affairs?'

'I think', said the other, '[that] whatsoever should bind, the multitude should hear, unless that they have resigned their power unto their commissioners, which they have not done, so far as I understand; for my Lord Justice Clerk heard them with one voice say that in no ways would they consent that anything should either here be voted or concluded.'

'I cannot tell', said Lethington, '[if] that my Lords that be here present, and that bear the burden of such matters, should be bound to their will. What say ye (said he), my Lords? Will ye vote [in] this matter or will ye not vote?'

After long reasoning, some that were made for the purpose said: 'Why may not the Lords vote, and then show unto the kirk whatsoever is done?'

'That appears to me', said John Knox, 'not only a backward order, but also a tyranny usurped upon the kirk. But for me, do as ye list (said he), for as I reason, so I vote; yet protesting as before that I dissent from all voting, till that the whole Assembly understand as well the questions as the reasonings.'

'Well', said Lethington, 'that cannot be done now, for the time is spent; and therefore, my Lord Chancellor (said he), ask ye the votes, and take every one of the ministers and [every] one of us.'

Mr John Douglas, rector.

And so was the rector of St Andrews commanded first to speak his conscience, who said: 'I refer to the superintendent of Fife, for I think we are both in one judgement; and yet (said he), if ye will that I speak first, my conscience is this: that if the Queen oppone herself to our religion, which is the only true religion, that in that case the nobility and estates of this realm, professors of the true doctrine, may justly oppone themselves unto her. But as concerning her own mass, I know it is idolatry, but yet I am not yet resolved whether that by violence we may take it from her or not.' The superintendent of Fife[28] said: 'That same is [my] conscience.' And so affirmed some of the nobility. But others voted frankly, and said: 'That as the mass was abomination, so was it just and right that it should be suppressed; and that in so doing men did no more wrong to the Queen's Majesty than they that should by force take from her a poisoned cup when she was going to drink it.'

Mr John Craig.

At last, Mr John Craig, fellow-minister with John Knox in the kirk of Edinburgh, was required to give his judgement and vote, who said: 'I will gladly show unto your Honours what I understand, but I greatly doubt whether my knowledge and conscience shall satisfy you, seeing ye have heard so many reasons and are so little moved by them. But yet I shall not conceal from you my judgement, adhering first to the protestation of my brother, to wit, that our voting prejudge not the liberty of the General Assembly. I was (said he) in the University of Bononia,[29] in the year of God 1554, wherein, in the place of the Black Friars of the same town, I saw in the time of their General Assembly this conclusion set forth; this same I heard reasoned, determined and concluded:

CONCLUSIO.

'"PRINCIPES omnes, tam supremi, quam inferiores, possunt et debent reformari, vel deponi per eos, per quos eliguntur, confirmantur, vel admittuntur ad officium, quoties a fide praestita subditis per juramentum deficiunt. Quoniam relatio juramenti subditorum et principum mutua est, et utrinque aequo jure servanda et reformanda, juxta legem et conditionem juramenti ab utraque parte facti.

[28] John Winram.
[29] That is, Bologna.

'"That is, all rulers, be they supreme or be they inferior, may and ought to be reformed or deposed by them by whom they are chosen, confirmed or admitted to their office, as often as they break that promise made by the oath to their subjects. Because that their prince is no less bound by oath to the subjects than is the subjects to their princes, and therefore ought to be kept and reformed equally, according to the law and condition of the oath that is made of other party."

'This conclusion, my Lords, I heard sustained and concluded, as I have said, in a most notable auditure. The sustainer was a learned man, M. Thomas de Finola, the rector of the University, a man famous in that country. Magister Vincentius de Placentia affirmed the conclusion to be most true and certain, agreeable both with the law of God and man.[30] The occasion of this disputation and conclusion was a certain disorder and tyranny that was attempted by the pope's governors, who began to make innovations in the country against the laws that were before established, alleging themselves not to be subject to such laws, by reason that they were not institute by the people, but by the pope, who was king of that country; and, therefore, they, having full commission and authority of the pope, might alter and change statutes and ordinances of the country without all consent of the people. Against this usurped tyranny, the learned and the people opponed themselves openly; and when that all reasons which the pope's governors could allege were heard and confuted, the pope himself was fain to take up the matter, and to promise to keep not only the liberty of the people, but also that he should neither abrogate[31] any law [or] statute, neither yet make any new law without their own consent. And, therefore, my Lord (said he), my vote and conscience is that princes are not only bound to keep laws and promises to their subjects, but also that in case they fail, they justly may be deposed; for the band betwixt the prince and the people is reciproce.'

Then start [up] a claw-back of that corrupt court, and said: 'Ye wat not what ye say; for ye tell us what was done in Bononia; we are a kingdom, and they are but a commonwealth.'

'My Lord', said he, 'my judgement is that every kingdom is, or at

[30] I have been unable to identify further Thomas de Finola, but Dr John Durkan has kindly informed me that a Dominican, Vincenzo Villa da Piacenza, was a teacher at the University of Bologna, becoming dean of the faculty of theology in 1548.

[31] Laing MS: have brought.

least should be, a commonwealth, albeit that every commonwealth be not a kingdom; and therefore I think that in a kingdom no less diligence ought to be taken that laws be not violated than is [in] a commonwealth; because that the tyranny of princes who continually ring[32] in a kingdom is more hurtful to the subjects than is the misgovernment of those that from year to year are changed in free commonwealths. But yet, my Lords, to assure you and all others further, that head was disputed by the uttermost; and then, in the end, it was concluded[33] that they spake not of such things as were done in diverse kingdoms and nations by tyranny and negligence of people. "But we conclude", said they, "what ought to be done in all kingdoms and commonwealths, according to the law of God, and unto the just laws of man. And if by the negligence of the people, or by tyranny of princes, contrary laws have been made, yet may that same people, or their posterity, justly crave all things to be reformed[34] according to the original institution of kings and commonwealths; and such as will not [do] so, deserve to eat the fruit of their own foolishness."'

Master James McGill, then Clerk of Register, perceiving the votes to be different, and hearing the bold plainness of the foresaid servant of God, said: 'I remember that this same question was long debated once before this in my house, and there, by reason that we were[35] not all of one mind, it was concluded that Mr Knox should in all our names have written to Mr Calvin for his judgement in the controversy.'

'Nay', said Mr Knox, 'my Lord Secretary would not consent that I should write, alleging that the greatest weight of the answer stood in the narrative, and therefore [promised that] he would write, and I should see it. But when (said he) that diverse times I required him to remember his promise, I found nothing but delay.'[36]

Whereto the Secretary did answer: 'True it is, I promised to write, and true it is that diverse times Mr Knox required me so to do. But when I had more deeply considered the weight of the matter, I began to find more doubts than that I did before, and this one among others:

[32] Laing MS: who continuing.
[33] Laing MS: not concluded.
[34] Laing MS: reasoned.
[35] Laing MS: are.
[36] For Knox's account of this earlier episode, occasioned by Mary's return to Scotland in 1561, see Laing, vol. II, pp. 291–2.

how I durst, I being a subject and the Queen's Majesty's Secretary, take upon me to seek resolution of controversies depending betwixt her Highness and her subjects without her own knowledge and consent.' Then was there an acclamation of the claw-backs of the court, as if Apollo had given his response: 'It was wisely and faithfully done.'

'Well', said John Knox, 'let worldly men praise worldly wisdom so highly as they please; I am assured that by such [shifts] idolatry is maintained and the truth of Jesus Christ is betrayed, whereof God one day will be revenged.' At this, and the like sharpness, many [were] offended, the voting ceased, and every faction began plainly to speak as affection moved them.

John Knox in the end was commanded yet to write to Mr Calvin, and to the learned in other kirks, to know their judgements in that question; which he refused, showing his reason: 'I myself am not only fully resolved in conscience, but also I have heard the judgements in this and all other things that I have affirmed within this realm of the most godly and most learned that be known in Europe. I came not to this realm without their resolution; and for my assurance I have the handwritings of many; and, therefore, if I should move the same question again, what should I do other but either show my own ignorance and forgetfulness or else inconstancy. And, therefore, it may please you to appardon me, albeit I write not. But I will teach you the surer way, which is that ye write and complain upon me, that I teach publicly and affirm constantly such doctrine as offends you, and so shall ye know their plain minds, and whether that I and they agree in judgement or not.'

Diverse said the offer was good, but no man was found that would be the secretary. And so did that Assembly in long reasoning break up. After the which time, the ministers, that were called precise, were holden of all the courtiers as monsters.

The end of the reasoning betwixt John Knox and the Secretary in June 1564.

Index of scriptural citations

Old testament

New testament

Index of proper names

(An asterisk denotes an entry in the Biographical notes; such entries are not otherwise indexed here.)

Index of subjects

Cambridge texts in the history of political thought

Titles published in the series thus far

Aristotle *The Politics* (edited by Stephen Everson)
Arnold *Culture and Anarchy and other writings* (edited by Stefan Collini)
Bakunin *Statism and Anarchy* (edited by Marshall Shatz)
Bentham *A Fragment on Government* (introduction by Ross Harrison)
Bernstein *The Preconditions of Socialism* (edited by Henry Tudor)
Bodin *On Sovereignty* (edited by Julian H. Franklin)
Bossuet *Politics Drawn from the Very Words of Holy Scripture* (edited by Patrick Riley)
Burke *Pre-Revolutionary Writings* (edited by Ian Harris)
Cicero *On Duties* (edited by M. T. Griffin and E. M. Atkins)
Constant *Political Writings* (edited by Biancamaria Fontana)
Diderot *Political Writings* (edited by John Hope Mason and Robert Wokler) and *The Dutch Revolt* (edited by Martin van Gelderen)
Filmer *Patriarcha and Other Writings* (edited by Johann P. Sommerville)
Harrington *A Commonwealth of Oceana* and *A System of Politics* (edited by J. G. A. Pocock)
Hegel *Elements of the Philosophy of Right* (edited by Allen W. Wood and H. B. Nisbet)
Hobbes *Leviathan* (edited by Richard Tuck)
Hooker *Of the Laws of Ecclesiastical Policy* (edited by A. S. McGrade)
John of Salisbury *Policraticus* (edited by Cary Nederman)
Kant *Political Writings* (edited by H. S. Reiss and H. B. Nisbet)
Knox *On Rebellion* (edited by Roger A. Mason)
Lawson *Politica sacra et civilis* (edited by Conal Condren)
Leibniz *Political Writings* (edited by Patrick Riley)
Locke *Two Treatises of Government* (edited by Peter Laslett) and *Luther and Calvin on Secular Authority* (edited by Harro Höpfl)
Machiavelli *The Prince* (edited by Quentin Skinner and Russell Price)
Malthus *An Essay on the Principle of Population* (edited by Donald Winch)
Marsiglio of Padua *Defensor minor* and *De translatione Imperii* (edited by Cary Nederman)
James Mill *Political Writings* (edited by Terence Ball)

J. S. Mill *On Liberty* with *The Subjection of Women* and *Chapters on Socialism* (edited by Stefan Collini)
Milton *Political Writings* (edited by Martin Dzelzainis)
Montesquieu *The Spirit of the Laws* (edited by Anne M. Cohler, Basia Carolyn Miller and Harold Samuel Stone)
More *Utopia* (edited by George M. Logan and Robert M. Adams)
Nicholas of Cusa *The Catholic Concordance* (edited by Paul E. Sigmund)
Paine *Political Writings* (edited by Bruce Kuklick)
Price *Political Writings* (edited by D. O. Thomas)
Priestley *Political Writings* (edited by Peter Miller)
Proudhon *What is Property?* (edited by Donald R. Kelley and Bonnie G. Smith)
Pufendorf *On the Duty of Man and Citizen according to Natural Law* (edited by James Tully)
The Radical Reformation (edited by Michael G. Baylor)
Herbert Spencer *Political Writings* (edited by John Offer)
Vitoria *Political Writings* (edited by Anthony Pagden and Jeremy Lawrance)
William of Ockham *A Short Discourse on Tyrannical Government* (edited by A. S. McGrade and John Kilcullen)